OSCAR

A Pictorial History of the Academy Awards

A NORBACK BOOK

BY THOMAS SIMONET
WITH THE
**EDITORS OF THE
ASSOCIATED PRESS**

Library

Contemporary Books, Inc.
Chicago

Library of Congress Cataloging in Publication Data

Main entry under title:

Oscar, a pictorial history of the Academy Awards.

Includes index.
1. Academy awards (Moving pictures)—History—
Pictorial works.   2. Moving-picture actors and actresses
—United States—Portraits.   3. Moving-picture producers
and directors—United States—Portraits.   I. Associated
Press.
PN1993.5.U6O88   1983   791.43'079   83-18949
ISBN 0-8092-5437-9
ISBN 0-8092-5572-3 (pbk.)

Photo research: Wendy Davis

Published by Contemporary Books, Inc.
180 North Michigan Avenue, Chicago, Illinois 60601
Manufactured in the United States of America
Library of Congress Catalog Card Number: 83-18949
International Standard Book Number: 0-8092-5437-9 (cloth)
0-8092-5572-3 (paper)

Published simultaneously in Canada by Beaverbooks, Ltd.
195 Allstate Parkway, Valleywood Business Park
Markham, Ontario L3R 4T8 Canada

Contents

Introduction

From their rather inauspicious inception — as a last-minute addition to the agenda of the Academy of Motion Picture Arts and Sciences at the first Academy banquet — the Academy Awards have become a true phenomenon. "Oscar" has become an internationally recognized symbol of motion picture achievement, while the award presentations continue to be spectacularly popular. With a yearly audience that numbers in millions, few people in the world are unfamiliar with Oscar.

What accounts for this tremendous success? Of course the celebrities themselves play a major role in the public's fascination with the Oscar telecast. Hundreds of usually bigger-than-life movie stars gather together, and frequently display emotional and personal reactions to the Academy's decisions. Superstar dispositions — sometimes super-gracious and sometimes super-tempered — are displayed on live television for the world to witness.

But the enduring popularity of the Academy Awards stems from much more than the delightful humanity of famous Academy members. The Awards recognize outstanding achievements in a myriad of fields, from the creative activities of acting and writing to the technological triumphs evident in camerawork and special effects. Well-crafted motion pictures result from extraordinarily successful marriages of technical prowess and artistic invention. The interdependence of these talents is never more apparent than during the Academy Awards presentation, where each craft and talent involved in creating a motion picture is recognized and rewarded.

We at the Associated Press, as longtime reporters of the Academy Awards, are acutely aware that lists alone, photographs alone, or text alone could not do justice to these multi-faceted, momentous occasions. We therefore combine all three elements to bring you this, the most comprehensive book available on the subject of the Academy Awards. Herein you will find, organized by award, lists of every award winner *and* every major nominee. We have included photographs of every major award winner — Best Pictures, Best Actors, Best Actresses, Best Supporting Actors. Best Supporting Actresses — as well as hundreds of other photographs: Directors, writers, songwriters, documentaries, foreign films, costume designers, and on and on. You will see candid shots taken during the Oscar ceremonies (including the 1974 streaker in mid-streak!) as well as hundreds of scenes from the films themselves.

In addition to all this is a multitude of history and historical commentary, with special attention paid to your Oscar favorites, such as Katharine Hepburn and Bob Hope. Finally, you will find special sections devoted to Oscar record-breakers, the Oscar jinx, award-winning musicals, acting directors, the great Oscar losers, and more.

So read on, and enjoy!

The Editors

CHAPTER 1

Hollywood's Golden Idol

*W*hen the Academy Awards were presented for the first time in 1929, few people thought the starkly elegant, then-unnamed statuette now known as Oscar would become the internationally recognized symbol of motion picture achievement that it is today.

Art director Cedric Gibbons (later a winner of 11 Academy Awards himself) designed the trophy in 1928. It stands 13½ inches tall and features a rather severe looking man holding a sword and standing atop a reel of film. The copyrighted statuette is cast of solid Britannia metal and electroplated with 18-karat gold. Its weight, which often surprises winners, is 8½ pounds. The Dodge Trophy Company of Carson, California — which has been manufacturing the statuettes since 1959 — charges the Academy of Motion Picture Arts and Sciences $200 per Oscar. To most winners, however, the award is priceless.

There are conflicting stories about how

Art director Cedric Gibbons, designer of the original Oscar

the prize came to be called Oscar. According to the official version, Academy Librarian, (and later Executive Director) Margaret Herrick exclaimed one day that the statuette looked like her Uncle Oscar. Two-time winner Bette Davis claims she named it when she observed that, from behind, it resembled her first husband, Harmon Oscar Nelson. Hollywood columnist Sidney Skolsky says he invented the name when he grew tired of referring to "the statuette" in his columns.

In the five decades since its creation, the Oscar has changed little physically, except for three years during World War II when it was made of plaster. (Wartime winners later received metal replace-ments.) But the award's visibility and significance have grown tremendously.

The idea of establishing the Academy and its awards arose in January 1927 at a small dinner party at the home of Louis B. Mayer, head of the Metro-Goldwyn-Mayer studios. At the time, the film industry was facing both economic disruption by organized labor and, with the coming of sound, technical disruption. Mayer believed that an all-industry association could help solve these and other troubles. That summer, the first banquet of the Academy of Motion Picture Arts and Sciences drew 300 people, and a statement of aims was published. Almost as an afterthought, the fifth objective put forth in this initial state-

Louis B. Mayer (far left), founder of the Academy, at the 1931 Academy Awards banquet. Also pictured: Governor James Rolph, Jr., Mayor John C. Porter, Vice President Curtis, Mrs. Dolly Gans, and Will Hays

ment said that the Academy "will encourage the improvement and advancement of the arts and sciences of the profession by the interchange of constructive ideas and by awards of merit for distinctive achievements."

The first Academy Awards presentation ceremony took place two years later, on the night of May 16, 1929, at the Hollywood Roosevelt Hotel. About 270 people attended. After a dinner of squab and lobster, guests spent the evening watching the presentation of 12 awards and hearing no less than nine after-dinner speeches, including one by Mayer himself.

Academy Award nominees were chosen by a committee of only 20 people; only five of these committee members then selected those first winners. Beginning in the third year, the Academy's entire membership (then 400) made the choices.

The first awards went to films released between August 1, 1927, and July 31, 1928. This split-year pattern was continued for six presentations through 1933. For the 1934 awards, the calendar year was used. This remains the practice, with the stipulation that a film must be shown for at least one week in a commercial theatre in the Los Angeles area for it to be eligible for nomination that year.

Until 1953, when the independent accounting firm of Price Waterhouse and Company began monitoring the voting, rumors of trade-offs and ballot-tampering were widespread, and the studios that dominated the Academy's leadership also dominated the awards. (For example, Academy founder Louis B. Mayer's Metro-Goldwyn-Mayer studios garnered 155 nominations and 33 Oscars in the first decade of the Awards' existence — twice as many as any other studio.) When Bette Davis failed to receive a Best Actress nomination for what was considered a brilliant performance in *Of Human Bondage,* many people in Hollywood viewed it as further

proof of vote fraud. Curiously enough, the first year that Price Waterhouse counted the votes, Davis won for her starring role in *Dangerous.*

Labor disputes diminished the Academy's membership drastically in the 1930s. Writers, directors, cameramen, and others who were joining the new craft guilds saw the Academy as pro-management, and they dropped out in droves. Director Frank Capra recalled a period when there were only 50 members, down from a high of 600. In 1935 Capra became Academy president and began the process of rebuilding the institution. In 1936 the officers had to donate money to pay for that year's awards. Then that year, an

Frank Capra, longtime Academy president, in 1937

Honorary Award, presented to influential and significant pioneer director D. W. Griffith, stirred interest. In the next few years the union battles were resolved with initial contracts, and the Academy's membership began to grow.

After 15 years the hotel banquets were dropped in favor of theatre presentations at Grauman's Chinese Theatre (1944-46), the Shrine Civic Auditorium (1947-48), the Academy Awards Theatre (1949), the RKO Pantages Theatre (1950-1960), the Santa Monica Civic Auditorium (1961-68), and the Dorothy Chandler Pavilion of the Los Angeles Music Center (1969 to the present).

Today, the responsibility for choosing the award nominees and winners falls to the Academy membership that numbers approximately 4,000. Each member is entitled to make five nominations for Best Picture and five for achievements in his or her own category. Performers nominate

Fans gathered early outside the Santa Monica Civic Auditorium, the 1961–1968 home of the Awards ceremonies.

performers, directors nominate directors, and so on, through 13 categories. Nominees do not have to be Academy members. The number of nominees in a particular category has varied through the years — up to as many as 14 for the best song of 1945. In the final balloting, members can vote in all categories though they must have seen all of the nominees for Foreign Language Film, Documentary, or Short Film awards to vote in each of those categories.

National telecasts, begun in 1953, added greatly to the Oscar's status and the Academy's wealth. Funding from the broadcasts (as much as $2 million a year) helps sponsor the Academy's other important work in research, film preservation, scholarships, and publications. At its Beverly Hills headquarters, the Academy operates the Margaret Herrick Library, one of the world's most respected collections of film resources, and the technologically innovative Samuel Goldwyn Theater.

While the Academy gains financial strength from its awards, Oscar winners can profit even more. There is no precise formula for how much the publicity and

Grauman's Chinese Theater, the first theater home of the Academy Awards

Oscar's current residence, the Los Angeles Music Center

Inside the Dorothy Chandler Pavilion of the Los Angeles Music Center during the 1971 Academy Awards show

respectability associated with winning an Oscar adds to a film's revenues. However, it is estimated that a Best Picture award today brings in an additional $12 to $20 million at the box office. A nomination alone is worth perhaps $1 million. *The French Connection*, voted Best Picture of 1971, quadrupled its take after receiving the award. The revenues of *The Deer Hunter* (1978) and *Ordinary People* (1980) doubled after their wins. *Variety* analyzed gross receipts of *One Flew over the Cuckoo's Nest* in 15 cities before and after it captured the top five 1975 awards (for picture, actor, actress, director, and screenplay). Revenues for *Cuckoo's Nest*, the first film to make a top-Oscar sweep since *It Happened One Night* in 1934, increased sharply everywhere, in some places by as much as 70 percent.

Awards and nominations outside of the Best Picture category also help their recipients, but with less certainty. Acting honors to Julie Christie (*Darling*, 1965) and Jack Lemmon (*Save the Tiger*, 1973) seemed to have had little impact at the box office. On the other hand, winning performers can command higher salaries for subsequent pictures. When George Kennedy won for

Best Supporting Actor in *Cool Hand Luke* (1967), his price per picture skyrocketed from $20,000 to $200,000. After Gene Hackman got the Oscar for Best Actor in *The French Connection* (1971), his price went from $200,000 a film to $500,000.

With so much at stake, it is not surprising that some moviemakers pursue the Oscars with costly advertising and public relations campaigns. "Reminder" ads in trade papers such as *Variety* and *The Hollywood Reporter* and wining and dining at private screenings sometimes involve expenses that the Academy itself has condemned as "outright, excessive, and vulgar solicitation of votes."

Leading Hollywood publicist Russell Birdwell spent more than $75,000 to help producer-director-star John Wayne's film *The Alamo* capture seven nominations for 1960. (The campaign strongly suggested that it would be unpatriotic for Academy voters not to support the film.) In the end, however, the movie received only one Oscar—for Sound Recording. In 1963 publicist Jay Bernstein spent $20,000 and secured a Supporting Actor nomination for his client, Nick Adams, in *Twilight of Honor* even though the actor appeared only briefly in reaction scenes in the film. In recent years, the costs have grown. Twentieth Century-Fox spent $68,950 on banquets alone before screenings of their 1980 releases; the studio received 25 nominations. In 1973 the total cost of Oscar campaigns was estimated to be $400,000. By 1982 that figure had increased tenfold to $4 million.

Outside observers have continuously chided the Academy for practices like these, as well as for the cronyism and sentimentality that allegedly affect some choices. They point out anomalous awards: Jimmy Stewart's for *The Philadelphia Story* (1940), they say, was to compensate for his failure to receive one for *Mr. Smith Goes to Washington* the previous year; Elizabeth Taylor's for *Butterfield 8* (1960) was said to represent a sympathy card after she'd suffered a serious illness. Some criticisms are harsher. Hollywood journalist Peter H. Brown has said, "The voters, the economic marketplace, and the force of greed control the Oscars."

In fact, the awards are unpredictable, and as frustrating as this may be to those who delight in second guessing, the unpredictability is part of the fascination of the Oscar process. And most critics do finally acknowledge grudging affection for the an-

Host Johnny Carson commented on the proliferation of awards shows as he introduced the 1982 Oscar ceremony.

nual award ceremonies. To quote journalist Steven V. Roberts: "Even the most violent critics agree that most of the winners are deserving, if not the most deserving, and that flagrant inequities are uncommon." *New York Times* film critic Vincent Canby, speaking on behalf of his fellow critics, said, "Few of us have missed an Oscar show in 20 years."

No one claims the Oscar system is perfect, but it is grounded in public respect and enormous popularity. George Cukor, winner of the Best Director award for *My Fair Lady* in 1964, said: "True popularity means something; it cannot be faked. If you look back over the history of the awards, in a curious way, the truth does come out; the choices of the Academy withstand the test of time."

The Oscars are accolades from the winners' peers, a fact that the recipients of the Awards repeatedly cite as the most gratifying aspect of the Academy Awards. When Orson Welles received an Honorary Award in 1971, he said: "As for the public, I hope that they will understand why this is the more precious just because it does not come to me from them, much less from the critics, but from movie people themselves, the ones who love movies most."

Johnny Carson introduced the 1982 Oscar ceremony, the 54th annual awards show, by joking, "By coincidence, this is also the 54th award show on television this year." Actually only a handful of other award shows are nationally televised, but 32 various organizations do give motion picture awards. Combining the fields of radio, television, theater, music, and dance, there are in fact 170 American organizations that bestow entertainment awards.

The medallions, scrolls, and winged figures may be multiplying, but the Oscar's preeminence has not been threatened. Alongside such prestigious awards as television's Emmys, the recording industry's Grammys, and Broadway's Tonys, the Oscar stands as the granddaddy of awards, the model for all that followed. "Despite the proliferation of awards these days," actress Maggie Smith said at the 1971 Academy Awards presentation, "Oscar remains the one symbol of achievement in the entertainment field that is recognized all over the world."

CHAPTER 2

The Oscars Televised

*O*n the evening of March 19, 1953, approximately 80 million Americans watching NBC-TV saw an exterior shot of the RKO Pantages Theatre on a rainswept Hollywood Boulevard and heard an unseen narrator, Ronald Reagan, introduce the 25th annual Academy Awards presentations. A new era for the Oscars was under way.

The ceremonies that originally had begun at private dinner parties during the 1920s had been covered by local radio since 1930. In 1944 radio coverage expanded to the networks. But it was the national telecast in 1953 that brought a quantum leap in audience attraction. While fewer than 300 people saw the first ceremonies, 300 *million* people in more than 50 countries avidly watch them today. Major television networks pay more than $2 million for the rights to a single show.

It was ironic that television should boost the Oscars. When the coast-to-coast Oscarcasts first began, television was Hollywood's nemesis. Between 1946 and 1953, movie attendance dropped an astonishing 45 percent as families shifted their entertainment focus to what was available in their own living rooms. Throughout these years it became a standing joke for Oscar hosts and presenters to lampoon their electronic rival.

"Television—that's where movies go when they die," Bob Hope joked on the first telecast, quoting Jack Warner's description of TV: "that furniture that stares back." In 1958 Jimmy Stewart said that the Oscar show was "brought to you in living black-and-white"—a reminder that Technicolor movies were years ahead of color television. (The first color telecast of the Academy Awards was in 1966, whereas the first Technicolor non-cartoon movie was *La Cucaracha* in 1934.)

Wide-screen formats were another

A stageful of past Academy Award winners gathered to celebrate "How Far We've Come" on Oscar's golden anniversary in 1978. It was the 26th Awards ceremony to be televised.

The first color telecast of the Academy Awards presentations was produced and directed by Richard Dunlap in the spring of 1966.

weapon the movies used to fight television. When Gary Cooper introduced a set of film clips during the Oscar show, he looked at the wide screen that was being put in place and called it a "20,418-inch TV set." Bob Hope even took gentle pot-shots at television's sacred advertisers. After one particularly long station break with several commercials, he reintroduced the show by saying, "Our sponsors have graciously given up some time so that we can continue with the Academy Awards."

Any hostility could not persist, for the relationship between the Oscars and television turned out to be mutually beneficial. Hollywood benefited from having its leading personalities visit millions of families in the intimacy of their living rooms. The stars were themselves, at least their public selves, instead of their celluloid images. Television viewers saw them embracing their spouses, thanking their parents, winning in tears, and losing with smiles. The Oscar telecasts reinforced a feeling of family that persists to this day

Award presenters and recipients mingled onstage during the finale of the 1979 Oscar ceremony.

Walter Matthau and Liza Minnelli rehearsed for the 52nd annual Awards show under the watchful eye of director Marty Pasetta (left) and producer Howard W. Koch (right). Rehearsals are essential to the smooth running of the live telecast.

among the American public and its Hollywood idols.

In 30 televised presentations (16 on ABC and 14 on NBC), the show's staging has become ever more elaborate and sophisticated. At first awkward moments were more than occasional, especially through 1957 when enormously risky live interconnections with a New York theater were incorporated into each show.

Even the business of handing out awards, which is still evolving today, looked difficult in the early shows. "Oh, there are two of you—I'm terribly sorry," Ginger Rogers said to a pair of winners for a technical award after she had announced only one name. When time was running short, recipients of less celebrated honors would be hustled off the stage so quickly that some almost did backbends trying to blurt out "thank you" into the microphone.

In the early shows the song and dance numbers were simply presented in front of a curtain. As time went on, the production numbers came to rival those of the glorious musicals of the 1930s—except that these were presented live. The opening of the 1978 show, commemorating Oscar's golden anniversary, was an extravagant celebration of "How Far We've Come." So many former Oscar winners were on the stage that the inimitable Hope quipped, "It looks like the road company of the Hollywood Wax Museum."

No amount of rehearsal and polish could anticipate the unexpected, often stridently political occurrences that marked several telecasts, particularly in the 1970s. Before the 1971 telecast, George C. Scott let it be known that, should he be named, he would not accept the Best Actor award

Goldie Hawn, presenter of the 1970 Best Actor award, could hardly believe that the winner was George C. Scott for his performance in *Patton*. Scott had let it be known that he would refuse the Oscar, scorning the Academy Awards as contrived and degrading.

for his performance in *Patton*. He was opposed to the whole idea of the Oscars and called the awards show a "meat parade." During the ceremony, presenter Goldie Hawn preceded the announcement of the winner with an unusual disclaimer. The award was not for the "best actor," she said. "It is the specific achievement that is being honored. That is a pertinent distinction to be kept in mind." When Hawn opened the envelope, she shrieked, "Oh my God!" and announced Scott's name. Producer Frank McCarthy accepted the award and said that it proved the Academy was unbiased in its choices.

The next person to refuse the Oscar was Marlon Brando, winner of the Best Actor award for his performance in *The Godfather* (1972). When his name was called, a native American, Sasheen Littlefeather, delivered part of a speech Brando had written in which he castigated the movie industry for its depiction of the American Indians. "The motion picture industry has been as responsible as any for degrading the Indian and making a mockery of his character, describing him as savage, hostile, and evil," he wrote. Later in the ceremony, Clint Eastwood sarcastically asked if anyone would like to say a word on behalf of all the cowboys that had been killed in Hollywood's scores of westerns.

The next year, in the midst of the streaking craze, a man named Bob Opel embarrassed the Academy's security people when he managed to get backstage with a fake press pass, take off all his clothes, and flash naked across the nation's television screens. David Niven, the emcee at the time, maintained his usual aplomb and blithely remarked, "Isn't it fascinating that probably the only laugh this man will ever get in his life is by stripping off his clothes and showing his shortcomings?"

Vietnam was the topic in 1975. Documentary winners Peter Davis and Bert Schneider accepted an Oscar for their controversial anti-war film *Hearts and Minds*. They read a telegram bearing "greetings of friendship" from a North Vietnamese

At the 45th Oscar ceremony, Sasheen Littlefeather explained why Marlon Brando would not accept the 1972 Oscar he won for his performance in *The Godfather*.

David Niven kept his cool when a streaker disrupted the telecast of the 1973 Academy Awards show.

leader. Emcee Frank Sinatra was later to throw cold water on this politicization of the Awards ceremony when he remarked: "We are not responsible for any political references made on this program tonight. And we are sorry that they were made."

A divisive appearance by Vanessa Redgrave in 1978 capped, at least temporarily, the political exploitation of the Oscars. She was a nominee for Best Supporting Actress in *Julia*, a film that depicted the struggle of the Jewish underground against Nazi Germany. More recently, she had appeared in *The Pales-tinian*, a film some people considered anti-Semitic. Protesters greeted her arrival outside the Dorothy Chandler Pavilion and speculation grew about what she would say if she won the Oscar. Redgrave did in fact win, and her acceptance speech included many controversial remarks.

Fewer sparks flew in the ensuing years. The Nielsen ratings continued to place the show high among the most-watched of the year. But in 1980, for the first time ever, the rating showed a slight decline. In 1981 it took a sizable dip—putting the audience size back to what it had been 20 years be-

John Travolta presented Vanessa Redgrave with the 1977 Oscar for her supporting role in *Julia*. To boos and catcalls from the audience, the actress delivered a controversial acceptance speech.

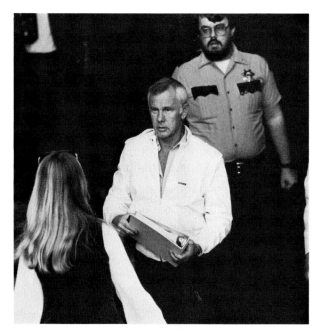 

Johnny Carson (left), host of the 53rd Academy Awards show, left the Los Angeles Music Center, and an Oscar statue (right) was removed from the center's grounds after organizers decided to postpone the ceremony for two days. The postponement resulted from the attempted assassination of President Ronald Reagan.

fore. Undoubtedly the 1981 rating was strongly affected by the two-day postponement of the Awards ceremony, which resulted from the attempted assassination of President Ronald Reagan. When the show did go on, it included Reagan's worldwide greeting in a prerecorded message.

Even when they are not controversial, the live Oscar telecasts maintain a spontaneity that makes them memorable: Red Buttons almost hyperventilating after a breathless run down the aisle to accept his Oscar for Best Supporting Actor in *Sayanara* (1957); Sarah Miles messing up her cue-card reading and then milking the bloopers for several laughs; a group of *Star Wars* technicians simply refusing to leave the stage before each one makes a thank you speech—despite the repeated efforts of the orchestra's conductor to drown them out with a few bars of John Williams' score.

Moments such as these have shown that movie people are human. They have helped build the special fondness and warmth that the public has for the Oscar and its recipients. Generally, all 31 telecasts have lived up to Bob Hope's introduction to the first show: "Welcome to 'Suspense.' This is television's most exciting giveaway show."

Bob Hope never received an Oscar for acting, but he received the Jean Hersholt Award for Humanitarian Service at the 1959 Oscar telecast—which he also hosted.

Bob Hope, Dorothy Lamour, and Bing Crosby in *The Road to Morocco* (1942), one of the seven "Road" pictures Hope did with Crosby

The court jester for U.S. presidents golfing with Gerald Ford

*B*ob Hope has been on hand to give out more Oscars than anyone in Oscar history. But he has received only one for his acting. It was given in 1946, and it was a joke — the statuette was one inch tall.

"I'm very happy to be here for my annual insult," he said when hosting his first Oscar ceremony in 1940. It became a running joke, one of his surest laugh getters. "Welcome to the Academy Awards — or as it's known at my house — Passover," he quipped in 1968.

Actually, the Academy has honored Hope with special awards five times. He received a silver plaque in 1940, a life membership in 1944, a statuette in 1952 ("for his contribution to the laughter of the world, his service to the motion picture industry and his devotion to the American premise"), the Jean Hersholt Humanitarian Award (see Chapter 15) in 1959, and a gold medal in 1965.

But for his acting, he's received nothing — as he loves reminding everyone, even when he dismisses the Oscar as a "bookend with a sneer." He mentioned his covetous desire for an Academy Award at each of the 16 ceremonies he hosted

Perennial Hope

(Left to right) Bob Hope in *The Road to Hong Kong* (1962), *Nothing but the Truth* (1941), and *The Pale Face* (1942).

or co-hosted, including the last one, at age 75, in 1978. Once he made a back-handed parody of an acceptance speech: "Now I haven't won an Academy Award in 15 years, and I've been trying very hard. And I just want to say to my producers, directors, and cameramen that I never could have done it alone. You all helped."

In his durable career, Hope has achieved enough success to last several lifetimes. He was a comic star of vaudeville, Broadway, radio, movies, television, and benefit shows; entertainer of U.S.O. troops from World War II to Vietnam; and court jester to American presidents from Roosevelt to Ford. He

would like "golfer" added to this list.

He specializes in topical monologues, rapid-fire barrages of jokes delivered at a merciless pace, timed in lockstep with the listener's pulsebeat. His radio monologues were so talked about that the Dow Jones news ticker carried excerpts the next morning. He can also ad lib, a technique that saved many an otherwise graceless moment in the Oscar shows.

Dick Cavett and Woody Allen, wholehearted admirers of Hope's confident comic style, have pointed out that his film acting is not bad either. Hope has appeared in 71 movies, including the seven "Road" pictures with Bing Crosby

and two movies in which he played serious roles (*The Seven Little Foys* in 1955 and *Beau James* in 1957). In 1979 his films were the subject of a retrospective tribute by the Film Society of Lincoln Center.

The nose that resembles a skateboard ramp, the slicked-back hair parted in the middle, the jutting jaw, and the sidelong, almost sneering, glances have become centerpieces of American entertainment, and the Oscar shows in particular. Millions of Oscar night television fans would like to repeat to Hope the simple title of his theme song (which is the Oscar-winning song from The Big Broadcast of 1938): "Thanks for the Memory."

CHAPTER 3

Best Picture Awards

*B*en Hur, Best Picture of 1959 and winner of 10 other Academy Awards, in many ways typifies the Best Picture winners of other years. It has a compelling story that is spectacularly told; its performances are Oscar-class; it has earned both critical acclaim and popularity; and the movie is as entertaining as it is uplifting.

It is the only Best Picture award winner set in Biblical times, but *Ben Hur* shares with other honored films a focus on enduring human concerns. Judah Ben Hur rises from galley slave, to adopted son of a powerful Roman, to devoted Christian. He learns that "forgiveness is greater and love more powerful than hatred." The message is woven into a series of spectacles, including a dignified tableau of the crucifixion of Jesus and an unforgettably exciting 8½-minute chariot race. Charlton Heston in the title role and Hugh Griffith as the Sheik Ilderim won Academy Awards for their performances. The movie

earned $36.6 million at the box office and was judged one of the best films of the year by *The New York Times*.

The Academy's other top winners have displayed similar qualities, beginning with the number one ingredient: a powerful story. Most of the winning movies have been serious treatments of significant topics. Some had the advantage of perfect timing, hitting the screen just when they were needed most. *The Best Years of Our Lives* (1946), the first postwar winner, dealt with adjustment to civilian life, an experience that was being shared at the time by thousands of GIs and their families. In 1968, the week that the Reverend Martin Luther King, Jr., was assassinated, the film named Best Picture of the preceding year was *In the Heat of the Night*, a study of racial prejudice.

Not that a Best Picture must be solemn. Nine of the winners have been musicals and seven have been comedies. But these,

The historical melodrama *Ben Hur* (1959) won 11 Oscars—the most ever. The big feast scene is shown here.

19

too, have generally been thoughtful and poignant, addressing significant social or personal issues—for instance, Robert Wise's *West Side Story* (1961) and Woody Allen's *Annie Hall* (1977).

The stories of most of the winners have been borrowed from other media; adaptations outnumber original screenplays four to one. Best pictures have been based on novels (such as *Ordinary People*, 1980), stage plays (such as *Cavalcade*, 1932-33), Broadway musicals (such as *My Fair Lady*, 1964) and—in one case—a television play (*Marty*, 1955). These stories were well polished by the time they were made into films, and their success in earlier forms lent respectability to the Academy's choices. Yet original screenplays have yielded many Best Picture awards that were equally memorable, such as *On The Waterfront* (1954), *Rocky* (1976), *Chariots of Fire* (1981), and *Gandhi* (1982).

Spectacle is another key ingredient; the Best Pictures simply provide more grand

The comedy-romance *Annie Hall* starred Diane Keaton and Woody Allen. The film's four 1977 Oscars included the Best Picture award.

sights than other movies. *Gone with the Wind* (1939), *Around the World in 80 Days* (1956), and *Lawrence of Arabia* (1962) are examples that fill the screen with visual feasts.

Many of the winners tend to have a long running time and be high-budget films. The Best Pictures are an average of 30 minutes longer than the standard movies and are costly to produce. Only *Marty*, made for $350,000, was a low-budget winner. On the other hand, super-extravagance is not necessarily rewarded: None of the 18 most expensive movies ever made won the Best Picture award.

The Academy voters like popular films, and after a film wins Best Picture, it becomes even more popular. According to *Variety*, 20 of the winners are among the 200 top box office attractions of all time. As for critical recognition, two-thirds of the Best Pictures have made *The New York Times* annual Ten Best Movies list.

Best Pictures can be foreign made. Four British productions—*Hamlet* (1948), *Oliver!* (1968), *Chariots of Fire* (1981) and *Gandhi* (1982)—have won. No foreign language film has done so, although three — *La Grande Illusion* (France, 1938), *Z* (Algeria, 1969), and *Cries and Whispers* (Sweden, 1973) — have been nominated.

No other film has matched *Ben Hur*'s record of 11 Academy Awards, but, as of 1982's awards, the Best Pictures of other years have averaged an additional 3.9 Oscars in other categories. Forty of the Best Pictures also won the Best Directing award, and 34 have been honored for their screenplays. In recognition of their visual achievements the Best Pictures have amassed 18 Oscars for art direction, 18 for film editing, and 16 for cinematography. Performances in Best Pictures have won 44 awards. Most of these have gone to men (19 for Best Actor and 11 for Best Supporting Actor, as opposed to eight for Best Supporting Actress and six for Best

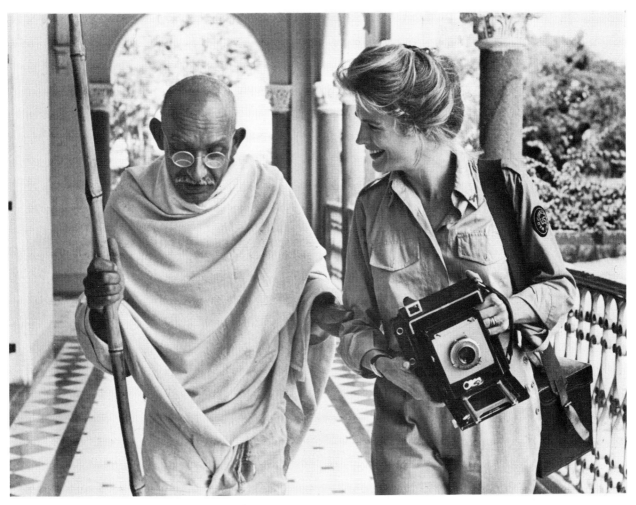

In the Best Picture of 1982, *Gandhi,* Candice Bergen played the famous *Life* magazine photographer Margaret Bourke-White, and Ben Kingsley played the Indian leader. Like most Best Pictures, *Gandhi* ran longer than average—188 minutes.

Actress), probably because so many winning films deal with war and other traditionally male-dominated adventures.

Each winning film is more than the sum of its Oscars, of course; it is a vehicle for ideas. Sam Spiegel, producer of three winners—*On the Waterfront* (1954), *The Bridge on the River Kwai* (1957), and *Law-*

rence of Arabia (1962)—put it this way: "The best motion pictures are those which reach you as entertainment, and, by the time you leave, have provoked thoughts. A picture that provokes no thoughts is usually not well conceived and does not entertain one anyway."

The war film *From Here to Eternity* was a look at army life at Pearl Harbor at the time of the Japanese attack.

In *The Best Years of Our Lives* (1946), a look at postwar America, Myrna Loy and Fredric March played a couple who were reunited after World War II.

*T*he first film ever to be named Best Picture, *Wings* (1927-28), contained several spectacular air battles of World War I. Since then the Academy Award for Best Picture of the Year has gone to 10 other films about war, thereby making it a leading subject of movies named Best Picture.

While elaborate military maneuvers are highlighted in some of the winning movies, what these films focus on are the effects of war on small groups of people. The six films dealing with World War II analyze how a number of individuals felt at various stages; collectively, the films reflect a great deal of the scope and chronology of the war. *From Here to Eternity* (1953) depicts barracks life in the days before Pearl Harbor. *Mrs. Miniver* (1942) follows a British family as its nation is drawn into war. *Patton* (1970) portrays a great general in victory and defeat. *Casablanca* (1942) uncovers a love triangle in a far-off corner of the war. *The Bridge on the River Kwai* (1957) examines life in a prisoner-of-war camp in an Asian jungle. *The Best Years of Our Lives* (1946) follows three servicemen going through the process of adapting to peace.

The Art of War

George C. Scott, Best Actor of 1970 for his role in *Patton,* developed deep admiration for the World War II hero during the making of the film.

The winning films generally stress the bitterness and ironies of war, rather than its glories. *All Quiet on the Western Front* (1929-30) and *The Deer Hunter* (1978) provide especially realistic pictures of World War I and Vietnam, respectively.

The longest Best Pictures are war films: *Lawrence of Arabia* (1962) runs 222 minutes and *Gone With the Wind* (1939) runs 220 minutes. While they are in-depth studies of their complex central characters—T. E. Lawrence and Scarlett O'Hara, respectively—these films also use the backgrounds of World War I and the Civil War to add violent grandeur to their epic stories.

Marlon Brando won the Best Actor Oscar for his portrayal of Vito Corleone, the title role in *The Godfather* (1972), a look at organized crime.

*M*essages are for Western Union," Samuel Goldwyn used to say. The Academy voters have disagreed, having chosen 11 "message films" in the Best Picture category. These movies boldly confront existing crucial problems that face society. The issues that are taken on read like a national agenda.

Winning films have examined alcoholism (*The Lost Weekend*, 1945); anti-Semitism (*Gentleman's Agreement*, 1947); political corruption (*All the King's Men*, 1949); labor violence (*On the Waterfront*, 1954); racial prejudice (*In the Heat of the Night*, 1967); drug trafficking (*The French Connection*, 1971); organized crime (*The Godfather*, 1972, and *The Godfather Part II*, 1974); mental disturbance (*One Flew over the Cuckoo's Nest*, 1975); child custody (*Kramer vs. Kramer*, 1979); and teenage suicide (*Ordinary People*, 1980).

Obviously, movies cannot cure social ills, but they can illuminate them and spur efforts to combat them. These winners have helped build a public awareness and an understanding of significant problems—the first step toward any solution.

Message Films

Kramer vs. Kramer, **an examination of the issue of child custody, was a big winner in 1979. The winners included (from left to right): actor Dustin Hoffman; supporting actress Meryl Streep; director Robert Benton; and producer Stanley Jaffe.**

To a Gershwin score, Gene Kelly and Leslie Caron danced and sang through Paris in the Best Picture of 1951, *An American in Paris*.

*M*usical films, with their opportunities for grandiose production numbers and ideally happy endings, have delighted moviegoers and Academy voters since *Broadway Melody* (1928-29), the first movie musical to have a completely original score and the first of nine to win Best Picture.

Broadway Melody (1929) and the second musical voted Best Picture, *The Great Ziegfeld* (1936), were back-stage musicals — shows about shows. Beginning with *Going My Way* (1944) and *An American in Paris* (1951), the winning musicals were set outside of theaters and therefore presented a far greater challenge when it came to integrating the songs into the story lines.

The heyday of the Oscar-winning musical was the decade from 1958 to 1968. Five of the 11 Best Pictures in that period were musicals: *Gigi* (1958), *West Side Story* (1961), *My Fair Lady* (1964), *The Sound of Music* (1965), and *Oliver!* (1968). No musical has won since.

The Best Picture musicals showcased Ira and George Gershwin's "I've Got Rhythm" in *An American in Paris*; Irving Berlin's "A Pretty Girl Is Like a

All Singin', All Dancin'

**Julie Andrews and Christopher Plummer (center) starred in the Best Picture of 1965, *The Sound of Music,*
one of the most popular musicals of all time. The Von Trapp family is shown singing at the Salzburg Music
Festival prior to their escape from the Nazis.**

Melody" in *The Great Ziegfeld*; Richard Rodgers and
Oscar Hammerstein II's
"Climb Every Mountain"
in *The Sound of Music*; and
Alan Jay Lerner and Fred-
erick Loewe's "I Could
Have Danced All Night" in
My Fair Lady. Such song titles encapsulate the attrib-
utes of the Academy's
favorite song-and-dance
films: rhythm, beauty, in-
spiration, and romance.

27-28 The silent film *Wings* (1927), starring Charles "Buddy" Rogers and Richard Arlen, won the first Best Picture award.

28-29 Anita Page and Bessie Love starred in the early musical *Broadway Melody*, the Best Picture of 1928–29.

Best Picture
1927-1982

29-30 Lew Ayres first gained screen prominence in *All Quiet on the Western Front,* the Best Picture of 1930.

30-31 *Cimarron,* the Best Picture of 1930-31, featured Irene Dunne's screen debut opposite Richard Dix.

31-32 *Grand Hotel* (1932) featured John Barrymore as a jewel thief and Greta Garbo as a lonely ballerina.

32-33 Diana Wynyard and Clive Davis appeared in *Cavalcade* (1933), adapted from Noel Coward's play of the same name.

34 Clark Gable and Claudette Colbert starred as the hard-bitten reporter and the runaway heiress in the screwball comedy *It Happened One Night* (1934).

35 Charles Laughton was the infamous Captain Bligh in the 1935 Best Picture, *Mutiny on the Bounty*.

36 William Powell had the title role in *The Great Ziegfeld*, the Best Picture of 1936.

37 Paul Muni was the fiery 19th-century French writer in *The Life of Emile Zola* (1937).

38 *You Can't Take It with You* won the 1938 Best Picture award and featured Jimmy Stewart and Jean Arthur as the young lovers.

39 Clark Gable and Vivien Leigh brought Margaret Mitchell's Rhett Butler and Scarlett O'Hara to the screen in *Gone with the Wind* (1939).

40 Laurence Olivier and Joan Fontaine engaged in a battle of wills in the Hitchcock thriller *Rebecca* (1940), one of only 15 films to win the Best Picture award but not the Best Director award.

41 Child star Roddy McDowall was a hit in the 1941 Best Picture, *How Green Was My Valley.*

42 *Mrs. Miniver,* a moving drama about a middle-class English family coping with the war, won Greer Garson (shown here with co-stars Walter Pidgeon and Richard Ney) the Best Actress award and was voted the Best Picture of 1942.

43 Humphrey Bogart and Ingrid Bergman joined the ranks of star-crossed screen lovers in *Casablanca* (1943).

44 Barry Fitzgerald and Bing Crosby teamed up in 1944's Best Picture, *Going My Way*.

45 Ray Milland starred in *The Lost Weekend* (1945), a landmark film about alcoholism.

46 Postwar America took the story of three returning World War II veterans to heart. It followed (left to right) Harold Russell, Teresa Wright, Dana Andrews, Myrna Loy, Hoagy Carmichael, and Fredric Marsh as they coped with the loss of *The Best Years of Our Lives* (1946).

47 Dorothy McGuire, Gregory Peck and John Garfield starred in the 1947 Best Picture, *Gentleman's Agreement*, a then-daring look at anti-Semitism.

48 Laurence Olivier produced, directed, and starred in the Best Picture of 1948, *Hamlet*.

49 *All the King's Men* (1949), starring Broderick Crawford, was based on Robert Penn Warren's thinly disguised novel about Huey Long.

50 In 1950 Gary Merrill, Anne Baxter, and Bette Davis starred in a cynical look at backstage maneuverings and the theatrical life in *All about Eve*.

51 Gene Kelly pondered a life of luxury with Nina Foch in the 1951 music and dance celebration *An American in Paris*.

52 Betty Hutton is shown here getting in shape for her role as an aerialist in *The Greatest Show on Earth* (1952).

53 The surfside embrace of Deborah Kerr and Burt Lancaster in *From Here to Eternity* (1953) was regarded as one of the most passionate love scenes in movie history.

54 Labor violence was one subject of the 1954 Best Picture, *On the Waterfront,* which starred (left to right) Karl Malden, Marlon Brando, Eva Marie Saint, and Arthur Keegan. The film won eight Oscars.

55 The relatively low-budget *Marty,* with Ernest Borgnine in the title role, captured four Academy Awards in 1955.

56 The Best Picture of 1956, *Around the World in 80 Days,* featured over 40 cameo appearances of show business figures. It starred (from left to right) Shirley MacLaine, David Niven, and Cantinflas.

57 Alec Guinness was the driven British colonel imprisoned by the Japanese in the Best Picture of 1957, *The Bridge on the River Kwai.*

58 Leslie Caron is shown here strolling through the Bois de Boulogne with Maurice Chevalier and Louis Jourdan in the 1958 musical *Gigi*.

59 Charlton Heston is shown pulling ahead in the famous 8½-minute chariot race scene of the 1959 Best Picture, *Ben Hur*.

60 Jack Lemmon coped with the bachelor life in *The Apartment* (1960).

61 In 1961's *West Side Story*, George Chakaris and gang claimed their turf in song and dance.

62 Peter O'Toole aimed at stardom with (but failed to receive an Oscar for) his portrayal of the enigmatic adventurer T. E. Lawrence in the Best Picture of 1962, *Lawrence of Arabia*.

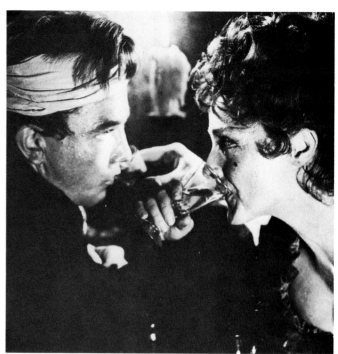

63 Albert Finney and Joyce Redman were featured in the lusty scene of seduction and feasting from 1963, *Tom Jones* (1963).

64 Rex Harrison and Audrey Hepburn are shown here awaiting their cue for the formal ballroom scene in *My Fair Lady* (1964).

65 Christopher Plummer and Julie Andrews wrestled with both love and the impending Nazi invasion of Austria in the popular 1965 Best Picture, *The Sound of Music*.

66 Fred Zinnemann won an Oscar (presented here by Rosalind Russell and Audrey Hepburn) for his direction of the Best Picture of 1966, *A Man for All Seasons*.

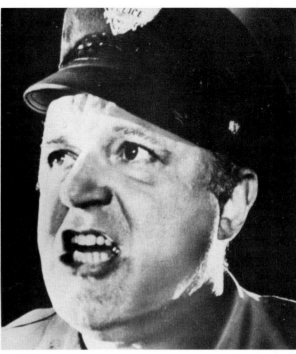

67 Rod Steiger, as a small-town southern cop, didn't want Sidney Poitier's help in solving a murder case in the Best Picture of 1967, *In the Heat of the Night*.

68 Ron Moody, as the rapacious Fagin, taught young Oliver (Mark Lester) the art of picking pockets in the musical, *Oliver!* (1968).

69 In the 1969 Best Picture, *Midnight Cowboy*, Joe Buck (Jon Voight) and Ratso Rizzo (Dustin Hoffman) struggled for survival in the seamy world of New York hustlers.

70 *Patton* starred George C. Scott and was the 1970 Best Picture in a multi-Oscar sweep.

71 Gene Hackman, as Popeye Doyle, shot a narcotics dealer (Marcel Bozzuffi) in the 1971 thriller, *The French Connection.*

72 *The Godfather* chronicled the lives of a Mafia don and his clan.

73 Con men Paul Newman and Robert Redford set up a scam operation in the 1973 winner, *The Sting*.

74 *The Godfather Part II* won seven Oscars, including Best Picture and Best Supporting Actor (Robert De Niro) in 1974.

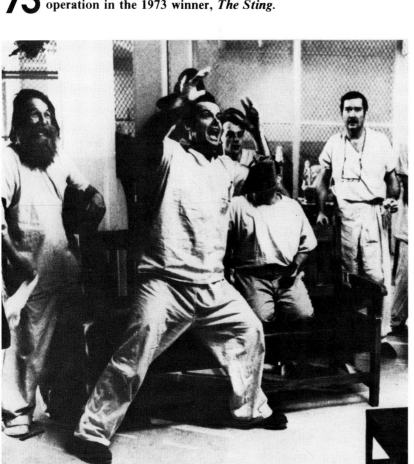

75 Jack Nicholson upset the routine of a mental hospital in the Best Picture of 1975, *One Flew over the Cuckoo's Nest*.

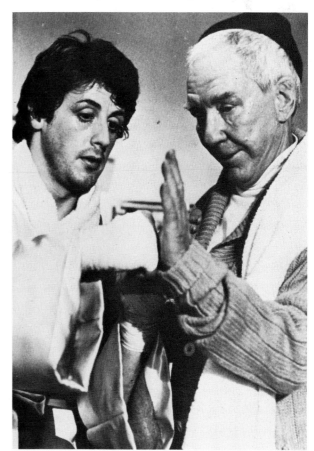

76 *Rocky* (1976) was a star-making hit for Sylvester Stallone, who played a boxer going after a dream with his trainer (Burgess Meredith).

77 Woody Allen, Diane Keaton, and Tony Roberts starred in the quirky autobiographical romance, *Annie Hall* (1977).

78 The intense and powerful Best Picture of 1978, *The Deer Hunter,* explored the effect of wartime duty in Vietnam on a group of friends.

79 Dustin Hoffman and Justin Henry starred in *Kramer vs. Kramer,* the 1979 film that chronicled a battle for child custody.

80 Mary Tyler Moore and Timothy Hutton were an alienated mother and son in *Ordinary People,* the Best Picture of 1980.

81 *Chariots of Fire* (1981) was a British film based on the true story of two athletes who ran in the 1924 Olympics.

82 Ben Kingsley was Mahatma Gandhi in the epic 1982 *Gandhi,* the story of one man's evolution into a spiritual leader and man of peace.

1927-28

Wings, Paramount
The Last Command, Paramount
The Racket, Paramount
Seventh Heaven, Fox
The Way of All Flesh, Paramount

1928-29

Broadway Melody, Metro-
    Goldwyn-Mayer
Alibi, Feature Prod., United Artists
Hollywood Revue, MGM
In Old Arizona, Fox
The Patriot, Paramount

1929-30

All Quiet on the Western Front, Uni-
    versal
The Big House, MGM
Disraeli, Warner Bros.
The Divorcee, MGM
The Love Parade, Paramount

1930-31

Cimarron, RKO Radio
East Lynne, Fox
The Front Page, UA
Skippy, Paramount
Trader Horn, MGM

1931-32

Grand Hotel, MGM
Arrowsmith, UA
Bad Girl, Fox
The Champ, MGM
Five Star Final, First National
One Hour with You, Paramount
Shanghai Express, Paramount
Smiling Lieutenant, Paramount

1932-33

Cavalcade, Fox
A Farewell to Arms, Paramount
Forty-Second Street, Warner Bros.
I Am a Fugitive from a Chain Gang,
    Warner Bros.
Lady for a Day, Columbia
Little Women, RKO Radio
The Private Life of Henry VIII, UA
    [British]
She Done Him Wrong, Paramount
Smilin' Thru, MGM
State Fair, Fox

1934

It Happened One Night, Columbia
The Barretts of Wimpole Street,
    MGM
Cleopatra, Paramount
Flirtation Walk, First National
The Gay Divorcee, RKO Radio
Here Comes the Navy, Warner Bros.
The House of Rothschild, United Art-
    ists

Imitation of Life, Universal
One Night of Love, Columbia
The Thin Man, MGM
Viva Villa, MGM
The White Parade, Fox

1935

Mutiny on the Bounty, MGM
Alice Adams, RKO Radio
Broadway Melody of 1936, MGM
Captain Blood, Warner Bros.-
    Cosmopolitan
David Copperfield, MGM
The Informer, RKO Radio
Les Miserables, 20th Century-UA
Lives of a Bengal Lancer, Paramount
A Midsummer Night's Dream, War-
    ner Bros.
Naughty Marietta, MGM
Ruggles of Red, Paramount
Top Hat, RKO Radio

1936

The Great Ziegfeld, MGM
Anthony Adverse, Warner Bros.
Dodsworth, Samuel Goldwyn
    Studios-UA
Libeled Lady, MGM
Mr. Deeds Goes to Town, Columbia
Romeo and Juliet, MGM
San Francisco, MGM
The Story of Louis Pasteur, Warner
    Bros.
A Tale of Two Cities, MGM
Three Smart Girls, Universal

1937

The Life of Emile Zola, Warner Bros.
The Awful Truth, Columbia
Captains Courageous, MGM
Dead End, UA
The Good Earth, MGM
In Old Chicago, 20th C.-Fox
Lost Horizon, Columbia
One Hundred Men and a Girl, Uni-
    versal
Stage Door, RKO Radio
A Star Is Born, UA

1938

You Can't Take It with You, Colum-
    bia
The Adventures of Robin Hood, War-
    ner Bros.
Alexander's Ragtime Band, 20th C.-
    Fox
Boys Town, MGM
The Citadel, MGM (British)
Four Daughters, Warner Bros.-First
    National
Grand Illusion, World Pictures
    (French)
Jezebel, Warner Bros.
Pygmalion, MGM (British)
Test Pilot, MGM

1939

Gone with the Wind, MGM
Dark Victory, Warner Bros.
Goodbye Mr. Chips, MGM (British)
Love Affair, RKO Radio
Mr. Smith Goes to Washington, Co-
    lumbia
Ninotchka, MGM
Of Mice and Men, UA
Stagecoach, UA
Wizard of Oz, MGM
Wuthering Heights, Goldwyn-UA

1940

Rebecca, UA
All This, and Heaven Too, Warner
    Bros.
Foreign Correspondent, UA
The Grapes of Wrath, 20th C.-Fox
The Great Dictator, UA
Kitty Foyle, RKO Radio
The Letter, Warner Bros.
The Long Voyage Home, UA
Our Town, UA
The Philadelphia Story, MGM

1941

How Green Was My Valley, 20th C.-
    Fox
Blossoms in the Dust, MGM
Citizen Kane, RKO Radio
Here Comes Mr. Jordan, Columbia
Hold Back the Dawn, Paramount
The Little Foxes, RKO Radio
The Maltese Falcon, Warner Bros.
One Foot in Heaven, Warner Bros.
Sergeant York, Warner Bros.
Suspicion, RKO Radio

1942

Mrs. Miniver, MGM
The Invaders, Columbia (British)
King's Row, Warner Bros.
The Magnificent Ambersons, RKO
    Radio
The Pied Piper, 20th C.-Fox
The Pride of the Yankees, Goldwyn-
    RKO Radio
Random Harvest, MGM
The Talk of the Town, Columbia
Wake Island, Paramount
Yankee Doodle Dandy, Warner Bros.

1943

Casablanca, Warner Bros.
For Whom the Bell Tolls, Paramount
Heaven Can Wait, 20th C.-Fox
The Human Comedy, MGM
In Which We Serve, UA (British)
Madame Curie, MGM
The More the Merrier, Columbia
The Ox-Bow Incident, 20th C.-Fox
The Song of Bernadette, 20th C.-Fox
Watch on the Rhine, Warner Bros.

Best Pictures

1944

Going My Way, Paramount
Double Indemnity, Paramount
Gaslight, MGM
Since You Went Away, UA
Wilson, 20th C.-Fox

1945

The Lost Weekend, Paramount
Anchors Aweigh, MGM
The Bells of St. Mary's, RKO Radio
Mildred Pierce, Warner Bros.
Spellbound, UA

1946

The Best Years of Our Lives,
  Goldwyn-RKO Radio
Henry V, UA (British)
It's a Wonderful Life, RKO Radio
The Razor's Edge, 20th C.-Fox
The Yearling, MGM

1947

Gentleman's Agreement, 20th C.-Fox
The Bishop's Wife, RKO Radio
Crossfire, RKO Radio
Great Expectations, Universal-
  International (British)
Miracle on 34th Street, 20th C.-Fox

1948

Hamlet, U-I (British)
Johnny Belinda, Warner Bros.
The Red Shoes, Eagle-Lion (British)
The Snake Pit, 20th C.-Fox
Treasure of Sierra Madre, Warner
  Bros.

1949

All the King's Men, Columbia
Battleground, MGM
The Heiress, Paramount
A Letter to Three Wives, 20th C.-Fox
Twelve O'Clock High, 20th C.-Fox

1950

All about Eve, 20th C.-Fox
Born Yesterday, Columbia
Father of the Bride, MGM
King Solomon's Mines, MGM
Sunset Boulevard, Paramount

1951

An American in Paris, MGM
Decision Before Dawn, 20th C.-Fox
A Place in the Sun, Paramount
Quo Vadis, MGM
A Streetcar Named Desire, Warner
  Bros.

1952

The Greatest Show on Earth, Para-
  mount
High Noon, UA
Ivanhoe, MGM
Moulin Rouge, UA
The Quiet Man, Republic

1953

From Here to Eternity, Columbia
Julius Caesar, MGM
The Robe, 20th C.-Fox
Roman Holiday, Paramount
Shane, Paramount

1954

On the Waterfront, Columbia
The Caine Mutiny, Columbia
The Country Girl, Paramount
Seven Brides for Seven Brothers,
  MGM
Three Coins in the Fountain, 20th C.-
  Fox

1955

Marty, UA
Love Is a Many-Splendored Thing,
  20th C.-Fox
Mister Roberts, Warner Bros.
Picnic, Columbia
The Rose Tattoo, Paramount

1956

Around the World in 80 Days, UA
Friendly Persuasion, Allied Artists
Giant, Warner Bros.
The King and I, 20th C.-Fox
The Ten Commandments, Para-
  mount

1957

The Bridge on the River Kwai, Co-
  lumbia
Peyton Place, 20th C.-Fox
Sayonara, Warner Bros.
12 Angry Men, UA
Witness for the Prosecution, UA

1958

Gigi, MGM
Auntie Mame, Warner Bros.
Cat on a Hot Tin Roof, MGM
The Defiant Ones, UA
Separate Tables, UA

1959

Ben Hur, MGM
Anatomy of a Murder, Columbia
The Diary of Anne Frank, 20th C.-
  Fox
The Nun's Story, Warner Bros.
Room at the Top, Continental Distr.,
  Inc. (British)

1960

The Apartment, UA
The Alamo, UA
Elmer Gantry, UA
Sons and Lovers, 20th C.-Fox
The Sundowners, Warner Bros.

1961

West Side Story, UA
Fanny, Warner Bros.
The Guns of Navarone, Columbia
The Hustler, 20th C.-Fox
Judgment at Nuremberg, UA

1962

Lawrence of Arabia, Columbia
The Longest Day, 20th C.-Fox
The Music Man, Warner Bros.
Mutiny on the Bounty, MGM
To Kill a Mockingbird, U-I

1963

Tom Jones, UA
America America, Warner Bros.
Cleopatra, 20th C.-Fox
How the West Was Won, MGM-
  Cinerama
Lilies of the Field, UA

1964

My Fair Lady, Warner Bros.
Becket, Paramount
*Dr. Strangelove or: How I Learned to
  Stop Worrying and Love the Bomb*,
  Columbia
Mary Poppins, Walt Disney Prod.
Zorba the Greek, International Clas-
  sics

1965

The Sound of Music, 20th C.-Fox
Darling, Embassy
Doctor Zhivago, MGM
Ship of Fools, Columbia
A Thousand Clowns, UA

1966

A Man for All Seasons, Columbia
Alfie, Paramount
The Russians Are Coming the Russians Are Coming, UA
The Sand Pebbles, 20th C.-Fox
Who's Afraid of Virginia Woolf? Warner Bros.

1967

In the Heat of the Night, UA
Bonnie and Clyde, Warner Bros.-Seven Arts
Doctor Dolittle, 20th C.-Fox
The Graduate, Embassy
Guess Who's Coming to Dinner, Columbia

1968

Oliver!, Columbia
Romeo & Juliet, Paramount
Funny Girl, Columbia
The Lion in Winter, Avco Embassy
Rachel, Rachel, Warner Bros.-Seven Arts

1969

Midnight Cowboy, UA
Anne of the Thousand Days, Universal
Butch Cassidy and the Sundance Kid, 20th C.-Fox
Hello, Dolly!, 20th C.-Fox
Z, Cinema V

1970

Patton, 20th C.-Fox
Airport, Universal
Five Easy Pieces, Columbia
Love Story, Paramount
*M*A*S*H*, 20th C.-Fox

1971

The French Connection, 20th C.-Fox
A Clockwork Orange, Warner Bros.
Fiddler on the Roof, UA
The Last Picture Show, Columbia
Nicholas and Alexandra, Columbia

1972

The Godfather, Paramount
Cabaret, Allied Artists
Deliverance, Warner Bros.
The Emigrants, Warner Bros.
Sounder, 20th C.-Fox

1973

The Sting, Universal
American Graffiti, Universal
Cries and Whispers, New World Pictures
The Exorcist, Warner Bros.
A Touch of Class, Avco Embassy

1974

The Godfather Part II, Paramount
Chinatown, Paramount
The Conversation, Paramount
Lenny, UA
The Towering Inferno, 20th C.-Fox-Warner Bros.

1975

One Flew over the Cuckoo's Nest, UA
Barry Lyndon, Warner Bros.
Dog Day Afternoon, Warner Bros.
Jaws, Universal
Nashville, Paramount

1976

Rocky, UA
All the President's Men, Warner Bros.
Bound for Glory, UA
Network, MGM-UA
Taxi Driver, Columbia

1977

Annie Hall, UA
The Goodbye Girl, MGM-Warner Bros.
Julia, 20th C.-Fox
Star Wars, 20th C.-Fox
The Turning Point, 20th C.-Fox

1978

The Deer Hunter, Universal
Coming Home, UA
Heaven Can Wait, Paramount
Midnight Express, Columbia (British)
An Unmarried Woman, 20th C.-Fox

1979

Kramer vs. Kramer, Columbia
All That Jazz, 20th C.-Fox
Apocalypse Now, UA
Breaking Away, 20th C.-Fox
Norma Rae, 20th C.-Fox

1980

Ordinary People, Paramount
Coal Miner's Daughter, Universal
The Elephant Man, Paramount
Raging Bull, UA
Tess, Columbia

1981

Chariots of Fire, Ladd Co./Warner Bros. (British)
Atlantic City, Paramount
On Golden Pond, Universal
Raiders of the Lost Ark, Paramount
Reds, Paramount

1982

Gandhi, Columbia (British)
E. T. — the Extra-Terrestrial, Universal
Missing, Universal
Tootsie, Columbia
The Verdict, 20th C.-Fox

The Shrine Civic Auditorium's stage was adorned with a giant Oscar at the 1948 awards ceremony. Best Supporting Actor Walter Huston is shown here receiving a congratulatory kiss from Celeste Holm.

CHAPTER 4

Best Actor Awards

*A*ctors frequently have said that their greatest joy in winning an Oscar was knowing that the tribute had come from their own peers. "Though the craft of acting is basically geared to a general audience acceptance," Jack Lemmon, best actor for *Save the Tiger* (1973), said, "there is still the understandable and special pride that the actor feels when his peers deem his efforts to be worthy of an Oscar. Long may that joy persist."

The Academy voters consider the depth of a performance — not only its technical quality but also its significance to an audience. Good looks and deep voices might be enough for some fans, but the Oscars go to uncommon acting talent in meaningful roles.

The words that John Wayne once suggested for his tombstone could apply to some of his fellow winners: "He was ugly, was strong, and had dignity." A group that includes Clark Gable and Fredric March is

hardly "ugly," but conventional romantic appeal is not necessarily a prerequisite for the award of Best Actor.

The faces in this chapter range from rough-hewn Ernest Borgnine to debonair David Niven. More than a certain look, the Best Actors have panache.

They portray strong, active protagonists. In battles large and small, from the River Kwai to the Golden Pond, these men win. Their strength is as insistent as Broderick Crawford's and as tough as Humphrey Bogart's.

The Best Actors have a generous supply of dignity as well. The winners play men who uphold their convictions and who have earned their self-respect: Think of a Gregory Peck, a Sidney Poitier. Their movies teach morality.

The Best Actors represent men with the moral fiber to fight for what they believe. They portray heroes of history from Paul Scofield's Sir Thomas More, to George C.

Henry Fonda in *On Golden Pond* in 1981

Ben Kingsley, in *Gandhi* (1982), fit the Best Actor mold: He played a man of history with strong ideals and moral fiber.

Scott's General Patton, to Ben Kingsley's Gandhi. They play priests (Spencer Tracy, Bing Crosby), kings (Charles Laughton, Yul Brynner), and ordinary men facing extraordinary personal problems (Ray Milland, Ronald Colman, Cliff Robertson).

The Best Actress and Best Actor of 1942, Greer Garson and James Cagney, happily embraced at the Academy Awards banquet.

Best Actress of 1959 Susan Hayward helped Best Actor David Niven cool off at the Pantages Theatre in Hollywood at the awards ceremony.

Their good fortune is to embody for a few moments — and have preserved forever on film — some great and human qualities. They must have been born right, for they boast the courage, ambition, and idealism needed to make it to the top.

Luck does play a part. Charlton Heston and Rex Harrison won their Oscars in roles that initially had been assigned to other actors. Each winner can be said to have played the right role at the right time. So to John Wayne's epitaph, add Clark Gable's. Without diminishing anyone's talent, it describes each of these remarkable men. As Gable put it: "He was lucky and he knew it."

Marlon Brando immortalized the new kind of hero both as Terry Malloy in *On the Waterfront* in 1954 and, in 1972, as *The Godfather* (photo on page 55).

*W*hen Marlon Brando won the 1954 Oscar for his portrayal of the tough misfit, Terry Malloy, in *On the Waterfront*, the Academy members recognized a new kind of leading man.

The traditional Oscar heroes had been virtuous in every way. Gary Cooper and James Stewart played men whose behavior was consistently proper. Dockworker Terry Malloy, on the other hand, was rebellious, inarticulate, and coarse. In the end, he displayed conviction, but for every strength in his character there was a shortcoming; for every admirable quality, a fault. He was a new kind of flawed protagonist, an antihero.

Brando did not invent these complex, fascinating characters, but he did make them popular. He immortalized them in two Oscar winning roles: Terry Malloy in *On the Waterfront* and the laryngitic Mafia don, Vito Corleone, in *The Godfather*.

Following in Brando's footsteps, 10 other leading and supporting players received nominations or Oscars for their portrayals of disreputable heroes: James Caan (*The Godfather*, 1972); James Dean (*East of Eden*, 1955, and *Giant*, 1956); Robert De Niro (*The Deer Hunter*, 1978, and *Raging Bull*, 1980); Dustin

A New Kind of Hero

Hoffman (*The Graduate,* 1967, *Midnight Cowboy,* 1969, and *Lenny,* 1974); Sal Mineo (*Rebel without a Cause,* 1955); Steve McQueen (*The Sand Pebbles,* 1966); Paul Newman *(Hud,* 1963, and *The Verdict,* 1982); Jack Nicholson *(Five Easy Pieces,* 1970); Al Pacino *(The Godfather II,* 1974); and Rod Steiger *(On the Waterfront,* 1954, and *In the Heat of the Night,* 1967).

These characters were flawed in many and varied ways, but they shared one appealing strength: They despised phoniness, hypocrisy, and pretention in all forms. They knew themselves, they were true to themselves, and they cared nothing about what others thought of them.

A new style of acting, again popularized by Brando, went along with the new character types. Stanislavski's technique, commonly termed "the Method," underlay the intense performances of most of these men. *On the Waterfront* director Elia Kazan and Actors' Studio head Lee Strasberg were the key American promoters of this naturalistic (some say "mumbling") style. It required actors to find the necessary emotions within themselves and "live" their roles, rather than enact them through stagy, artificial mannerisms.

Both the style and the character flaws contributed to believability. Even though the characters were sometimes offensive in many ways, they were also strangely attractive. The men that Cooper, Peck, and Stewart had played were inspiring. On the other hand, the men that De Niro, Hoffman, and Nicholson played were neither loved nor hated, but audiences could identify in these characters certain aspects of themselves.

The Academy recognized that, for actors, the roles of flawed characters were peculiarly demanding. Saintly heroes and wicked villains could be consistent, but because of the nature of their complex roles, antiheroes had to provide messages that were disturbingly mixed.

*A*ctors often win Oscars late in their careers, and when they do the triumph seems especially poignant.

"I have spent nearly 50 years chasing this elusive fellow with good performances and bad," John Wayne said, "so I was extremely delighted when he was handed to me by Barbra Streisand." Wayne was 62 when he was named Best Actor in 1969 for *True Grit*. It was his 84th film. Surely the Duke had been as good or even better in some of his earlier films, but comparisons were irrelevant. Among other things, the Academy's tribute acknowledged that he had become an institution in Hollywood and throughout the nation.

Actresses win their awards earlier and more often. Seven women have won for their first time on screen, but only one man has — Ben Kingsley for *Gandhi* (1982). The average Best Actress is nine years younger and has 10 fewer films to her credit than the average Best Actor. Nine women have won the award for Best Actress more than once, but only four men have done the same.

For many actors, the Oscars more often represent recognition of an enduring presence on the screen. The awards crown their careers. Humphrey Bogart was 53, a veteran of 61 films, when

he received his Oscar for *The African Queen* (1951). It was four years before his death. Earlier he had won praise for *Casablanca* (1942), for which he was nominated; *Key Largo* (1948); *The Treasure of Sierra Madre* (1948); and *The Maltese Falcon* (1941). When he finally won the Oscar, he said in his tough, understated way, "It's a long way from the Belgian Congo to the Pantages Theatre, but I'd rather be here than there."

The award can come after death, as it did for Peter Finch for his role in *Network* (1976). His earlier credits included 48 films made in Australia, England, and the United States. Posthumous nominations also went to Spencer Tracy for *Guess Who's Coming to Dinner?* (1967) and to a much younger man, James Dean, who was nominated twice after he died — for *East of Eden* (1955) and for *Giant* (1956).

The oldest man to win was Henry Fonda at 76. He received the Oscar for Best Actor in 1981 from a hospital bed a few months before his death. Critics were unanimous in praising his last performance in *On Golden Pond*, but many added they thought he had earned an award several times before. Fonda had made 83 films and had been nominated only once — for

Stagecoach (1939), with Claire Trevor, was one of John Wayne's earliest films.

The Duke acted in 84 films before receiving the Best Actor award for *True Grit* in 1969.

Better Late . . .

Although he won praise for his earlier films—including *Casablanca* (1942) with Ingrid Bergman—Humphrey Bogart didn't receive an Oscar until 1951.

Art Carney, Ed Norton on TV's *The Honeymooners,* won an Oscar at the age of 57 for *Harry and Tonto* (1974).

Peter Finch, Spencer Tracy, and James Dean were all nominated posthumously. Finch's Oscar for *Network* (1976) was accepted by his wife, Eletha Finch.

The Grapes of Wrath in 1940. The awards for Best Actor are tributes to endurance as well as quality, and luckily Fonda was both a strong artist and a strong survivor.

The young Henry Fonda was nominated as Best Actor for *Grapes of Wrath* in 1940, but he didn't win the Best Actor award until he was 76 years old.

27-28 Emil Jannings received the first Best Actor award in 1928 for his performance in both *The Last Command* and *The Way of All Flesh*.

28-29 Warner Baxter won an Oscar in 1929 for his role in *In Old Arizona*.

29-30 George Arliss was the 1930 winner for his portrayal of the great British statesman, *Disraeli* (1929).

30-31 For his performance in *A Free Soul* (1931), Lionel Barrymore won an Oscar.

31-32 Wallace Beery (left) and Fredric March tied for the Best Actor award of 1931-32. They won for roles in *The Champ* (1931) and *Dr. Jekyll and Mr. Hyde* (1931), respectively.

Best Actor
1927-1982

32-33 Charles Laughton played the 16th-century British monarch in *The Private Life of Henry VIII* in 1933.

34 Clark Gable called himself "lucky" when he won his Oscar for *It Happened One Night* (1934).

35 For his portrayal of a hard-drinking Irishman in *The Informer*, Victor McLaglen won the 1935 Oscar.

36 Paul Muni portrayed the famous French scientist in *The Story of Louis Pasteur* in 1936.

37 Best Actor of 1937 Spencer Tracy starred in *Captains Courageous.*

38 Spencer Tracy won the Best Actor award in 1938 as well, this year for *Boys Town.* A young Mickey Rooney (left) co-starred.

39 In *Goodbye, Mr. Chips* (1939) Robert Donat played a shy British schoolmaster.

40 Jimmy Stewart was a reporter who fell in love with society girl Katharine Hepburn in *The Philadelphia Story* (1940).

41 In 1941 Gary Cooper was *Sergeant York,* a pacifist who became a World War I hero.

42 James Cagney's performance in *Yankee Doodle Dandy* in 1942 included singing and dancing.

43 *Watch on the Rhine,* adapted from Lillian Hellman's play, starred Paul Lukas, the Best Actor of 1943.

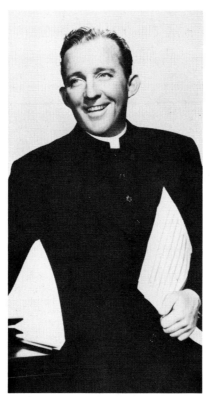

44 Things went Bing Crosby's way on Oscar night for his role in the 1944 film *Going My Way.*

45 Ray Milland portrayed an alcoholic on a binge in *The Lost Weekend* (1945).

46 Fredric March won his second Oscar for playing a World War II veteran in the timely film, *The Best Years of Our Lives* (1946).

47 In 1947 Ronald Colman played an actor whose roles affected his real life in *Double Life.*

48 Laurence Olivier captured the 1948 Oscar for his performance in the British film, *Hamlet.*

49 Broderick Crawford played venal politician Willie Stark in *All the King's Men* (1949).

50 Jose Ferrer had the title role in *Cyrano De Bergerac* (1950).

51 In 1951 Humphrey Bogart won his only Oscar for his portrayal of a crusty riverboat pilot in *The African Queen*.

52 Gary Cooper was the sheriff of a small western town in *High Noon* (1952).

53 William Holden won for his role in *Stalag 17* (1953), a World War II movie.

54 Marlon Brando scored a major screen triumph in 1954's *On the Waterfront*.

55 Ernest Borgnine won an Oscar for his heart-tugging portrayal of a lonely man in the Best Picture of 1955, *Marty.*

56 Yul Brynner was the stubborn King of Siam in the 1956 musical, *The King and I.*

57 Alec Guinness is shown reading a telegram telling him that he was chosen as Best Actor of 1957 for *The Bridge on the River Kwai.*

58 Debonair David Niven's only Oscar was for *Separate Tables* in 1958.

59 Charlton Heston won an Oscar for his performance in the blockbuster *Ben Hur,* which swept the 1959 Awards.

60 Burt Lancaster was a winner in the filmization of Sinclair Lewis's story, *Elmer Gantry* (1960).

61 Maximilian Schell (far right) won the 1961 Best Actor award for his role in *Judgment at Nuremberg*. He's shown here with George Chakiris, Greer Garson, and Rita Moreno at the 1961 Oscar ceremony.

62 In *To Kill a Mockingbird* (1962) lawyer Gregory Peck defended a black man accused of rape in a small southern town.

63 Sidney Poitier received an Oscar for *Lilies of the Field* in 1963.

64 As Henry Higgins in *My Fair Lady*, British actor Rex Harrison captured the 1964 award.

65 Lee Marvin won in 1965 for his role as a drunken gunfighter in *Cat Ballou*. On Oscar night, he thanked his horse.

66 The *Man for All Seasons* in 1966 was Paul Scofield, who had played Sir Thomas More on stage.

67 In 1967 Rod Steiger played a redneck police chief in *In the Heat of the Night*.

68 Cliff Robertson proved himself in a demanding role as a mentally retarded person in *Charly* (1968).

69 *True Grit* brought John Wayne his only Oscar in 1969.

70 George C. Scott starred as *Patton* in 1970. He turned down the Oscar but it stayed on the books.

71 In *The French Connection* (1971) Gene Hackman played Popeye Doyle, a tough narcotics cop.

72 The title role in *The Godfather* (1972) went to Marlon Brando.

73 Jack Lemmon played a garment executive facing a crisis at midlife in 1973's *Save the Tiger.*

74 After a long career on stage and television, Art Carney won the 1974 Oscar for *Harry and Tonto,* his fourth film.

75 Jack Nicholson was a free-spirited mental patient in *One Flew over the Cuckoo's Nest* (1975).

76 Peter Finch studied television anchorpersons to prepare for his role in *Network,* for which he won the 1976 award posthumously.

77 Richard Dreyfuss co-starred with Marsha Mason in *The Goodbye Girl* in 1977.

1975

Jack Nicl
  Cucko
Walter M
  Boys, N
Al Pacinc
  Warne
Maximili
  Glass I
  tre Dis
James W
  Harry!

1976

Peter Fi:
Robert L
  Colum
Giancarl
  ties, C
William
  UA
Sylveste

1977

Richard
  Girl,
Woody

78 As a Vietnam war casualty, Jon Voight won in *Coming Home* (1978), as did co-star Jane Fonda.

79 Dustin Hoffman portrayed a father fighting for custody of his son in *Kramer vs. Kramer* (1979).

80 Robert De Niro won for his portrayal of prizefighter Jake La Motta in *Raging Bull* (1980).

81 Henry Fonda and youthful co-star Doug McKeon showed how generations touch each other in *On Golden Pond* (1981).

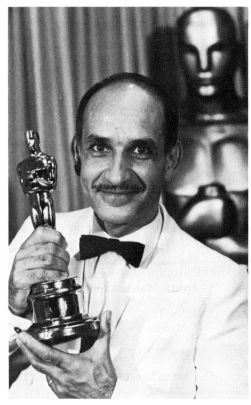

82 Stage actor Ben Kingsley won an Oscar for his first film appearance, as the Indian spiritual and political leader *Gandhi* (1982).

CHAPTER 5

Best Actress Awards

Winners of the Best Actress award project a quality suggested by the title of one of Glenda Jackson's winning films: *A Touch of Class* (1972).

The appeal they share has many components. One of Ingrid Bergman's first directors observed some of them in her performances: "She always moved with wonderful grace and self-control. She spoke her lines beautifully and her radiant beauty struck me the first time I saw her. She appreciated compliments, accepted them shyly, but never altered the three totally original characteristics of her work: truth, naturalness, and fantasy."

Consider the other winning actresses, particularly those who, like Bergman and Jackson, won more than once: Bette Davis, Olivia De Havilland, Jane Fonda, Katharine Hepburn, Vivien Leigh, Luise Rainer, and Elizabeth Taylor. They radiate the same stylish appeal. It is a quality that is much more than sensual. The Jean Har-

lows and Marilyn Monroes have not been nominated. Even such actresses as heartbreakingly beautiful as Audrey Hepburn have needed more than looks to win Academy Awards.

"Women, I think, liked me before men," Bergman once said. "And men identified me with their wives, their mothers, their sisters." She was reflecting on the early part of her career when she won the first of three Oscars (two as Best Actress, one as Best Supporting Actress). Her fellow winners shared her dazzling ability to strike chords and win friends throughout various segments of the audience.

While some of the Best Actors were traversing deserts and sailing heavy seas, many of the Best Actresses were exploring the more subtle terrain of the human mind. They fought to retain their sanity or to help someone else find peace in a turbulent world. Joan Fontaine (*Suspicion*, 1941), Ingrid Bergman (*Gaslight*, 1944),

Six-time nominee Greer Garson won her only Oscar for *Mrs. Miniver* (1942).

Luise Rainer won two consecutive Best Actress Oscars for her work in *The Great Ziegfeld* (1936) and *The Good Earth* (1937).

Joanne Woodward (*The Three Faces Of Eve*, 1957), Louise Fletcher (*One Flew Over the Cuckoo's Nest*, 1975), and Meryl Streep (*Sophie's Choice*, 1982) played characters whose vulnerabilities were exposed and whose strengths were rallied in psychological wars.

Others won for portraying women as diverse as a factory worker (Sally Field), a Southern belle (Vivien Leigh), a cabaret singer (Liza Minnelli), and a saint (Jennifer Jones). Each role demanded high intelligence and rare grace.

A dozen women have been awarded the Best Actress honor after the age of 40, and nine have won more than once. Many have enjoyed careers that have been as long as they have been prosperous. In their own personalities, as well as in the characters they portray, the Best Actresses prove strong-willed, capable, and self-reliant.

"In this business you go on to the next film, or play, or whatever, and it's almost like starting from scratch every time," said winner Faye Dunaway (*Network*, 1976). "Winning an Oscar doesn't mean you can

Ingrid Bergman's won many laurels for her acting, including two Best Actress awards (for *Gaslight* and *Anastasia*) and a Best Supporting Actress award (for *Murder on the Orient Express*) from the Academy.

Oscar-winning actress Jennifer Jones as she appeared in the 1955 classic, *Love Is a Many Splendored Thing*

Coal Miner's Daughter, the rags-to-riches biography of country singer Loretta Lynn, turned Sissy Spacek into 1981's Best Actress. Spacek was also nominated in 1976 for *Carrie.*

rest on your laurels. . . . An Oscar is something that becomes part of your record, a tangible acknowledgment that your efforts have made a difference."

Ann Magnani gleefully displayed a telegram from the Academy informing her that she had been named the Best Actress of 1955 for her role in *The Rose Tattoo.*

The 1958 classic, *I Want to Live!*, was based on the true story of convicted murderess Barbara Graham and won Susan Hayward her first Oscar in a leading role.

*J*anet Gaynor won the first award for Best Actress in 1927-28 for playing a woman of questionable virtue in *Seventh Heaven*. She appeared to be a prostitute but, given a chance, she proved to be virtuous. She was the first Oscar-winning "good bad girl." The type has fascinated audiences and Academy voters for decades. Winning roles for women often involve the complex issue of sexuality. Prostitutes with hearts of gold and adulterers with good intentions have proved to be favorite roles of the Academy voters.

Jane Fonda, Susan Hayward, and Elizabeth Taylor won for sympathetic portrayals of prostitutes. Judy Holliday and Simone Signoret played mistresses. Julie Christie and Glenda Jackson depicted women who were involved in affairs.

Always, these "sinners" had redeeming grace. Many psychologists have contended that the noble but seductive woman combines two male fantasies: the woman who is good in bed and the woman who is morally good as well.

From Hollywood's standpoint, this image was not entirely sexist. The

The Good Bad Girls

Elizabeth Taylor, as a high-class prostitute wanting to go straight, was romanced by Laurence Harvey in the 1960 film, *Butterfield 8.*

In 1961 Laurence Harvey did some seducing of his own with Simone Signoret in *Room at the Top.*

Glenda Jackson and George Segal were an unlikely couple in *A Touch of Class,* but the film brought Jackson the Best Actress award of 1973.

Cloris Leachman portrayed an adultress in *The Last Picture Show* in 1971.

multi-dimensional women refused to be passive victims; they took responsibility for their lives. But the moviemakers had an even simpler motive for creating "good bad girl" types: It was a neat way to slip a spicy plot past the censors.

"The Great Kate" during a rare, relaxed moment in her Seattle hotel room in 1951

Arriving in London in 1958, Hepburn turned to the photographer and said, "You must have made an awful lot of pictures of this raincoat in the last 25 years."

As an Oscar-winning performer, Katharine Hepburn is the champion, unequaled, and many would say, unrivaled. In a career that has spanned a half-century, she has captured four Best Actress awards and eight other Best Actress nominations.

Hepburn's style is an elegant sort of tough femininity. She wears tennis shoes and pants; she lives independently; and she emphatically chooses career instead of family. But her cultivated accent and graceful gestures forever mark her as a lady.

In two score films she has handled with authority roles ranging from screwball comedy to costume spectacle. Her arrogant dignity puts her in charge of every scene in which she appears. The essence of her art is control.

"I hope I'm like old wood," Hepburn told an interviewer from *Look*. "Some people are like boxes made out of jewels or of beads. I prefer things made of plainer materials. . . . I suppose it's nice to see things gussied up for a change, but only for a change. I think the same is true of acting, don't you?"

She co-starred with her longtime friend, Spencer

The Great Kate

Although she's won four Best Actress Oscars and nine other nominations, Hepburn's first appearance at the Academy Awards was in 1974 to present the Irving G. Thalberg Award to producer Lawrence Weingarten.

Hepburn and director George Cukor are shown taking a stroll on location near London while filming *The Corn Is Green*. Hepburn and Cukor have been making films together since 1932.

Always the free spirit, Hepburn is shown here in 1968 departing for the studio on her bicycle in southern France.

Tracy, in nine films. In two of her nominated roles, *The African Queen* (1951) and *Summertime* (1955), she excelled in portrayals of unmarried women who conveyed the strength—though of course not the superstardom—of her own unmarried status.

Tracy received nine nominations and two Oscars himself, but the two friends were nominated for the same film only once. It was *Guess Who's Coming to Dinner* (1967), completed only weeks before Tracy's death.

Hepburn missed the Oscar ceremonies that honored her for *Morning Glory* (1932-33), *Guess Who's Coming to Dinner* (1967), *The Lion in Winter* (1968), and *On Golden Pond* (1981). Her one appearance at the awards came in 1974. She wanted to honor Thalberg Award winner Lawrence Weingarten, who had produced *Adam's Rib* (1950). At the very sight of Hepburn, a special thrill seemed to sweep through the audience, as it gave a long standing ovation to a living legend.

"I couldn't, except with laughter, think of myself as a legend," Hepburn once said. "If I've lasted damn near 50 years now in the movie business—and that's quite a triumph—well, then I say I think I was born at a time that was enormously suitable for my personality."

27–28 Janet Gaynor won for *Seventh Heaven* (1927), *Sunrise* (1927), and *Street Angel* (1928). Her *Seventh Heaven* co-star was Charles Farrell.

28–29 "America's Sweetheart," Mary Pickford, won for *Coquette* in 1929.

29–30 In 1930 Norma Shearer received an Oscar for her performance in *The Divorcee*.

30–31 Marie Dressler won for *Min and Bill* (1930), an early talkie.

31–32 Academy founder Louis B. Mayer presented Helen Hayes with the 1932 Best Actress award for *The Sin of Madelon Claudet*.

Best Actress

1927-1982

32-33 Katharine Hepburn received the first of 12 nominations in 1933 and her first Oscar—for *Morning Glory*, co-starring with Adolphe Menjou.

34 Runaway heiress Claudette Colbert fell in love with tough reporter Clark Gable in *It Happened One Night* (1934).

35 Bette Davis received a 1935 Oscar for *Dangerous* at the same banquet at which Victor McLaglen received his for *The Informer*.

36 Luise Rainer co-starred with William Powell in the 1936 musical, *The Great Ziegfeld.*

37 Luise Rainer won again in 1937, this time for *The Good Earth,* in which she co-starred with Paul Muni (right).

38 Bette Davis won her second Oscar as the tempestuous southern belle, *Jezebel* (1938).

39 Vivien Leigh played a different tempestuous southern belle, Scarlett O'Hara, in *Gone with the Wind* (1939). Evelyn Keyes (left) played Scarlett's sister, Sue Ellen.

40 Ginger Rogers was *Kitty Foyle* in the 1940 love story.

41 Joan Fontaine competed with her sister, Olivia De Havilland, for the 1941 Oscar. Fontaine won it for the Hitchcock film, *Suspicion*.

42 Greer Garson co-starred with Walter Pidgeon in *Mrs. Miniver*, the story of an English family coping with World War II.

43 For her performance in *The Song of Bernadette*, Jennifer Jones received the 1943 Oscar.

44 Ingrid Bergman was Best Actress of 1944 for her portrayal of a wife being driven crazy by dastardly Charles Boyer in *Gaslight*.

45 Joan Crawford was successful businesswoman *Mildred Pierce* in 1945.

46 Olivia De Havilland's Oscar for *To Each His Own* (1946) was presented to her by Ray Milland.

47 Loretta Young was Best Actress of 1947 for the comedy, *The Farmer's Daughter*.

48 The challenging role of a young deaf mute earned Jane Wyman the award for *Johnny Belinda* (1948).

49 Olivia De Havilland won her second Oscar for her portrayal of *The Heiress* in 1949.

50 Judy Holliday was the quintessential dumb blonde in *Born Yesterday* (1950).

51 Vivien Leigh earned her second Oscar for *A Streetcar Named Desire* (1951).

52 Stage veteran Shirley Booth captured the Oscar for her performance in *Come Back, Little Sheba* in 1952.

53 In *Roman Holiday* (1953) Audrey Hepburn was a princess who yearned for a normal life.

54 Grace Kelly won the 1954 Oscar for *The Country Girl.*

55 Anna Magnani was a widow who fell for Burt Lancaster in the 1955 film, *The Rose Tattoo.*

56 In 1956 Ingrid Bergman co-starred with Yul Brynner in *Anastasia* and won her second Oscar.

57 Playing a schizophrenic earned Joanne Woodward the 1957 Oscar for *The Three Faces of Eve.*

58 Susan Hayward was framed and sentenced to death in the 1958 film, *I Want to Live!*

59 Simone Signoret co-starred with Laurence Harvey in *Room at the Top*.

60 Elizabeth Taylor won her first Oscar for her role as a high-class prostitute in *Butterfield 8* (1960).

61 Sophia Loren starred as an Italian mother raped by Allied soldiers in World War II in *Two Women* (1961).

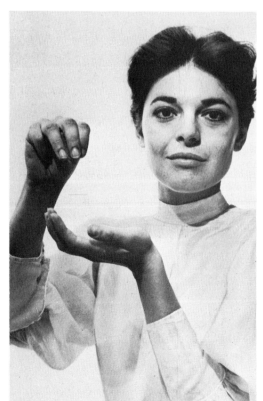

62 Anne Bancroft recreated for the screen her Broadway role in *The Miracle Worker* and won the 1962 Oscar.

63 Best Actress honors went to Patricia Neal in 1963 for her performance in *Hud*.

64 Julie Andrews was the perfect nanny as *Mary Poppins* in 1964.

65 British actress Julie Christie, winner for her performance in *Darling*, posed with Best Actor winner Lee Marvin at the 1965 awards ceremony.

66 In 1966 Elizabeth Taylor co-starred with then-husband Richard Burton in *Who's Afraid of Virginia Woolf?*, a film that broke Hollywood taboos for adult material.

67 Katharine Hepburn and Spencer Tracy (right) teamed up a final time in *Guess Who's Coming to Dinner* (1967). Also pictured are Sidney Poitier and Katharine Houghton.

68 Katharine Hepburn, co-starring with Peter O'Toole as Eleanor of Aquitaine in *Lion in Winter*, and Barbra Streisand, as *Funny Girl*, tied for the Best Actress award in 1968.

69 For playing an Edinburgh schoolteacher in *The Prime of Miss Jean Brodie*, Maggie Smith was Best Actress of 1969.

70 Glenda Jackson's first Oscar came for *Women in Love* (1970).

71 In 1971 Jane Fonda played a prostitute in *Klute* and won her first Oscar.

72 Liza Minnelli belted out songs in the 1972 film *Cabaret,*, which was based on the Broadway musical.

73 *A Touch of Class* is what Glenda Jackson had in the 1973 film.

74 Ellen Burstyn and Kris Kristofferson teamed up in *Alice Doesn't Live Here Anymore* in 1974.

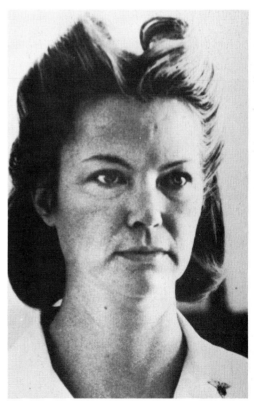

75 Louise Fletcher won as the villainous Nurse Ratched in *One Flew over the Cuckoo's Nest* (1975).

76 In 1976 Faye Dunaway was a ruthless programming executive in *Network.*

77 Woody Allen's real-life girlfriend Diane Keaton was *Annie Hall (1977).* The Allen movie won four Oscars.

78 Jane Fonda fell for a paraplegic Vietnam veteran (Jon Voight) in *Coming Home* (1978) and won her second Oscar.

79 In 1979 Sally Field won for her portrayal of union activist *Norma Rae.*

80 Sissy Spacek was *The Coal Miner's Daughter* (1980), a film based on country singer Loretta Lynn's autobiography.

81 Katharine Hepburn won her fourth Best Actress award in 1981, this time for *On Golden Pond*.

82 Meryl Streep was highly praised for her 1982 portrayal of a Catholic Pole who survived a Nazi prison camp in *Sophie's Choice*. She's shown here on Oscar night with two other winners, Richard Attenborough and Ben Kingsley.

1927-28

Janet Gaynor in *Seventh Heaven*,
Fox
Janet Gaynor in *Street Angel*, Fox
Janet Gaynor in *Sunrise*, Fox
Louise Dresser in *A Ship Comes In*,
RKO Radio
Gloria Swanson in *Sadie Thompson*,
United Artists

1928-29

Mary Pickford in *Coquette*, UA
Ruth Chatterton in *Madame X*,
Metro-Goldwyn-Mayer
Betty Compson in *The Barker*, First
National
Jeanne Eagels in *The Letter*, Para-
mount
Bessie Love in *The Broadway
Melody*, MGM

1929-30

Norma Shearer in *The Divorcee*,
MGM
Nancy Carroll in *The Devil's
Holiday*, Paramount
Ruth Chatterton in *Sarah and Son*,
Paramount
Greta Garbo in *Anna Christie*, MGM
Greta Garbo in *Romance*, MGM
Norma Shearer in *Their Own Desire*,
MGM
Gloria Swanson in *The Trespasser*,
UA

1930-31

Marie Dressler in *Min and Bill*,
MGM
Marlene Dietrich in *Morocco*, Para-
mount
Irene Dunne in *Cimarron*, RKO
Radio
Ann Harding in *Holiday*, RKO-Pathe
Norma Shearer in *A Free Soul*,
MGM

1931-32

Helen Hayes in *The Sin of Madelon
Clauder*, MGM
Marie Dressler in *Emma*, MGM
Lynn Fontanne in *The Guardsman*,
MGM

1932-33

Katharine Hepburn in *Morning
Glory*, RKO Radio
May Robson in *Lady for a Day*, Co-
lumbia
Diana Wynyard in *Cavalcade*, Fox

1934

Claudette Colbert in *It Happened
One Night*, Columbia
Grace Moore in *One Night of Love*,
Columbia
Norma Shearer in *The Barretts of
Wimpole Street*, MGM

1935

Bette Davis in *Dangerous*, Warner
Bros.
Elisabeth Bergner in *Escape Me Nev-
er*, UA (British)
Claudette Colbert in *Private Worlds*,
Paramount
Katharine Hepburn in *Alice Adams*,
RKO Radio
Merle Oberon in *The Dark Angel*,
Samuel Goldwyn Studios-UA

1936

Luise Rainer in *The Great Ziegfeld*,
MGM
Irene Dunne in *Theodora Goes Wild*,
Columbia
Gladys George in *Valiant Is the
Word for Carrie*, Paramount
Carole Lombard in *My Man Godfrey*,
Universal
Norma Shearer in *Romeo and Juliet*,
MGM

1937

Luise Rainer in *The Good Earth*,
MGM
Irene Dunne in *The Awful Truth*, Co-
lumbia
Greta Garbo in *Camille*, MGM
Janet Gaynor in *A Star Is Born*, UA
Barbara Stanwyck in *Stella Dallas*,
Goldwyn-UA

1938

Bette Davis in *Jezebel*, Warner Bros.
Fay Bainter in *White Banners*, War-
ner Bros.
Wendy Hiller in *Pygmalion*, MGM
(British)
Norma Shearer in *Marie Antoinette*,
MGM
Margaret Sullavan in *Three Com-
rades*, MGM

1939

Vivien Leigh in *Gone with the Wind*,
MGM
Bette Davis in *Dark Victory*, Warner
Bros.
Irene Dunne in *Love Affair*, RKO
Radio

Greta Garbo in *Ninotchka*, MGM
Greer Garson in *Goodbye, Mr. Chips*,
MGM (British)

1940

Ginger Rogers in *Kitty Foyle*, RKO
Radio
Bette Davis in *The Letter*, Warner
Bros.
Joan Fontaine in *Rebecca*, UA
Katharine Hepburn in *The Philadel-
phia Story*, MGM
Martha Scott in *Our Town*, UA

1941

Joan Fontaine in *Suspicion*, RKO
Radio
Bette Davis in *The Little Foxes*,
Goldwyn-RKO Radio
Olivia De Havilland in *Hold Back
the Dawn*, Paramount
Greer Garson in *Blossoms in the
Dust*, MGM
Barbara Stanwyck in *Ball of Fire*,
Goldwyn-RKO Radio

1942

Greer Garson in *Mrs. Miniver*, MGM
Bette Davis in *Now, Voyager*, War-
ner Bros.
Katharine Hepburn in *Woman of the
Year*, MGM
Rosalind Russell in *My Sister Eileen*,
Columbia
Theresa Wright in *The Pride of the
Yankees*, Goldwyn-RKO Radio

1943

Jennifer Jones in *The Song of Ber-
nadette*, 20th C.-Fox
Jean Arthur in *The More the Merrier*,
Columbia
Ingrid Bergman in *For Whom the
Bell Tolls*, Paramount
Joan Fontaine in *The Constant
Nymph*, Warner Bros.
Greer Garson in *Madame Curie*,
MGM

1944

Ingrid Bergman in *Gaslight*, MGM
Claudette Colbert in *Since You Went
Away*, UA
Bette Davis in *Mr. Skeffington*, War-
ner Bros.
Greer Garson in *Mrs. Parkington*,
MGM
Barbara Stanwyck in *Double In-
demnity*, Paramount

Best Actresses

1945

Joan Crawford in *Mildred Pierce*, Warner Bros.
Ingrid Bergman in *The Bells of St. Mary's*, RKO Radio
Greer Garson in *The Valley of Decision*, MGM
Jennifer Jones in *Love Letters*, Paramount
Gene Tierney in *Leave Her to Heaven*, 20th C.-Fox

1946

Olivia De Havilland in *To Each His Own*, Paramount
Celia Johnson in *Brief Encounter*, Universal-International (British)
Jennifer Jones in *Duel in the Sun*, Selznick International
Rosalind Russell in *Sister Kenny*, RKO Radio
Jane Wyman in *The Yearling*, MGM

1947

Loretta Young in *The Farmer's Daughter*, RKO Radio
Joan Crawford in *Possessed*, Warner Bros.
Susan Hayward in *Smash Up—the Story of a Woman*, U-I
Dorothy McGuire in *Gentleman's Agreement*, 20th C.-Fox
Rosalind Russell in *Mourning Becomes Electra*, RKO Radio

1948

Jane Wyman in *Johnny Belinda*, Warner Bros.
Ingrid Bergman in *Joan of Arc*, RKO Radio
Olivia De Havilland in *The Snake Pit*, 20th C.-Fox
Irene Dunne in *I Remember Mama*, RKO Radio
Barbara Stanwyck in *Sorry, Wrong Number*, Paramount

1949

Olivia De Havilland in *The Heiress*, Paramount
Jeanne Crain in *Pinky*, 20th C.-Fox
Susan Hayward in *My Foolish Heart*, RKO Radio
Deborah Kerr in *Edward, My Son*, MGM
Loretta Young in *Come to the Stable*, 20th C.-Fox

1950

Judy Holliday in *Born Yesterday*, Columbia
Anne Baxter in *All about Eve*, 20th C.-Fox
Bette Davis in *All about Eve*, 20th C.-Fox
Eleanor Parker in *Caged*, Warner Bros.
Gloria Swanson in *Sunset Boulevard*, Paramount

1951

Vivien Leigh in *A Streetcar Named Desire*, Warner Bros.
Katharine Hepburn in *The African Queen*, UA
Eleanor Parker in *Detective Story*, Paramount
Shelley Winters in *A Place in the Sun*, Paramount
Jane Wyman in *The Blue Veil*, RKO Radio

1952

Shirley Booth in *Come Back Little Sheba*, Paramount
Joan Crawford in *Sudden Fear*, RKO Radio
Bette Davis in *The Star*, 20th C.-Fox
Julie Harris in *The Member of the Wedding*, Columbia
Susan Hayward in *With a Song in My Heart*, 20th C.-Fox

1953

Audrey Hepburn in *Roman Holiday*, Paramount
Leslie Caron in *Lili*, MGM
Ava Gardner in *Mogamba*, MGM
Deborah Kerr in *From Here to Eternity*, Columbia
Maggie McNamara in *The Moon Is Blue*, UA

1954

Grace Kelly in *The Country Girl*, Paramount
Dorothy Dandridge in *Carmen Jones*, 20th C.-Fox
Judy Garland in *A Star Is Born*, Warner Bros.
Audrey Hepburn in *Sabrina*, Paramount
Jane Wyman in *The Magnificent Obsession*, U-I

1955

Anna Magnani in *The Rose Tattoo*, Paramount
Susan Hayward in *I'll Cry Tomorrow*, MGM
Katharine Hepburn in *Summertime*, UA
Jennifer Jones in *Love Is a Many Splendored Thing*, 20th C.-Fox
Eleanor Parker in *Interrupted Melody*, MGM

1956

Ingrid Bergman in *Anastasia*, 20th C.-Fox
Carroll Baker in *Baby Doll*, Warner Bros.
Katharine Hepburn in *The Rainmaker*, Paramount
Nancy Kelly in *The Bad Seed*, Warner Bros.
Deborah Kerr in *The King and I*, 20th C.-Fox

1957

Joanne Woodward in *The Three Faces of Eve*, 20th C.-Fox
Deborah Kerr in *Heaven Knows, Mr. Allison*, 20th C.-Fox
Anna Magnani in *Wild Is the Wind*, Paramount
Elizabeth Taylor in *Raintree Country*, MGM
Lana Turner in *Peyton Place*, 20th C.-Fox

1958

Susan Hayward in *I Want to Live!*, UA
Deborah Kerr in *Separate Tables*, UA
Shirley MacLaine in *Some Came Running*, MGM
Rosalind Russell in *Auntie Mame*, Warner Bros.
Elizabeth Taylor in *Cat on a Hot Tin Roof*, MGM

1959

Simone Signoret in *Room at the Top*, Continental Dist., Inc. (British)
Doris Day in *Pillow Talk*, U-I
Audrey Hepburn in *The Nun's Story*, Warner Bros.
Katharine Hepburn in *Suddenly, Last Summer*, Columbia
Elizabeth Taylor in *Suddenly, Last Summer*, Columbia

1960

Elizabeth Taylor in *Butterfield 8*, MGM
Greer Garson in *Sunrise at Campobello*, Warner Bros.
Deborah Kerr in *The Sundowners*, Warner Bros.
Shirley MacLaine in *The Apartment*, UA
Melina Mercouri in *Never on Sunday*, Lopert Pictures Corp. (Greek)

1961

Sophia Loren in *Two Women*, Embassy Pictures Corp. (Italo-French)
Audrey Hepburn in *Breakfast at Tiffany's*, Paramount
Piper Laurie in *The Hustler*, 20th C.-Fox
Geraldine Page in *Summer and Smoke*, Paramount
Natalie Wood in *Splendor in the Grass*, Warner Bros.

1962

Anne Bancroft in *The Miracle Worker*, UA
Bette Davis in *What Ever Happened to Baby Jane?*, Warner Bros.
Katharine Hepburn in *Long Day's Journey into Night*, Embassy Pictures
Geraldine Page in *Sweet Bird of Youth*, MGM
Lee Remick in *Days of Wine and Roses*, Warner Bros.

1963

Patricia Neal in *Hud*, Paramount
Leslie Caron in *The L-Shaped Room*, Columbia
Shirley MacLaine in *Irma La Douce*, UA
Rachel Roberts in *This Sporting Life*, Walter Reade-Sterling-Continental Dist.
Natalie Wood in *Love with the Proper Stranger*, Paramount

1964

Julie Andrews in *Mary Poppins*, Walt Disney Productions
Anne Bancroft in *The Pumpkin Eater*, Royal Films International
Sophia Loren in *Marriage Italian Style*, Embassy Pictures
Debbie Reynolds in *The Unsinkable Molly Brown*, MGM
Kim Stanley in *Seance on a Wet Afternoon*, Artixo Prods., Ltd.

1965

Julie Christie in *Darling*, Embassy
Julie Andrews in *The Sound of Music*, 20th C.-Fox
Samantha Eggar in *The Collector*, Columbia
Elizabeth Hartman in *A Patch of Blue*, MGM
Simone Signoret in *Ship of Fools*, Columbia

1966

Elizabeth Taylor in *Who's Afraid of Virginia Woolf?*, Warner Bros.
Anouk Aimee in *A Man and a Woman*, Allied Artists
Ida Kaminska in *The Shop on Main Street*, Prominent Films
Lynn Redgrave in *Georgy Girl*, Columbia
Vanessa Redgrave in *Morgan*, Cinema V

1967

Katharine Hepburn in *Guess Who's Coming to Dinner*, Columbia
Anne Bancroft in *The Graduate*, Embassy
Faye Dunaway in *Bonnie and Clyde*, Warner Bros.-Seven Arts
Dame Edith Evans in *The Whisperers*, UA
Audrey Hepburn in *Wait until Dark*, Warner Bros.-Seven Arts

1968

Katharine Hepburn in *The Lion in Winter*, Avco Embassy (*tie*)
Barbra Streisand in *Funny Girl*, Columbia (*tie*)
Patricia Neal in *The Subject Was Roses*, MGM
Vanessa Redgrave in *Isadora*, Universal
Joanne Woodward in *Rachel, Rachel*, Warner Bros.-Seven Arts

1969

Maggie Smith in *The Prime of Miss Jean Brodie*, 20th C.-Fox
Genevieve Bujold in *Anne of the Thousand Days*, Universal
Jane Fonda in *They Shoot Horses, Don't They?*, Cinerama
Liza Minnelli in *The Sterile Cuckoo*, Paramount
Jean Simmons in *The Happy Ending*, UA

1970

Glenda Jackson in *Women in Love*, UA
Jane Alexander in *The Great White Hope*, 20th C.-Fox
Ali MacGraw in *Love Story*, Paramount
Sarah Miles in *Ryan's Daughter*, MGM
Carrie Snodgrass in *Diary of a Mad Housewife*, Universal

1971

Jane Fonda in *Klute*, Warner Bros.
Julie Christie in *McCabe & Mrs. Miller*, Warner Bros.
Glenda Jackson in *Sunday Bloody Sunday*, UA
Vanessa Redgrave in *Mary, Queen of Scots*, Universal
Janet Suzman in *Nicholas and Alexandra*, Columbia

1972

Liza Minnelli in *Cabaret*, Allied Artists
Diana Ross in *Lady Sings the Blues*, Paramount
Maggie Smith in *Travels with My Aunt*, MGM
Cicely Tyson in *Sounder*, 20th C.-Fox
Liv Ullmann in *The Emigrants*, Warner Bros.

1973

Glenda Jackson in *A Touch of Class*, Avco Embassy
Ellen Burstyn in *The Exorcist*, Warner Bros.
Marsha Mason in *Cinderella Liberty*, 20th C.-Fox
Barbra Streisand in *The Way We Were*, Columbia
Joanne Woodward in *Summer Wishes, Winter Dreams*, Columbia

1974

Ellen Burstyn in *Alice Doesn't Live Here Anymore*, Warner Bros.
Diahann Carroll in *Claudine*, 20th C.-Fox
Faye Dunaway in *Chinatown*, Paramount
Valerie Perrine in *Lenny*, UA
Gena Rowlands in *A Woman under the Influence*, Faces International Films

1975

Louise Fletcher in *One Flew over the Cuckoo's Nest*, UA
Isabelle Adjani in *The Story of Adele H.*, New World Pictures
Ann-Margret in *Tommy*, Columbia
Glenda Jackson in *Hedda*, Brut Productions
Carol Kane in *Hester Street*, Midwest Film Productions

1976

Faye Dunaway in *Network*, MGM
Marie-Christine Barrault in *Cousin, Cousine*, Northal Film Distributors Ltd. (French)
Talia Shire in *Rocky*, UA
Sissy Spacek in *Carrie*, UA
Liv Ullmann in *Face to Face*, Paramount

1977

Diane Keaton in *Annie Hall*, UA
Anne Bancroft in *The Turning Point*, 20th C.-Fox
Jane Fonda in *Julia*, 20th C.-Fox

Shirley MacLaine in *The Turning Point*, 20th C.-Fox
Marsha Mason in *The Goodbye Girl*, Warner Bros.

1978

Jane Fonda in *Coming Home*, UA
Ingrid Bergman in *Autumn Sonata*
Ellen Burstyn in *Same Time Next Year*
Geraldine Page in *Interiors*, UA
Jill Clayburgh in *An Unmarried Woman*, 20th C.-Fox

1979

Sally Field in *Norma Rae*, 20th C.-Fox
Jill Clayburgh in *Starting Over*
Jane Fonda in *The China Syndrome*
Marsha Mason in *Chapter Two*
Bette Midler in *The Rose*

1980

Sissy Spacek in *Coal Miner's Daughter*, Universal
Ellen Burstyn in *Resurrection*

Goldie Hawn in *Private Benjamin*
Mary Tyler Moore in *Ordinary People*, Paramount
Gena Rowlands in *Gloria*

1981

Katharine Hepburn in *On Golden Pond*, Universal
Diane Keaton in *Reds*, Paramount
Marsha Mason in *Only When I Laugh*
Susan Sarandon in *Atlantic City*, Paramount
Meryl Streep in *The French Lieutenant's Woman*

1982

Meryl Streep in *Sophie's Choice*
Julie Andrews in *Victor/Victoria*
Jessica Lange in *Frances*
Sissy Spacek in *Missing*, Universal
Debra Winger in *An Officer and a Gentleman*

A young Jane Wyman was honored for her performance of the role of a young deaf mute in *Johnny Belinda* (1948).

CHAPTER 6

Best Director Awards

Those who have won the Oscar for Best Director, have been winners at the box office as well as winners at the awards ceremonies. Their movies are clear and to the point. They consistently connect with audiences.

Like four-time winner John Ford, most of the winning directors spurned artsy tricks and philosophical theories about technique. "Directing is a craft," Ford said. "If a director's films do not make money, he cannot expect to retain the confidence and good will of the men who put up with the wherewithal." A string of commercially successful films brought Ford the freedom to do a project that was dear to his heart. "I waited four years to do *The Informer* (1935) and got the chance only after every sort of hesitation," he said. This personally expressive film brought him his first Oscar.

Like Ford, several other successful directors have been repeatedly successful.

Thirteen others have won the Directing award more than once: Frank Borzage, Frank Capra, Elia Kazan, David Lean, Frank Lloyd, Joseph L. Mankiewicz, Leo McCarey, Lewis Milestone, George Stevens, Billy Wilder, Robert Wise, William Wyler, and Fred Zinnemann. Together they have earned 32 Best Director awards and a total of 40 nominations. There are more repeat winners in Directing than in any other Oscar category.

The Best Directors directed films of many and various genres. Frank Capra directed sentimental comedies (*It Happened One Night* in 1934, *Mr. Deeds Goes to Washington* in 1936, and *You Can't Take It with You* in 1938). Elia Kazan dealt with social issue dramas in *Gentleman's Agreement* in 1947 and *On the Waterfront* in 1954. David Lean's spectacles, *The Bridge on the River Kwai* in 1957 and *Lawrence of Arabia* in 1962, won the Directing award, as did Robert Wise's musicals,

A four-time winner in the Best Director category, John Ford received his first Oscar in 1935 for *The Informer*.

Director George Stevens is shown rehearsing a scene from *The Diary of Anne Frank* (1959) with actress Millie Perkins. He was nominated for his work on this film, and received Academy Awards for two earlier films, *A Place in the Sun* (1951) and *Giant* (1956).

Director Robert Wise won the Best Director Oscar for two musicals—*West Side Story* (1961) and *The Sound of Music* (1965).

Three-time winner William Wyler was nominated four times before receiving three Oscars for Best Director—for *Mrs. Miniver (1942), The Best Years of Our Lives* (1946), and *Ben Hur* (1959). He is shown here during the shooting of desert scenes for *Ben Hur*.

With one Oscar already under his belt, Fred Zinnemann (left) went on to be voted the Best Director of 1966 for *A Man for All Seasons*. Paul Scofield starred as Sir Thomas More.

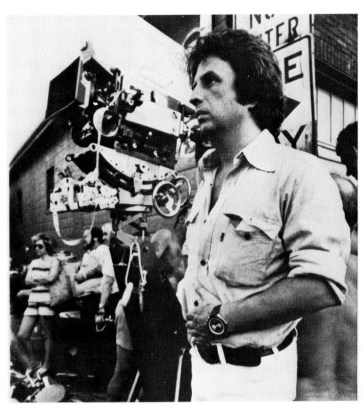

Michael Cimino's directorial work on *The Deer Hunter* brought him a 1978 Oscar. Cimino co-wrote and co-produced as well as directed the film, which was also named Best Picture of 1978.

The director of the Best Picture usually wins the Best Director Award, and 1982 was no exception. At the 55th annual Academy Awards ceremony, Richard Attenborough was named Best Director and his film, *Gandhi,* was named Best Picture.

West Side Story in 1961 and *The Sound of Music* in 1965.

While many top-grossing films have won, box office receipts alone will not guarantee the prestigious statuette. Nor is critical praise from the reviewers enough. It takes a winning combination.

The secret is a significant message, clearly expressed. Most of the time the Directing award has gone to the director of the Best Picture. Only 15 times in Oscar history and only twice since 1957 (in 1972 and 1981) has someone other than the director of the Best Picture been given the award.

If the Best Picture and the Best Director awards are often redundant, the Academy wants it to be so. The honors to directors signify special, individual recognition that the Academy members want to give to the skilled craftsmen/managers/artists who bring the movies together.

"The Academy Award is most valuable because it is dearly won," George Cukor, the winning director of *My Fair Lady* (1964), said. "It is an expert, professional judgment, at once the most merciless and, sometimes, the most amazingly generous. . . . Mine seemed to be an inordinately long time coming but when at last I got it, it meant more to me than any other award I have ever received."

Annie Hall (1977), **which Woody Allen directed, co-wrote, and starred in, won both Best Picture and Best Directing awards. Allen avoided the awards ceremony, however, in favor of Michael's Pub on New York's East Side, where he often sits in on the clarinet.**

*M*any actors believe they can direct a picture better than a director. And some can. At least the Academy voters have thought so three times since 1977 when they selected as best directors men widely known as actors.

Comic Woody Allen won the Best Director award for *Annie Hall* (1977), the movie he directed. He was nominated again the next year for *Interiors.*

Robert Redford won the Best Director Oscar for the first film he directed, *Ordinary People* (1980). Only one other director, Delbert Mann (*Marty,* 1955), has won for a first effort.

Warren Beatty won for his second directorial effort, *Reds* (1981). For his first, *Heaven Can Wait* (1978), he had been nominated in four categories—writing, producing, directing and acting—matching Orson Welles' four nominations for *Citizen Kane* (1941).

As different as these actor-directors are, they do share two instinctive gifts: They know how to pick the right cast, and they know how to elicit fine performances from their fellow actors. In addition to winning Best Director Oscars, *Annie Hall, Ordinary*

Acting Directors

Warren Beatty both starred in and directed *Reds* in 1981. Beatty and co-star Diane Keaton (left) were both nominated for their performances in leading roles (as John Reed and Louise Bryant), and Beatty joyfully accepted the Best Director Oscar for his first directorial effort.

Mary Tyler Moore called Robert Redford the best director she'd ever worked with. He directed her in the 1980 film, *Ordinary People.*

People, and *Heaven Can Wait* received a total of nine nominations for acting excellence.

Most directors have had some acting experience whether on stage, like Oscar winner Mike Nichols (*The Graduate*, 1967), or in the movies, like John Huston (*Key Largo*, 1948). A few, such as Alfred Hitchcock, have made a point of appearing briefly in their own films. A very small number, such as Charlie Chaplin, have written, directed, *and* starred in their own films.

Robert Redford had acted in 23 films and had begun to feel "reduced" by his pretty-boy image, he said, when he took on the challenge of directing *Ordinary People.* For 10 years he had been thinking about directing—and being critical of those who were directing him. "I don't respond to direction," he said, "and, with only a few exceptions, I have not gotten direction that was inspiring." But Redford himself proved inspiring, according to Mary Tyler Moore, one of the stars of *Ordinary People.* She felt "mutual respect" on the set and called him "the best director I've ever worked with."

The number of actors working behind the cameras grew in the 1970s and included stars Clint Eastwood, Burt Reynolds, and Sylvester Stallone. Those who succeeded brought to their job a special sensitivity they had gained as performers.

1927-28

Frank Borzage for *Seventh Heaven*, Fox
Herbert Brenon for *Sorrell and Son*, United Artists
King Vidor for *The Crowd*, Metro-Goldwyn-Mayer
Comedy Direction (not given after this year):
Lewis Milestone for *Two Arabian Knights*, UA
Charles Chaplin for *The Circus*, UA
Ted Wilde for *Speedy*, Paramount

1928-29

Frank Lloyd for *The Divine Lady*, First National
Lionel Barrymore for *Madame X*, MGM
Harry Beaumont for *Broadway Melody*, MGM
Irving Cummings for *In Old Arizona*, Fox
Frank Lloyd for *Weary River*, First National
Frank Lloyd for *Drag*, First National
Ernst Lubitsch for *The Patriot*, Paramount

1929-30

Lewis Milestone for *All Quiet on the Western Front*, Universal
Clarence Brown for *Anna Christie*, MGM
Clarence Brown for *Romance*, MGM
Robert Leonard for *The Divorcee*, MGM
Ernst Lubitsch for *The Love Parade*, Paramount
King Vidor for *Hallelujah*, MGM

1930-31

Norman Taurog for *Skippy*, Paramount
Clarence Brown for *A Free Soul*, MGM
Lewis Milestone for *The Front Page*, UA
Wesley Ruggles for *Cimarron*, RKO Radio
Josef Von Sternberg for *Morocco*, Paramount

1931-32

Frank Borzage for *Bad Girl*, Fox
King Vidor for *The Champ*, MGM
Josef Von Sternberg for *Shanghai Express*, Paramount

Director Frank Lloyd, one of the founders of the Academy, won two early Oscars: one for the 1929 film, *The Divine Lady*, and one for the 1933 film, *Calvacade*.

1932-33

Frank Lloyd for *Cavalcade*, Fox
Frank Capra for *Lady for a Day*, Columbia
George Cukor for *Little Women*, RKO Radio

1934

Frank Capra for *It Happened One Night*, Columbia
Victor Schertzinger for *One Night of Love*, Columbia
W. S. Van Dyke for *The Thin Man*, MGM

1935

John Ford for *The Informer*, RKO Radio
Henry Hathaway for *Lives of a Bengal Lancer*, Paramount
Frank Lloyd for *Mutiny on the Bounty*, MGM

At the fifth Academy Awards banquet in 1932: Best Director Frank Borzage (for *Bad Girl*), Best Actress Helen Hayes (for *The Sin of Madelon Claudet*), and Best Actor Fredric March (for *Dr. Jekyll and Mr. Hyde*).

Best Directors

1936

Frank Capra for *Mr. Deeds Goes to Town*, Columbia
Gregory La Cava for *My Man Godfrey*, Universal
Robert Z. Leonard for *The Great Ziegfeld*, MGM
W. S. Van Dyke for *San Francisco*, MGM
William Wyler for *Dodsworth*, UA

1937

Leo McCarey for *The Awful Truth*, Columbia
William Dieterle for *The Life of Emile Zola*, Warner Bros.
Sidney Franklin for *The Good Earth*, MGM
Gregory La Cava for *Stage Door*, RKO Radio
William Wellman for *A Star Is Born*, UA

1938

Frank Capra for *You Can't Take It with You*, Columbia
Michael Curtiz for *Angels with Dirty Faces*, Warner Bros.
Michael Curtiz for *Four Daughters*, Warner Bros.
Norman Taurog for *Boys Town*, MGM
King Vidor for *The Citadel*, MGM

1939

Victor Fleming for *Gone with the Wind*, MGM
Frank Capra for *Mr. Smith Goes to Washington*, Columbia
John Ford for *Stagecoach*, UA
Sam Wood for *Goodbye, Mr. Chips*, MGM (British)
William Wyler for *Wuthering Heights*, UA

1940

John Ford for *The Grapes of Wrath*, Fox
George Cukor for *The Philadelphia Story*, MGM
Alfred Hitchcock for *Rebecca*, UA
Sam Wood for *Kitty Foyle*, RKO Radio
William Wyler for *The Letter*, Warner Bros.

1941

John Ford for *How Green Was My Valley*, 20th Century-Fox
Alexander Hall for *Here Comes Mr. Jordan*, Columbia
Howard Hawks for *Sergeant York*, Warner Bros.
Orson Welles for *Citizen Kane*, RKO Radio
William Wyler for *The Little Foxes*, RKO Radio

1942

William Wyler for *Mrs. Miniver*, MGM
Michael Curtiz for *Yankee Doodle Dandy*, Warner Bros.
John Farrow for *Wake Island*, Paramount
Mervyn Leroy for *Random Harvest*, MGM
Sam Wood for *King's Row*, Warner Bros.

1943

Michael Curtiz for *Casablanca*, Warner Bros.
Clarence Brown for *The Human Comedy*, MGM
Henry King for *The Song of Bernadette*, 20th C.-Fox
Ernst Lubitsch for *Heaven Can Wait*, 20th C.-Fox
George Stevens for *The More the Merrier*, Columbia

1944

Leo McCarey for *Going My Way*, Paramount
Alfred Hitchcock for *Lifeboat*, 20th C.-Fox
Henry King for *Wilson*, 20th C.-Fox
Otto Preminger for *Laura*, 20th C.-Fox
Billy Wilder for *Double Indemnity*, Paramount

1945

Billy Wilder for *The Lost Weekend*, Paramount
Clarence Brown for *National Velvet*, MGM
Alfred Hitchcock for *Spellbound*, UA
Leo McCarey for *The Bells of St. Mary's*, RKO Radio
Jean Renoir for *The Southerner*, UA

1946

William Wyler for *The Best Years of Our Lives*, RKO Radio
Clarence Brown for *The Yearling*, MGM
Frank Capra for *It's a Wonderful Life*, RKO Radio
David Lean for *Brief Encounter*, U-I (British)
Robert Siodmak for *The Killers*, Universal

1947

Elia Kazan for *Gentleman's Agreement*, 20th C.-Fox
George Cukor for *A Double Life*, U-I
Edward Dmytryk for *Crossfire*, RKO Radio
Henry Koster for *The Bishop's Wife*, RKO Radio
David Lean for *Great Expectations*, U-I (British)

1948

John Huston for *The Treasure of the Sierra Madre*, Warner Bros.
Anatole Litvak for *The Snake Pit*, 20th C.-Fox
Jean Negulesco for *Johnny Belinda*, Warner Bros.
Laurence Olivier for *Hamlet*, U-I (British)
Fred Zinnemann for *The Search*, MGM (Swiss)

1949

Joseph L. Mankiewicz for *A Letter to Three Wives*, 20th C.-Fox
Carol Reed for *The Fallen Idol*, SRO (British)
Robert Rossen for *All the King's Men*, Columbia
William A. Wellman for *Battleground*, MGM
William Wyler for *The Heiress*, Paramount

1950

Joseph L. Mankiewicz for *All about Eve*, 20th C.-Fox
George Cukor for *Born Yesterday*, Columbia
John Huston for *The Asphalt Jungle*, MGM
Carol Reed for *The Third Man*, SRO (British)
Billy Wilder for *Sunset Boulevard*, Paramount

1951

George Stevens for *A Place in the Sun*, Paramount
John Huston for *The African Queen*, UA
Elia Kazan for *A Streetcar Named Desire*, Warner Bros.
Vincente Minnelli for *An American in Paris*, MGM
William Wyler for *Detective Story*, Paramount

1952

John Ford for *The Quiet Man*, Republic
Cecil B. De Mille for *The Greatest Show on Earth*, Paramount
John Huston for *Moulin Rouge*, UA
Joseph L. Mankiewicz for *Five Fingers*, 20th C.-Fox
Fred Zinnemann for *High Noon*, UA

1953

Fred Zinnemann for *From Here to Eternity*, Columbia
George Stevens for *Shane*, Paramount
Charles Walters for *Lili*, MGM
Billy Wilder for *Stalag 17*, Paramount
William Wyler for *Roman Holiday*, Paramount

1954

Elia Kazan for *On the Waterfront*, Columbia
Alfred Hitchcock for *Rear Window*, Paramount
George Seaton for *The Country Girl*, Paramount
William Wellman for *The High and the Mighty*, Warner Bros.
Billy Wilder for *Sabrina*, Paramount

1955

Delbert Mann for *Marty*, UA
Elia Kazan for *East of Eden*, Warner Bros.
David Lean for *Summertime*, UA (Anglo-American)
Joshua Logan for *Picnic*, Columbia
John Sturges for *Bad Day at Black Rock*, MGM

1956

George Stevens for *Giant*, Warner Bros.
Michael Anderson for *Around the World in 80 Days*, UA
Walter Lang for *The King and I*, 20th C.-Fox
King Vidor for *War and Peace*, Paramount (Italo-American)
William Wyler for *Friendly Persuasion*, Allied Artists

1957

David Lean for *The Bridge on the River Kwai*, Columbia
Joshua Logan for *Sayonara*, Warner Bros.
Sidney Lumet for *12 Angry Men*, UA
Mark Robson for *Peyton Place*, 20th C.-Fox
Billy Wilder for *Witness for the Prosecution*, UA

1958

Vincente Minnelli for *Gigi*, MGM
Richard Brooks for *Cat on a Hot Tin Roof*, MGM
Stanley Kramer for *The Defiant Ones*, UA
Mark Robson for *The Inn of the Sixth Happiness*, 20th C.-Fox
Robert Wise for *I Want to Live!*, UA

1959

William Wyler for *Ben Hur*, MGM
Jack Clayton for *Room at the Top*, Romulus Films, Ltd. (British)
George Stevens for *The Diary of Anne Frank*, 20th C.-Fox
Billy Wilder for *Some Like It Hot*, UA
Fred Zinnemann for *The Nun's Story*, Warner Bros.

1960

Billy Wilder for *The Apartment*, UA
Jack Cardiff for *Sons and Lovers*, 20th C.-Fox
Jules Dassin for *Never on Sunday*, Lopert Pictures Corp. (Greek)
Alfred Hitchcock for *Psycho*, Paramount
Fred Zinnemann for *The Sundowners*, Warner Bros.

1961

Jerome Robbins and **Robert Wise** for *West Side Story*, UA
Federico Fellini for *La Dolce Vita*, Astor Pictures, Inc. (Italian)
Stanley Kramer for *Judgment at Nuremberg*, UA
Robert Rossen for *The Hustler*, 20th C.-Fox
J. Lee Thompson for *The Guns of Navarone*, Columbia

1962

David Lean for *Lawrence of Arabia*, Columbia
Pietro Germi for *Divorce — Italian Style*, Embassy Pictures
Robert Mulligan for *To Kill a Mockingbird*, U-I
Arthur Penn for *The Miracle Worker*, UA
Frank Perry for *David and Lisa*, Continental

1963

Tony Richardson for *Tom Jones*, UA-Lopert Pictures
Federico Fellini for *Federico Fellini's 8½*, Embassy Pictures
Elia Kazan for *America America*, Warner Bros.
Otto Preminger for *The Cardinal*, Columbia
Martin Ritt for *Hud*, Paramount

1964

George Cukor for *My Fair Lady*, Warner Bros.
Michael Cacoyannis for *Zorba the Greek*, Intl. Classics
Peter Glenville for *Becket*, Paramount
Stanley Kubrick for *Dr. Strangelove or: How I Learned to Stop Worrying and Love the Bomb*, Columbia
Robert Stevens for *Mary Poppins*, Walt Disney Prods.

1965

Robert Wise for *The Sound of Music*, 20th C.-Fox
David Lean for *Doctor Zhivago*, MGM
John Schlesinger for *Darling*, Embassy
Hiroshi Teshigahara for *Woman in the Dunes*, Pathe Contemporary Films
William Wyler for *The Collector*, Columbia

1966

Fred Zinnemann for *A Man for All Seasons*, Columbia
Michelangelo Antonioni for *Blow-Up*, Premier Productions
Richard Brooks for *The Professionals*, Columbia
Claude Lelouch for *A Man and a Woman*, Allied Artists
Mike Nichols for *Who's Afraid of Virginia Woolf?*, Warner Bros.

Tony Richardson (at right, on the front of the truck) is shown here making what turned out to be the Best Picture of 1963, *Tom Jones*. Richardson won the Best Director award for the film. The crew is shown here preparing to shoot close-ups of Peter Bull (at left) that will appear as if the actor is on a horse and galloping to the hunt. *Tom Jones* received four Oscars.

1967

Mike Nichols *for The Graduate*, Embassy
Richard Brooks for *In Cold Blood*, Columbia
Norman Jewison for *In the Heat of the Night*, UA
Stanley Kramer for *Guess Who's Coming to Dinner*, Columbia
Arthur Penn for *Bonnie and Clyde*, Warner Bros.-Seven Arts

1968

Carol Reed for *Oliver!*, Columbia
Anthony Harvey for *The Lion in Winter*, Avco Embassy
Stanley Kubrick for *2001: A Space Odyssey*, MGM
Gillo Pentecorvo for *The Battle of Algiers*, Allied Artists
Franco Zeffirelli for *Romeo & Juliet*, Paramount

1969

John Schlesinger for *Midnight Cowboy*, UA
Costa-Gavras for *Z*, Cinema V
George Roy Hill for *Butch Cassidy and the Sundance Kid*, 20th C.-Fox
Arthur Penn for *Alice's Restaurant*, UA
Sydney Pollack for *They Shoot Horses, Don't They?*, Cinerama

1970

Franklin J. Schaffner for *Patton*, 20th C.-Fox
Robert Altman for *M*A*S*H*, 20th C.-Fox
Federico Fellini for *Fellini Satyricon*, UA
Arthur Hiller for *Love Story*, Paramount
Ken Russell for *Women in Love*, UA

1971

William Friedkin for *The French Connection*, 20th C.-Fox
Peter Bogdanovich for *The Last Picture Show*, Columbia
Norman Jewison for *Fiddler on the Roof*, UA
Stanley Kubrick for *A Clockwork Orange*, Warner Bros.
John Schlesinger for *Sunday Bloody Sunday*, UA

1972

Bob Fosse for *Cabaret*, Allied Artists
John Boorman for *Deliverance*, Warner Bros.
Francis Ford Coppola for *The Godfather*, Paramount
Joseph L. Mankiewicz for *Sleuth*, 20th C.-Fox
Jan Troell for *The Emigrants*, Warner Bros.

1973

George Roy Hill for *The Sting*, Universal
Ingmar Bergman for *Cries and Whispers*, New World Pictures
Bernardo Bertolucci for *Last Tango in Paris*, UA
William Friedkin for *The Exorcist*, Warner Bros.
George Lucas for *American Graffiti*, Universal

1974

Francis Ford Coppola for *The Godfather Part II*, Paramount
John Cassavetes for *A Woman under the Influence*, Faces Intl. Films
Bob Fosse for *Lenny*, UA
Roman Polanski for *Chinatown*, Paramount
Francois Truffaut for *Day for Night*, Warner Bros.

1975

Milos Forman for *One Flew over the Cuckoo's Nest*, UA
Robert Altman for *Nashville*, Paramount
Federico Fellini for *Amarcord*, New World Pictures
Stanley Kubrick for *Barry Lyndon*, Warner Bros.
Sidney Lumet for *Dog Day Afternoon*, Warner Bros.

1976

John G. Avildsen for *Rocky*, UA
Ingmar Bergman for *Face to Face*, Paramount
Sidney Lumet for *Network*, MGM-UA
Alan J. Pakula for *All the President's Men*, Warner Bros.

1977

Woody Allen for *Annie Hall*, UA
Steven Speilberg for *Close Encounters of the Third Kind*, Columbia
Fred Zinnemann for *Julia*, 20th C.-Fox
George Lucas for *Star Wars*, 20th C.-Fox
Herbert Ross for *The Turning Point*, 20th C.-Fox

1978

Michael Cimino for *The Deer Hunter*, Universal
Woody Allen for *Interiors*, UA
Hal Ashby for *Coming Home*, UA
Warren Beatty and Buck Henry for *Heaven Can Wait*, Paramount
Alan Parker for *Midnight Express*, Columbia (British)

John Avildsen won the Best Director Oscar for the 1976 film, *Rocky*.
Rocky, **a low-budget hit, was nominated for nine Academy Awards and won three—for Best Picture and Best Film Editing as well as Best Director. Writer–leading actor Sylvester Stallone was nominated for two awards but won none.**

1979

Robert Benton for *Kramer vs. Kramer*, Columbia

Francis Ford Coppola for *Apocalypse Now*, UA

Bob Fosse for *All That Jazz*, 20th C.-Fox

Edouard Molinaro for *La Cage aux Folles*

Peter Yates for *Breaking Away*, 20th C.-Fox

1980

Robert Redford for *Ordinary People*, Paramount

David Lynch for *The Elephant Man*

Roman Polanski for *Tess*, Columbia

Richard Rush for *The Stunt Man*

Martin Scorsese for *Raging Bull*, Columbia

1981

Warren Beatty for *Reds*, Paramount

Hugh Hudson for *Chariots of Fire*, Warner Bros.

Louis Malle for *Atlantic City*, Paramount

Mark Rydell for *On Golden Pond*, Universal

Steven Spielberg for *Raiders of the Lost Ark*, Paramount

1982

Richard Attenborough for *Gandhi*, Columbia

Sidney Lumet for *The Verdict*, 20th C.-Fox

Wolfgang Petersen for *Das Boot*

Sydney Pollack for *Tootsie*, Columbia

Steven Spielberg for *E. T.—the Extra-Terrestrial*, Universal

CHAPTER 7

Best Supporting Role Awards

Rising stars and falling stars, fleeting comets and enduring lights: The best supporting players make a strange constellation. The Best Supporting Actor and Actress Oscars were first awarded in 1936, the ninth year of the Academy Awards. Winners include names that have become household words, like Frank Sinatra and Goldie Hawn, and names that only movie buffs remember, like Josephine Hull and Beatrice Straight.

The character roles that win supporting Oscars often call for ethnic looks and accents, and the winners supply all sorts. If they ever were gathered together, it would look like a United Nations meeting.

Seventeen Best Supporting Actors and Actresses were foreign-born: in Austria (Joseph Schildkraut); England (Sir John Gielgud, Dame Wendy Hiller, John Mills, Vanessa Redgrave, Dame Margaret Rutherford, and Peter Ustinov); Greece (Katina Paxinou); Japan (Miyoshi Umeki); Mexico (Anthony Quinn); Romania (John Houseman, to Alsatian and British parents); Russia (Lila Kedrova and, to British parents, George Sanders); Scotland (Donald Crisp); Sweden (Ingrid Bergman); and Wales (Hugh Griffith and Edmund Gwenn).

Another seven supporting award winners were born in America to immigrant parents: Ed Begley, George Chakiris, Melvyn Douglas, Celeste Holm, Karl Malden, Walter Matthau, and Frank Sinatra. America's largest minorities were represented by winners Hattie McDaniel, a black actress, and Puerto Rican Rita Moreno.

Both unknowns and seasoned veterans have won in supporting roles. Their careers have been as varied as their backgrounds. Some of the character actors showed versatility, while others were typecast in film after film (often in B pictures) as suave or villainous, as motherly or seductive.

In 1982, Lou Gossett, Jr.'s Best Sup-

Jason Robards, two-time Best Supporting Actor (1976 and 1977)

porting Actor award for his portrayal of a tough drill sergeant in *An Officer and a Gentleman* made him only the third black performer to win an Oscar. (Sidney Poitier had won Best Actor for *Lilies of the Field* in 1963, and Hattie McDaniel was the Best Supporting Actress for her role in *Gone with the Wind* in 1939.)

Best Supporting Actress of 1982 Jessica Lange (for *Tootsie*) was also nominated that year for Best Actress for her role in *Frances*. She was only the third performer to be nominated for two roles in the same year. (The others were Fay Bainter in 1938 and Teresa Wright in 1942.)

Several of the winners faded from the screen after receiving their Oscar. Following *A Tree Grows in Brooklyn* (1945), James Dunn made only five films in the last 22 years of his life. Miyoshi Umeki

Lou Gossett, Jr., accepting the 1982 Best Supporting Actor award

Melvyn Douglas won his most recent supporting Oscar for *Being There* (1979) at the age of 78, and Margaret Rutherford won her Oscar at the age of 72.

has made only four since *Sayonara* in 1957.

Katina Paxinou spent more time on stage than on the screen after winning the Best Supporting Actress award. Shirley Jones and Patty Duke appeared mostly on TV. The careers of Anne Revere and Kim Hunter eclipsed because they were blacklisted during the era of McCarthy's witch-hunt. Some commentators blamed the "Oscar jinx" for the fizzled careers of others (see pages 244–45).

Meanwhile some winners enjoyed unusually long careers. Jane Darwell's credits spanned 51 years. Donald Crisp acted in 79 films and directed 50. John Mills appeared in 84 films, Mary Astor in 115, and Walter Brennan in 119.

For all their diversity, the supporting players share a special talent: the ability to take a small role and make it sing. They stole many a scene from leading performers. Their names might have been forgettable, but their performances were certainly not.

Only Shelley Winters has received more than one Supporting Actress award, but two actresses (Helen Hayes and Ingrid Bergman) have won Oscars in both the Best Actress and the Best Supporting Actress categories.

The 1947 supporting award winners, Edmund Gwenn (left) and Celeste Holm (second from right), congratulated the 1948 winners, Walter Huston and Claire Trevor, at the 21st annual awards ceremony.

Jack Lemmon and Robert De Niro are the only actors ever to win the Best Supporting Actor award first and then the Best Supporting Actor award. Lemmon was the 1973 Best Actor for *Save the Tiger (left)*, and De Niro was the 1981 Best Actor for *Raging Bull* (right).

*J*ack Lemmon and Robert De Niro moved up the ladder as Oscar winners. Early in their careers they won the Best Supporting Actors award, and later they received awards for their outstanding performances in leading roles.

The progression from a supporting to a leading role is not the usual path that Oscar winners take. In fact, Lemmon and De Niro are the only actors who followed it, and Meryl Streep is the only actress. But seven performers have moved the other way. Ingrid Bergman, Helen Hayes, and Maggie Smith first won awards for Best Actress, then for Best Supporting Actress. Wendy Hiller, Vanessa Redgrave, Shelly Winters, and Walter Huston won for secondary roles after having been nominated for leading roles.

Four upwardly mobile men—Melvyn Douglas, Walter Matthau, Anthony Quinn, and Frank Sinatra—went part of the way up the Oscar ladder. They each won an Oscar for Best Supporting Actor and then were nominated for Best Actor. In the actress categories, Anne Baxter also progressed this way.

A move from leading Oscars to supporting Oscars

Moving Up (and Down)

Meryl Streep is the only actress ever to progress from winning an Academy Award for a supporting role (*Kramer vs. Kramer* in 1979) to winning an Academy Award for a leading role (*Sophie's Choice*) in 1982.

Anne Baxter won the Best Supporting Actress award (for *The Razor's Edge* in 1946) and then proceeded to win a nomination for Best Actress (for *All about Eve*) in 1950.

does not necessarily mean that an actor's or actress's talent has declined. Often character parts go to older players, and in these assignments, past glories can help win votes.

Hollywood reporter Peter H. Brown once observed that for supporting Oscars, "the voters, having to choose between established names and dazzling newcomers, almost always pick the old favorites."

George Burns, Melvyn Douglas, John Gielgud, Ruth Gordon, John Houseman, Helen Hayes, and Dame Margaret Rutherford were all over 70 years old and beloved in Hollywood when they were chosen to win Oscars for their supporting roles.

Not that every winner is old. The youngest person ever to win an Oscar for best performance was 10-year-old Tatum O'Neal, who won in the Supporting Actress category for her role in *Paper Moon* (1973). She had plenty of career time ahead to move up the ladder to leading roles.

Barry Fitzgerald, nominated for both the Best Actor and the Best Supporting Actor awards for the same performance in 1944, accepted the Best Supporting Actor Oscar from 1943 winner Charles Coburn.

A strange situation occurred in 1944. Barry Fitzgerald was nominated both as Best Actor and as Best Supporting Actor for the same performance in *Going My Way.* When the confusion cleared, Fitzgerald won the Best Supporting Actor award. Bing Crosby won the Best Actor award.

Current rules prohibit two nominations for one role. The Academy has acknowledged the impossibility of writing ironclad definitions of leading and supporting roles, and so has decided not to do so. Instead, Voting Rule Seven states, "The determination as to whether a role is a lead or support shall be made individually by members of the [actors'] branch at the time of balloting."

This is the nomination stage: Eligible voters in the actors' branch each nominate five people in each of the four acting categories. If someone's name comes up in two categories, a "preferential tabulation process" decides which category the person will be in.

This lack of definition of what constitutes a supporting and leading role can thus result in apparently arbitrary categorizations.

In 1963 Melvyn Douglas

What Is a Supporting Role?

Timothy Hutton, shown here with director Robert Redford, was the nucleus of *Ordinary People*, but he was nominated (and won) for Best Supporting Actor rather than Best Actor in 1980.

Susan Sarandon was nominated for Best Actress of 1980 but nominated herself in the Best Supporting Actress category.

played the father of the title character in *Hud*, and Patricia Neal played the housekeeper. While Neal's role was no larger than Douglas's, she won the Best Actress award and he won the Best Supporting Actor award.

If billing were the key to defining the categories, Candice Bergen would have been nominated as Jill Clayburgh's equal in *Starting Over* (1979) rather than in the Best Supporting Actress category. If critical attention were the criterion, Walter Matthau's role in *The Fortune Cookie* (1966)

would have been considered a lead rather than a supporting role. In reality, no single factor determines whether a performance is categorized as leading or supporting; rather, each role must be determined on an individual basis.

Katharine Hepburn's second Best Actress Oscar, for *Guess Who's Coming to Dinner* (1967), was awarded for one of the smallest roles she ever played.

In 1980, Judd Hirsch and eventual winner Timothy Hutton were both nominated as Best Supporting Actor for their perfor-

mances in *Ordinary People*. Hirsch had a relatively small part, but Hutton's was the nucleus of the film. It was a role at least as important as that of his mother, played by Mary Tyler Moore, who was nominated as Best Actress.

The same year, actress Susan Sarandon expressed great surprise when she was nominated as Best Actress for her role in *Atlantic City*. She had expected, if nominated, to be in the Supporting Actress category. Ironically, even she had voted that way herself.

36 The first Best Supporting Actor award went to Walter Brennan for his performance in *Come and Get It* in 1936.

37 Joseph Schildkraut played the wrongly accused Captain Dreyfus in the 1937 production of *The Life of Emile Zola.*

38 Walter Brennan's second Oscar was for *Kentucky* in 1938. 7D(1939)

39 Spencer Tracy handed Thomas Mitchell his Oscar for his portrayal of a drunken doctor in John Ford's classic western, *Stagecoach* (1939).

40 Walter Brennan won his third Oscar in five years—a record yet to be broken—for playing Judge Bean in *The Westerner* in 1940.

41 The 1941 award went to Donald Crisp in *How Green Was My Valley.*

42 Van Heflin (a lieutenant) won the 1942 Oscar for *Johnny Eager.*

43 Charles Coburn received the Supporting Actor award for *The More the Merrier* (1943).

44 Barry Fitzgerald wound up with the Best Supporting Actor award of 1944, while his co-star Bing Crosby received the Best Actor award.

Best Supporting Actor

1936–1982

45 Best Supporting Actor of 1945 James Dunn (for *A Tree Grows in Brooklyn*) joined the Oscar ranks along with Peggy Ann Garner (left), Ann Revere, and Ray Milland.

46 Harold Russell, a handless veteran-turned-actor won for his role in *The Best Years of Our Lives* (1946). Congratulating him are Olivia De Havilland (left), Cathy O'Donnell, and Anne Baxter.

47 Edmund Gwenn played Kris Kringle in *Miracle on 34th Street* (1947).

48 Walter Huston (left) won an Oscar for *Treasure of the Sierra Madre*, a film directed by his son, John Huston.

49 In 1950 Dean Jagger and Mercedes McCambridge both won for their supporting roles, his in *Twelve O'Clock High*.

50 George Sanders (second from right) played cynical theatre critic Addison De Witt in the 1950 film *All about Eve*. From left are Dean Jagger, Josephine Hull, and Helen Hayes.

51 Karl Malden won for his performance in *A Streetcar Named Desire* in 1951.

52 Anthony Quinn, shown here with actress Pat Van Iver, was a winner in 1952 for *Viva Zapata!*

53 Frank Sinatra, co-starring with Robert Montgomery and Burt Lancaster, was Best Supporting Actor of 1953 for *From Here to Eternity*.

54 Donna Reed announced that Edmond O'Brien was the 1954 winner for his performance in *The Barefoot Contessa*.

55 In 1955 Jack Lemmon (center) put in an award-winning performance appearing with William Powell (left) and Henry Fonda in *Mister Roberts*.

56 Anthony Quinn earned a second Oscar for his supporting role in *Lust for Life*.

57 For his role in *Sayonara*, Red Buttons accepted the 1957 Oscar from Lana Turner.

58 In 1958 burly ballad singer Burl Ives won an Oscar for *The Big Country*.

59 British actor Hugh Griffiths captured the 1959 Oscar for his performance in *Ben Hur*.

118

60 Peter Ustinov's 1961 Oscar was for his role in *Spartacus*. It was presented to him by actress Eva Marie Saint.

61 George Chakiris won the Oscar in 1961 for playing Bernardo in *West Side Story*.

62 Ed Begley portrayed a boss of a corrupt southern town in *Sweet Bird of Youth* (1962).

63 Melvyn Douglas was Paul Newman's uncompromising father in the 1963 film, *Hud*.

64 Peter Ustinov's second Best Supporting Actor award was for *Topkapi* in 1964.

65 Martin Balsam was a winner in *A Thousand Clowns* (1965).

66 Walter Matthau was voted Best Supporting Actor in 1966 for his role in *The Fortune Cookie*. Shelley Winters presented the Oscar.

67 As a dim-witted convict, his first nonvillainous role, George Kennedy won the 1967 Oscar for *Cool Hand Luke*.

68 *The Subject Was Roses* (1968) brought Jack Albertson his Supporting Actor Oscar. Frank Sinatra presented the award.

69 Gig Young was the promoter of the marathon dance in *They Shoot Horses, Don't They?* (1969).

70 John Mills had a challenging role, as a village idiot who never spoke a word, in *Ryan's Daughter* (1970).

71 Ben Johnson was the Best Supporting Actor of 1971 for his performance in *The Last Picture Show*.

72 Joel Grey recreated his Broadway role in *Cabaret* (1972).

73 John Houseman immortalized the character of a tyrannical law professor in *The Paper Chase*. (1973).

74 Robert De Niro—shown here in *Mean Streets* (1973)—won the Best Supporting Actor award for his portrayal of the young Vito Corleone in *The Godfather Part II* (1974).

75 At 80 George Burns was the oldest Best Supporting Actor ever. He won for *The Sunshine Boys* (1975).

76 Jason Robards played *Washington Post* editor Ben Bradlee in the Watergate drama, *All the President's Men* (1976).

77 For the second year in a row, the Oscar went to Jason Robards, this time for his performance as Dashiell Hammett in *Julia* (1977).

78 Christopher Walken earned his 1978 award for *The Deer Hunter*.

79 Melvyn Douglas captured his second supporting Oscar for *Being There* (1979).

80 Although some argued that he had a leading role, Timothy Hutton won the Oscar for Best Supporting Actor for *Ordinary People*.

81 Veteran British actor Sir John Gielgud won the supporting Oscar in 1981 for *Arthur*.

82 In 1982 Lou Gossett, Jr., won for playing a tough-as-nails sergeant in *An Officer and a Gentleman*.

36 The first Best Supporting Actress award went to Gale Sondergaard for her performance in *Anthony Adverse*

37 Alice Brady played Mrs. O'Leary in *In Old Chicago* (1937).

38 Fay Bainter won Best Supporting Actress for *Jezebel* the same year she was nominated for Best Actress in *White Banners*, 1938.

39 Fay Bainter presented the 1939 award to Hattie McDaniel, who won for her role as Mammy in *Gone with the Wind*.

40 Her performance as Ma Joad in *The Grapes of Wrath* (1940) brought Jane Darwell an Oscar.

41 Mary Astor was Best Supporting Actress of 1941 for *The Great Lie*.

42 Teresa Wright won the Best Supporting Actress of 1942 for *Mrs. Miniver*. She was nominated for the Best Actress award for *The Pride of the Yankees* that same year.

43 Katina Paxinou led a guerrilla band in *For Whom the Bell Tolls* (1943).

44 Ethel Barrymore won an Oscar for her first appearance on the screen in 12 years—in *None but the Lonely* (1944) with Cary Grant.

Best Supporting Actress

1936–1982

45 The 1945 award went to Anne Revere for her role in *National Velvet*.

46 Anne Baxter earned an Oscar for *The Razor's Edge* (1946).

47 Celeste Holm received the 1947 award for *Gentleman's Agreement*. At left are a representative of Price Waterhouse and Co. and actor Warde Ogden.

48 Claire Trevor is shown accepting her 1948 Oscar for *Key Largo* as master of ceremonies Robert Montgomery approves.

49 *All the King's Men* (1949) was Mercedes McCambridge's first film, but she won an Oscar for it.

50 Josephine Hull won for *Harvey* in 1950.

51 Actor Jose Ferrer (left) presented the 1951 Best Supporting Actress award to Kim Hunter for her performance in *A Streetcar Named Desire*.

52 Gloria Grahame won for her performance in *The Bad and the Beautiful* (1952).

53 Donna Reed won for *From Here to Eternity* (1953). Her co-star, Montgomery Clift, was nominated as Best Actor.

54 In 1954 Eva Marie Saint received a Best Supporting Actress Oscar for her first film, *On the Waterfront*.

55 Jo Van Fleet was Best Supporting Actress of 1955 for *East of Eden*.

56 Dorothy Malone portrayed a nymphomaniac in the 1956 film, *Written on the Wind*.

57 Miyoshi Umeki played the Japanese wife of GI Red Buttons in *Sayonara*. Both won Oscars for supporting roles.

58 British actress Wendy Hiller was happy to hear she was chosen for a 1958 Oscar for *Separate Tables*.

59 Shelley Winters was Mrs. Van Daan, ever fearful of Nazi arrest, in *The Diary of Anne Frank* (1959). Lou Jacobi played her husband.

60 Shirley Jones, who had usually portrayed a sweet, old-fashioned girl, won the 1960 Best Supporting Actress award for her portrayal of a prostitute in the film *Elmer Gantry*.

61 Both Rita Moreno and George Chakiris won Oscars for their supporting roles in the 1961 musical, *West Side Story*.

64 Winner Patty Duke, who played Helen Keller in *The Miracle Worker*, is shown with Best Supporting Actor Ed Begley at the 1962 awards.

62 Veteran British actress Margaret Rutherford played a dowdy duchess in *The V.I.P.s* (1963).

63 Lila Kedrova was a dying prostitute in *Zorba the Greek* (1964).

65 Shelley Winters is the only actress to earn two Best Supporting Actress awards. Her second was for *A Patch of Blue* in 1965.

66 Sandy Dennis is shown receiving congratulations for her Best Supporting Actress Oscar for *Who's Afraid of Virginia Woolf?* (1966).

67 Walter Matthau presented the 1967 Oscar to Estelle Parsons for her performance in *Bonnie and Clyde*.

68 Ruth Gordon won an Oscar at the age of 71 for *Rosemary's Baby*.

69 Goldie Hawn appeared with Walter Matthau and Ingrid Bergman in the 1969 comedy, *Cactus Flower*.

70 After a 12-year absence from the screen, Helen Hayes returned in 1970 as a little old lady stowaway in *Airport*.

71 The 1971 Oscar went to Cloris Leachman in *The Last Picture Show*.

72 Eileen Heckart received an Oscar for playing an overprotective mother in *Butterflies Are Free* (1972).

73 Ten-year-old Tatum O'Neal was the youngest winner in any acting category. She won for *Paper Moon* in 1973.

74 In her acceptance speech, Ingrid Bergman said that the younger actress Valentina Cortese (in *Day for Night*) "should have won." Bergman won for her role in *Murder on the Orient Express* (1974).

75 On her third nomination, Lee Grant won the Best Supporting Actress award for 1975 with her performance in *Shampoo*.

76 Beatrice Straight received the 1976 Oscar from Sylvester Stallone and Muhammad Ali. She won for *Network*.

77 Vanessa Redgrave was a controversial choice for the 1977 Oscar. She won for *Julia*.

126

78 In 1978, Maggie Smith won for her performance in *California Suite*.

79 In *Kramer vs. Kramer* (1979), Meryl Streep played a wife who walks out on her husband and son.

80 Mary Steenburgen was presented with the 1980 Oscar for her performance in *Melvin and Howard*.

81 Maureen Stapleton was nominated for a supporting role for the third time in 1981; this time she won for her portrayal of Emma Goldman in *Reds*.

82 Jessica Lange was chosen Best Supporting Actress for *Tootsie* in 1982. That same year, she was also nominated as Best Actress for her leading role in *Frances*.

1936

Walter Brennan in *Come and Get It*, Samuel Goldwyn Studios-United Artists

Mischa Auerin in *My Man Godfrey*, Universal

Stuart Erwin in *Pigskin Parade*, 20th Century-Fox

Basil Rathbone in *Romeo and Juliet*, Metro-Goldwyn-Mayer

Akim Tamiroff in *The General Died at Dawn*, Paramount

1937

Joseph Schildkraut in *The Life of Emile Zola*, Warner Brothers

Ralph Bellamy in *The Awful Truth*, Columbia

Thomas Mitchell in *Hurricane*, Goldwyn-UA

H. B. Warner in *Lost Horizon*, Columbia

Roland Young in *Topper*, MGM

1938

Walter Brennan in *Kentucky*, 20th C.-Fox

John Garfield in *Four Daughters*, Warner Bros.

Gene Lockhart in *Algiers*, UA

Robert Morley in *Marie Antoinette*, MGM

Basil Rathbone in *If I Were King*, Paramount

1939

Thomas Mitchell in *Stagecoach*, UA

Brian Aherne in *Juarez*, Warner Bros.

Harry Carey in *Mr. Smith Goes to Washington*, Columbia

Brian Donlevy in *Beau Geste*, Paramount

Claude Rains in *Mr. Smith Goes to Washington*, Columbia

1940

Walter Brennan in *The Westerner*, Goldwyn-UA

Albert Basserman in *Foreign Correspondent*, UA

William Gargan in *They Knew What They Wanted*, RKO Radio

Jack Oakie in *The Great Dictator*, UA

James Stephenson in *The Letter*, Warner Bros.

1941

Donald Crisp in *How Green Was My Valley*, 20th C.-Fox

Walter Brennan in *Sergeant York*, Warner Bros.

Charles Coburn in *The Devil and Miss Jones*, RKO Radio

James Gleason in *Here Comes Mr. Jordan*, Columbia

Sydney Greenstreet in *The Maltese Falcon*, Warner Bros.

1942

Van Heflin in *Johnny Eager*, MGM

William Bendix in *Wake Island*, Paramount

Walter Huston in *Yankee Doodle Dandy*, Warner Bros.

Frank Morgan in *Tortilla Flat*, MGM

Henry Travers in *Mrs. Miniver*, MGM

1943

Charles Coburn in *The More the Merrier*, 20th C.-Fox

Charles Bickford in *The Song of Bernadette*, 20th C.-Fox

J. Carrol Naish in *Sahara*, Columbia

Claude Rains in *Casablanca*, Warner Bros.

Akim Tamiroff in *For Whom the Bell Tolls*, Paramount

1944

Barry Fitzgerald in *Going My Way*, Paramount

Hume Cronyn in *The Seventh Cross*, MGM

Claude Rains in *Mr. Skeffington*, Warner Bros.

Clifton Webb in *Laura*, 20th C.-Fox

Monty Woolley in *Since You Went Away*, UA

1945

James Dunn in *A Tree Grows in Brooklyn*, 20th C.-Fox

Michael Chekhov in *Spellbound*, UA

John Dall in *The Corn Is Green*, Warner Bros.

Robert Mitchum in *G.I. Joe*, UA

J. Carrol Naish in *A Medal for Benny*, Paramount

1946

Harold Russell in *The Best Years of Our Lives*, RKO Radio

Charles Coburn in *The Green Years*, MGM

William Demarest in *The Jolson Story*, Columbia

Claude Rains in *Notorious*, RKO Radio

Clifton Webb in *The Razor's Edge*, 20th C.-Fox

1947

Edmund Gwenn in *Miracle on 34th Street*, 20th C.-Fox

Charles Bickford in *The Farmer's Daughter*, RKO Radio

Thomas Gomez in *Ride the Pink Horse*, Universal

Robert Ryan in *Crossfire*, RKO Radio

Richard Widmark in *Kiss of Death*, 20th C.-Fox

1948

Walter Huston in *The Treasure of the Sierra Madre*, Warner Bros.

Charles Bickford in *Johnny Belinda*, Warner Bros.

Jose Ferrer in *Joan of Arc*, RKO Radio

Oscar Homolka in *I Remember Mama*, RKO Radio

Cecil Kellaway in *The Luck of the Irish*, 20th C.-Fox

1949

Dean Jagger in *Twelve O'Clock High*, 20th C.-Fox

John Ireland in *All the King's Men*, Columbia

Arthur Kennedy in *Champion*, UA

Ralph Richardson in *The Heiress*, Paramount

James Whitmore in *Battleground*, MGM

1950

George Sanders in *All about Eve*, 20th C.-Fox

Jeff Chandler in *Broken Arrow*, 20th C.-Fox

Edmund Gwenn in *Mister 880*, 20th C.-Fox

Sam Jaffe in *The Asphalt Jungle*, MGM

Erich von Stroheim in *Sunset Boulevard*, Paramount

Best Supporting Actors

1951

Karl Malden in *A Streetcar Named Desire*, Warner Bros.
Leo Genn in *Quo Vadis*, MGM
Kevin McCarthy in *Death of a Salesman*, Columbia
Peter Ustinov in *Quo Vadis*, MGM
Gig Young in *Come Fill the Cup*, Warner Bros.

1952

Anthony Quinn in *Viva Zapata!*, 20th C.-Fox
Richard Burton in *My Cousin Rachel*, 20th C.-Fox
Arthur Hunnicut in *The Big Sky*, RKO Radio
Victor McLaglen in *The Quiet Man*, Republic
Jack Palance in *Sudden Fear*, RKO Radio

1953

Frank Sinatra in *From Here to Eternity*, Columbia
Eddie Albert in *Roman Holiday*, Paramount
Brandon De Wilde in *Shane*, Paramount
Jack Palance in *Shane*, Paramount
Robert Strauss in *Stalag 17*, Paramount

1954

Edmond O'Brien in *The Barefoot Contessa*, UA
Lee J. Cobb in *On the Waterfront*, Columbia
Karl Malden in *On the Waterfront*, Columbia
Rod Steiger in *On the Waterfront*, Columbia
Tom Tully in *The Caine Mutiny*, Columbia

1955

Jack Lemmon in *Mister Roberts*, Warner Bros.
Arthur Kennedy in *Trial*, MGM
Joe Mantell in *Marty*, UA
Sal Mineo in *Rebel without a Cause*, Warner Bros.
Arthur O'Connell in *Picnic*, Columbia

1956

Anthony Quinn in *Lust for Life*, MGM
Don Murray in *Bus Stop*, 20th C.-Fox
Anthony Perkins in *Friendly Persuasion*, Allied Artists
Mickey Rooney in *The Bold and the Brave*, RKO Radio
Robert Stack in *Written on the Wind*, Universal

1957

Red Buttons in *Sayonara*, Warner Bros.
Vittorio de Sica in *A Farewell to Arms*, 20th C.-Fox
Sessue Hayakawa in *The Bridge on the River Kwai*, Columbia
Arthur Kennedy in *Peyton Place*, 20th C.-Fox
Russ Tamblin in *Peyton Place*, 20th C.-Fox

1958

Burl Ives in *The Big Country*, UA
Theodore Bikel in *The Defiant Ones*, UA
Lee J. Cobb in *The Brothers Karamazov*, MGM
Arthur Kennedy in *Some Came Running*, MGM
Gig Young in *Teacher's Pet*, Paramount

1959

Hugh Griffith in *Ben-Hur*, MGM
Arthur O'Connell in *Anatomy of a Murder*, Columbia
George C. Scott in *Anatomy of a Murder*, Columbia
Robert Vaughn in *The Young Philadelphians*, Warner Bros.
Ed Wynn in *The Diary of Anne Frank*, 20th C.-Fox

1960

Peter Ustinov in *Spartacus*, Universal
Peter Falk in *Murder, Inc.*, 20th C.-Fox
Jack Kruschen in *The Apartment*, UA
Sal Mineo in *Exodus*, UA
Chill Wills in *The Alamo*, UA

1961

George Chakiris in *West Side Story*, UA
Montgomery Clift in *Judgment at Nuremberg*, UA
Peter Falk in *Pocketful of Miracles*, UA
Jackie Gleason in *The Hustler*, 20th C.-Fox
George C. Scott in *The Hustler*, 20th C.-Fox

1962

Ed Begley in *Sweet Bird of Youth*, MGM
Victor Buono in *What Ever Happened to Sweet Baby Jane?*, Warner Bros.
Telly Savalas in *Bird Man of Alcatraz*, UA
Omar Sharif in *Lawrence of Arabia*, Columbia
Terence Stamp in *Billy Budd*, Allied Artists

1963

Melvyn Douglas in *Hud*, Paramount
Nick Adams in *Twilight of Honor*, MGM
Bobby Darin in *Captain Newman*, Universal
Hugh Griffith in *Tom Jones*, UA-Lopert Pictures
John Huston in *The Cardinal*, Columbia

1964

Peter Ustinov in *Topkapi*, UA
John Gielgud in *Becket*, Paramount
Stanley Holloway in *My Fair Lady*, Warner Bros.
Edmond O'Brien in *Seven Days in May*, Paramount
Lee Tracy in *The Best Man*, UA

1965

Martin Balsam in *A Thousand Clowns*, UA
Ian Bannen in *The Flight of the Phoenix*, 20th C.-Fox
Tom Courtenay in *Doctor Zhivago*, MGM
Michael Dunn in *Ship of Fools*, Columbia
Frank Finlay in *Othello*, Warner Bros.

1966

Walter Matthau in *The Fortune Cookie*, UA
Mako in *The Sand Pebbles*, 20th C.-Fox
James Mason in *Georgy Girl*, Columbia
George Segal in *Who's Afraid of Virginia Woolf?*, Warner Bros.
Robert Shaw in *A Man for All Seasons*, Columbia

1967

George Kennedy in *Cool Hand Luke*, Warner Bros.-Seven Arts
John Cassavetes in *The Dirty Dozen*, MGM
Gene Hackman in *Bonnie and Clyde*, Warner Bros.-Seven Arts
Cecil Kellaway in *Guess Who's Coming to Dinner*, Columbia
Michael J. Pollard in *Bonnie and Clyde*, Warner Bros.-Seven Arts

1968

Jack Albertson in *The Subject Was Roses*, MGM
Seymour Cassel in *Faces*, Walter Reade-Continental Distributing
Daniel Massey in *Star!*, 20th C.-Fox
Jack Wild in *Oliver!*, Columbia
Gene Wilder in *The Producers*, Avco Embassy

1969

Gig Young in *They Shoot Horses, Don't They?*, Cinerama
Rupert Crosse in *The Reivers*, National General
Elliott Gould in *Bob & Carol & Ted & Alice*, Columbia
Jack Nicholson in *Easy Rider*, Columbia
Anthony Quayle in *Anne of the Thousand Days*, Universal

1970

John Mills in *Ryan's Daughter*, MGM
Richard Castellano in *Lovers and Other Strangers*, Cinerama
Chief Dan George in *Little Big Man*, National General
Gene Hackman in *I Never Sang for My Father*, Columbia
John Marley in *Love Story*, Paramount

1971

Ben Johnson in *The Last Picture Show*, Columbia
Jeff Bridges in *The Last Picture Show*, Columbia
Leonard Frey in *Fiddler on the Roof*, UA
Richard Jaeckel in *Sometimes a Great Notion*, Universal
Roy Scheider in *The French Connection*, 20th C.-Fox

1972

Joel Grey in *Cabaret*, Allied Artists
Eddie Albert in *The Heartbreak Kid*, 20th C.-Fox
James Caan in *The Godfather*, Paramount
Robert Duvall in *The Godfather*, Paramount
Al Pacino in *The Godfather*, Paramount

1973

John Houseman in *The Paper Chase*, 20th C.-Fox
Vincent Gardenia in *Bang the Drum Slowly*, Paramount
Jack Gilford in *Save the Tiger*, Paramount
Jason Miller in *The Exorcist*, Warner Bros.
Randy Quaid in *The Last Detail*, Columbia

1974

Robert De Niro in *The Godfather Part II*, Paramount
Fred Astaire in *The Towering Inferno*, 20th C.-Fox/Warner Bros.
Jeff Bridges in *Thunderbolt and Lightfoot*, UA
Michael V. Gazzo in *The Godfather Part II*, Paramount
Lee Strasberg in *The Godfather Part II*, Paramount

1975

George Burns in *The Sunshine Boys*, MGM
Brad Dourif in *One Flew over the Cuckoo's Nest*, UA
Burgess Meredith, *The Day of the Locust*, Paramount
Chris Sarandon in *Dog Day Afternoon*, Warner Bros.
Jack Warden in *Shampoo*, Columbia

1976

Jason Robards in *All the President's Men*, Warner Bros.
Ned Beatty in *Network* , MGM-UA
Burgess Meredith in *Rocky*, UA
Laurence Olivier in *Marathon Man*, Paramount
Burt Young in *Rocky*, UA

1977

Jason Robards in *Julia*, 20th C.-Fox
Mikhail Baryshnikov in *The Turning Point*, 20th C.-Fox
Peter Firth in *Equus*, UA
Alec Guinness in *Star Wars*, 20th C.-Fox
Maximilian Schell in *Julia*, 20th C.-Fox

1978

Christopher Walken in *The Deer Hunter*, Universal
Bruce Dern in *Coming Home*, UA
Richard Farnsworth in *Comes a Horseman*
John Hurt in *Midnight Express*, Columbia (British)
Jack Warden in *Shampoo*

1979

Melvyn Douglas in *Being There*
Robert Duvall in *Apocalypse Now*, UA
Frederick Forrest in *The Rose*
Justin Henry in *Kramer vs. Kramer*, Columbia
Mickey Rooney in *The Black Stallion*

1980

Timothy Hutton in *Ordinary People*, Paramount
Judd Hirsch in *Ordinary People*, Paramount
Michael O'Keefe in *The Great Santini*
Joe Pesci in *Raging Bull*, UA
Jason Robards in *Melvin and Howard*

1981

John Gielgud in *Arthur*
James Coco in *Only When I Laugh*
Ian Holm in *Chariots of Fire*, Warner Bros.
Jack Nicholson in *Reds*, Paramount
Howard E. Rollins, Jr., in *Ragtime*

1982

Lou Gossett, Jr., in *An Officer and a Gentleman*
Charles Durning in *The Best Little Whorehouse in Texas*
John Lithgow in *The World According to Garp*
James Mason in *The Verdict*, 20th C.-Fox
Robert Preston in *Victor/Victoria*

Veteran performer Jack Albertson proudly displayed the Oscar he won for his supporting role in *The Subject Was Roses* (1968).

1936

Gale Sondergaard in *Anthony Adverse*, Warner Brothers
Beulah Bond in *The Gorgeous Hussy*, Metro-Goldwyn-Mayer
Alice Brady in *My Man Godfrey*, Universal
Bonita Granville in *These Three*, Samuel Goldwyn Studios-United Artists
Maria Ouspenskaya in *Dodsworth*, UA

1937

Alice Brady in *In Old Chicago*, 20th Century-Fox
Andrea Leeds in *Stage Door*, RKO Radio
Anne Shirley in *Stella Dallas*, UA
Claire Trevor in *Dead End*, UA
Dame May Whitty in *Night Must Fall*, MGM

1938

Fay Bainter in *Jezebel*, Warner Bros.
Beulah Bond in *Of Human Hearts*, MGM
Billie Burke in *Merrily We Live*, MGM
Spring Byington in *You Can't Take It with You*, Columbia
Miliza Korjus in *The Great Waltz*, MGM

1939

Hattie McDaniel in *Gone with the Wind*, MGM
Olivia De Havilland in *Gone with the Wind*, MGM
Geraldine Fitzgerald in *Wuthering Heights*, UA
Edna May Oliver in *Drums along the Mohawk*, 20th C.-Fox
Maria Ouspenskaya in *Love Affair*, RKO Radio

1940

Jane Darwell in *The Grapes of Wrath*, 20th C.-Fox
Judith Anderson in *Rebecca*, UA
Ruth Hussey in *The Philadelphia Story*, MGM
Barbara O'Neill in *All This, and Heaven Too*, Warner Bros.
Marjorie Rambeau in *Primrose Path*, RKO Radio

1941

Mary Astor in *The Great Lie*, Warner Bros.
Sara Allgood in *How Green Was My Valley*, 20th C.-Fox
Patricia Collinge in *The Little Foxes*, RKO Radio
Teresa Wright in *The Little Foxes*, Goldwyn-RKO Radio
Margaret Wycherly in *Sergeant York*, Warner Bros.

1942

Teresa Wright in *Mrs. Miniver*, MGM
Gladys Cooper in *Now, Voyager*, Warner Bros.
Agnes Moorehead in *The Magnificent Ambersons*, RKO Radio
Susan Peters in *Random Harvest*, MGM
Dame May Whitty in *Mrs. Miniver*, MGM

1943

Katina Paxinou in *For Whom the Bell Tolls*, Paramount
Gladys Cooper in *The Song of Bernadette*, 20th C.-Fox
Paulette Goddard in *So Proudly We Hail*, Paramount
Anne Revere in *The Song of Bernadette*, 20th C.-Fox
Lucille Watson in *Watch on the Rhine*, Warner Bros.

1944

Ethel Barrymore in *None but the Lonely Heart*, RKO Radio
Jennifer Jones in *Since You Went Away*, UA
Angela Lansbury in *Gaslight*, MGM
Aline McMahon in *Dragon Seed*, MGM
Agnes Moorehead in *Mrs. Parkington*, MGM

1945

Anne Revere in *National Velvet*, MGM
Eve Arden in *Mildred Pierce*, Warner Bros.
Ann Blyth in *Mildred Pierce*, Warner Bros.
Angela Lansbury in *The Picture of Dorian Gray*, MGM
Joan Lorring in *The Corn Is Green*, Warner Bros.

1946

Anne Baxter in *The Razor's Edge*, 20th C.-Fox
Ethel Barrymore in *The Spiral Staircase*, RKO Radio
Lillian Gish in *Duel in the Sun*, Selznick International
Flora Robson in *Saratoga Trunk*, Warner Bros.
Gale Sondergaard in *Anna and the King of Siam*, 20th C.-Fox

1947

Celeste Holm in *Gentleman's Agreement*, 20th C.-Fox
Ethel Barrymore in *The Paradine Case*, Selznick Intl.
Gloria Grahame in *Crossfire*, RKO Radio
Marjorie Main in *The Egg and I*, Universal
Anne Revere in *Gentleman's Agreement*, 20th C.-Fox

1948

Claire Trevor in *Key Largo*, Warner Bros.
Barbara Bel Geddes in *I Remember Mama*, RKO Radio
Ellen Corby in *I Remember Mama*, RKO Radio
Agnes Moorehead in *Johnny Belinda*, Warner Bros.
Jean Simmons in *Hamlet*, Universal

1949

Mercedes McCambridge in *All the King's Men*, Columbia
Ethel Barrymore in *Pinky*, 20th C.-Fox
Celeste Holm in *Come to the Stable*, 20th C.-Fox
Elsa Lanchester in *Come to the Stable*, 20th C.-Fox
Ethel Waters in *Pinky*, 20th C.-Fox

1950

Josephine Hull in *Harvey*, Universal-International
Hope Emerson in *Caged*, Warner Bros.
Celeste Holm in *All about Eve*, 20th C.-Fox
Nancy Olson in *Sunset Boulevard*, Paramount
Thelma Ritter in *All about Eve*, 20th C.-Fox

Best Supporting Actresses

1951

Kim Hunter in *A Streetcar Named Desire*, Warner Bros.
Joan Blondell in *The Blue Veil*, RKO Radio
Mildred Dunnock in *Death of a Salesman*, Columbia
Lee Grant in *Detective Story*, Paramount
Thelma Ritter in *The Mating Season*, Paramount

1952

Gloria Grahame in *The Bad and the Beautiful*, MGM
Jean Hagen in *Singin' in the Rain*, MGM
Colette Marchand in *Moulin Rouge*, UA
Terry Moore in *Come Back, Little Sheba*, Paramount
Thelma Ritter in *With a Song in My Heart*, 20th C.-Fox

1953

Donna Reed in *From Here to Eternity*, Columbia
Grace Kelly in *Mogambo*, MGM
Geraldine Page in *Hondo*, Warner Bros.
Marjorie Rambeau in *Torch Song*, MGM
Thelma Ritter in *Pickup on South Street*, 20th C.-Fox

1954

Eva Marie Saint in *On the Waterfront*, Columbia
Nina Foch in *Executive Suite*, MGM
Katy Jurado in *Broken Lance*, 20th C.-Fox
Jan Sterling in *The High and the Mighty*, Warner Bros.
Claire Trevor in *The High and the Mighty*, Warner Bros.

1955

Jo Van Fleet in *East of Eden*, Warner Bros.
Betsy Blair in *Marty*, UA
Peggy Lee in *Pete Kelly's Blues*, Warner Bros.
Marisa Pavan in *The Rose Tattoo*, Paramount
Natalie Wood in *Rebel without a Cause*, Warner Bros.

1956

Dorothy Malone in *Written on the Wind*, U-I
Mildred Dunnock in *Baby Doll*, Warner Bros.
Eileen Heckart in *The Bad Seed*, Warner Bros.
Mercedes McCambridge in *Giant*, Warner Bros.
Patty McCormack in *The Bad Seed*, Warner Bros.

1957

Miyoshi Umeki in *Sayonara*, Warner Bros.
Carolyn Jones in *The Bachelor Party*, UA
Elsa Lanchester in *Witness for the Prosecution*, UA
Hope Lange in *Peyton Place*, 20th C.-Fox
Diane Varsi in *Peyton Place*, 20th C.-Fox

1958

Wendy Hiller in *Separate Tables*, UA
Peggy Cass in *Auntie Mame*, Warner Bros.
Martha Hyer in *Some Came Running*, MGM
Maureen Stapleton in *Lonelyhearts*, UA
Cara Williams in *The Defiant Ones*, UA

1959

Shelley Winters in *The Diary of Anne Frank*, 20th C.-Fox
Hermione Baddeley in *Room at the Top*, Continental Distributing, Inc. (British)
Susan Kohner in *Imitation of Life*, U-I
Juanita Moore in *Imitation of Life*, U-I
Thelma Ritter in *Pillow Talk*, U-I

1960

Shirley Jones in *Elmer Gantry*, UA
Glynis Johns in *The Sundowners*, Warner Bros.
Shirley Knight in *The Dark at the Top of the Stairs*, Warner Bros.
Janet Leigh in *Psycho*, Paramount
Mary Ure in *Sons and Lovers*, 20th C.-Fox

1961

Rita Moreno in *West Side Story*, UA
Fay Bainter in *The Children's Hour*, UA
Judy Garland in *Judgment at Nuremberg*, UA
Lotte Lenya in *The Roman Spring of Mrs. Stone*, Warner Bros.
Una Merkel in *Summer and Smoke*, Paramount

1962

Patty Duke in *The Miracle Worker*, UA
Mary Badham in *To Kill a Mockingbird*, U-I
Shirley Knight in *Sweet Bird of Youth*, MGM
Angela Lansbury in *The Manchurian Candidate*, UA
Thelma Ritter in *Bird Man of Alcatraz*, UA

1963

Margaret Rutherford in *The V.I.P.s*, MGM
Diane Cilento in *Tom Jones*, UA-Lopert Pictures
Dame Edith Evans in *Tom Jones*, UA-Lopert Pictures
Joyce Redman in *Tom Jones*, UA-Lopert Pictures
Lilia Skala in *Lilies of the Field*, UA

1964

Lila Kedrova in *Zorba the Greek*, International Classics
Gladys Cooper in *My Fair Lady*, Warner Bros.
Dame Edith Evans in *The Chalk Garden*, Universal
Grayson Hall in *The Night of the Iguana*, MGM
Agnes Moorehead in *Hush . . . Hush, Sweet Charlotte*, 20th C.-Fox

1965

Shelley Winters in *A Patch of Blue*, MGM
Ruth Gordon in *Inside Daisy Clover*, Warner Bros.
Joyce Redman in *Othello*, Warner Bros.
Maggie Smith in *Othello*, Warner Bros.
Peggy Wood in *The Sound of Music*, 20th C.-Fox

1966

Sandy Dennis in *Who's Afraid of Virginia Woolf?*, Warner Bros.
Wendy Hiller in *A Man For All Seasons*, Columbia
Jocelyne Lagarde in *Hawaii*, UA
Vivien Merchant in *Alfie*, Paramount
Geraldine Page in *You're a Big Boy Now*, Seven Arts

1967

Estelle Parsons in *Bonnie and Clyde*, Warner Bros.-Seven Arts
Carol Channing in *Thoroughly Modern Millie*, Universal
Mildred Natwick in *Barefoot in the Park*, Paramount
Beah Richards in *Guess Who's Coming to Dinner*, Columbia
Katharine Ross in *The Graduate*, Embassy

1968

Ruth Gordon in *Rosemary's Baby*, Paramount
Lynn Carlin in *Faces*, Walter Reade-Continental Distr.
Sondra Locke in *The Heart Is a Lonely Hunter*, Warner Bros.-Seven Arts
Kay Medford in *Funny Girl*, Columbia
Estelle Parsons in *Rachel, Rachel*, Warner Bros.-Seven Arts

1969

Goldie Hawn in *Cactus Flower*, Columbia
Catherine Burns in *Last Summer*, Allied Artists
Dyan Cannon in *Bob & Carol & Ted & Alice*, Columbia
Sylvia Miles in *Midnight Cowboy*, UA
Susannah York in *They Shoot Horses, Don't They?*, Cinerama

1970

Helen Hayes in *Airport*, Universal
Karen Black in *Five Easy Pieces*, Columbia
Lee Grant in *The Landlord*, UA

Sally Kellerman in *M*A*S*H*, 20th C.-Fox
Maureen Stapleton in *Airport*, Universal

1971

Cloris Leachman in *The Last Picture Show*, Columbia
Ellen Burstyn in *The Last Picture Show*, Columbia
Barbara Harris in *Who Is Harry Kellerman and Why Is He Saying Those Terrible Things about Me?*, National General
Margaret Leighton in *The Go-Between*, Columbia
Ann-Margret in *Carnal Knowledge*, Avco Embassy

1972

Eileen Heckart in *Butterflies Are Free*, Columbia
Jeannie Berlin in *The Heartbreak Kid*, 20th C.-Fox
Geraldine Page in *Pete 'n' Tillie*, Universal
Susan Tyrrell in *Fat City*, Columbia
Shelley Winters in *The Poseidon Adventure*, 20th C.-Fox

1973

Tatum O'Neal in *Paper Moon*, Paramount
Linda Blair in *The Exorcist*, Warner Bros.
Candy Clark in *American Graffiti*, Universal
Madeline Kahn, *Paper Moon*, Paramount
Sylvia Sidney in *Summer Wishes, Winter Dreams*, Columbia

1974

Ingrid Bergman in *Murder on the Orient Express*, Paramount
Valentina Cortese in *Day for Night*, Warner Bros.
Madeline Kahn in *Blazing Saddles*, Warner Bros.
Diane Ladd in *Alice Doesn't Live Here Anymore*, Warner Bros.
Talia Shire in *The Godfather Part II*, Paramount

1975

Lee Grant in *Shampoo*, Columbia
Ronee Blakley in *Nashville*, Paramount
Sylvia Miles in *Farewell, My Lovely*, Avco Embassy
Lily Tomlin in *Nashville*, Paramount
Brenda Vaccaro in *Jacqueline Susann's Once Is Not Enough*, Paramount

1976

Beatrice Straight in *Network*, MGM-UA
Jane Alexander in *All the President's Men*, Warner Bros.
Jodie Foster in *Taxi Driver*, Columbia Pictures
Lee Grant in *Voyage of the Damned*, Avco Embassy
Piper Laurie in *Carrie*, UA

1977

Vanessa Redgrave in *Julia*, 20th C.-Fox
Leslie Browne in *The Turning Point*, 20th C.-Fox
Quinn Cummings in *The Goodbye Girl*, MGM-Warner Bros.
Melinda Dillon in *Close Encounters of the Third Kind*, Columbia
Tuesday Weld in *Looking for Mr. Goodbar*, Paramount

1978

Maggie Smith in *California Suite*
Dyan Cannon in *Heaven Can Wait*, Paramount
Penelope Milford in *Coming Home*, UA
Maureen Stapleton in *Interiors*, UA
Meryl Streep in *The Deer Hunter*, Universal

1979

Meryl Streep in *Kramer vs. Kramer*, Columbia
Jane Alexander in *Kramer vs. Kramer*, Columbia
Barbara Barrie in *Breaking Away*, 20th C.-Fox
Candice Bergen in *Starting Over*
Mariel Hemingway in *Manhattan*, UA

1980

Mary Steenburgen in *Melvin and Howard*
Eileen Brennan in *Private Benjamin*
Eva Le Gallienne in *Resurrection*
Cathy Moriarty in *Raging Bull*, UA
Diana Scarwid in *Inside Moves*

1981

Maureen Stapleton in *Reds*, Paramount
Melinda Dillon in *Absence of Malice*
Jane Fonda in *On Golden Pond*, Universal
Joan Hackett in *Only When I Laugh*
Elizabeth McGovern in *Ragtime*

1982

Jessica Lange in *Tootsie*, Columbia
Glenn Close in *The World According to Garp*
Teri Garr in *Tootsie*, Columbia
Kim Stanley in *Frances*
Lesley Ann Warren in *Victor/Victoria*

At the RKO Pantages Theatre, Edmund Gwenn, Best Supporting Actor of 1947, presented Gloria Grahame with her 1952 Oscar for her supporting role in *The Bad and the Beautiful.*

CHAPTER 8

Best Writing Awards

"From time immemorial, Hollywood producers have been obsessed by the problem of how to make pictures without using writers," Oscar-winning screenwriter S. J. Perelman once mused. "They tried every imaginable device, such as employing the half-dozen apes reputed to have tapped out all the plays of Shakespeare. In final desperation, they sometimes wrote the screenplays themselves—but these grossed even less than the chimpanzee version."

Of course, writers could never be dispensed with, but they could go unappreciated. One studio executive called writers "a necessary evil," and another said, "Writers clutter up a story conference."

Given fans' worship of stars and movie buffs' adoration of directors, there is no one left to love the writers. "Writing a good movie brings about as much fame as riding a bicycle," complained Academy

Award winning writer Ben Hecht.

A few enlightened souls begged to differ. Samuel Goldwyn, known for his caustic barbs as well as his malapropisms, surprisingly enough wrote this in the *Saturday Evening Post*: "Just as water can't rise above its source, so a picture can't rise higher than its story. The bigger the stars, the director and the producer, the harder they fall on a bad story."

The Oscars have indeed provided recognition for writers, though sometimes in such vague and changing categories that the public could be excused for not being sure who had done what. Since Oscar's inception, the Academy has changed the names of the writing awards an average of once every three years.

The problem has been sorting out writers who create original screenplays from those who adapt works, such as novels and plays, by others. Original authors working in other media never win Oscars unless they adapt their own works.

Bo Goldman has won two Academy Awards for his writing—one as co-author of *One Flew over the Cuckoo's Nest* (1975) and one for *Melvin and Howard* (1980).

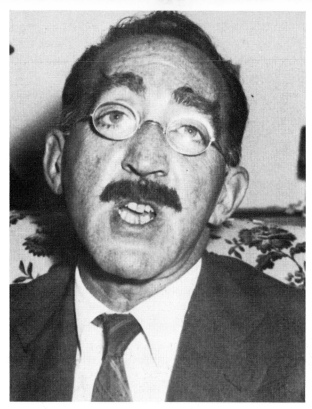

Humor writer S. J. Perelman complained about an American ailment, "decay of the funny bone." He won an Oscar for co-writing the adapted screenplay *Around the World in 80 Days* (1956).

Ben Hecht, Oscar winner for writing the early films *Underworld* (1927–28) and *The Scoundrel* (1935), thought writers should receive greater recognition for their work.

Writer Dudley Nichols, a militant member of the Screen Writers Guild, was the first person to refuse an Academy Award. He refused to accept the Best Writing award for *The Informer* in 1935.

Playright Robert Bolt rewrote his Broadway drama, *A Man for All Seasons,* for the screen. The 1966 film brought Bolt an Academy Award for writing.

Woody Allen teamed up with Marshall Brickman to write *Annie Hall*, and they each won an Oscar for their screenplay.

When it comes to voting on adaptations, it has never been explained how Academy voters sorted out the adapter's contributions from the original author's—without taking the two texts and comparing them word for word. Controversies have been plentiful in the writing categories. A hassle with the Screen Writers Guild, arguments over who really deserved credit for various scripts, and confusion over two films with the same title (*High Society,* 1956) all caused friction.

The most deeply felt disputes concerned the infamous political blacklisting of the 1950s, which affected many liberal-leaning writers. Despite studio pressures, blacklisted writers received 17 nominations and eight Oscars, Hollywood journalist Peter H. Brown calculated. In 1956, during the McCarthy era, the winner was the pseudonymous "Robert Rich" (for *The Brave One*), later identified as the blacklisted writer Dalton Trumbo.

More significant than they are familiar, the names and faces in this chapter are of men and women who make their absolutely essential contributions to the movies far behind the scenes.

Leo McCarey with Best Director Oscar for *The Awful Truth* (1937)

*L*eo McCarey is one of only five men to double up and win both writing and directing Oscars for the same film. He did it with *Going My Way* (1944), the third feature for which he had worn both hats. The screenwriter-directors with the hyphens in their titles stand out in American film-making as having a special claim to the hallowed French term for the person who is the guiding force and single mind behind a film—the *auteur*.

Moviemaking always requires collaboration, of course. But the hyphenates obviously have additional and expanded opportunity to put their personal imprint on a picture.

Billy Wilder (*The Lost Weekend*, 1945), John Huston (*The Treasure of Sierra Madre*, 1948), Francis Ford Coppola (*The Godfather Part II*, 1974), and Woody Allen (*Annie Hall*, 1977) have matched McCarey's achievement. Others came close. William Wellman (*A Star Is Born*, 1937), Orson Welles (*Citizen Kane*, 1941), and Claude Lelouch (*A Man and a Woman*, 1966), received writing awards and directing nominations for their films.

McCarey boasted one more hyphenation in his

McCarey the Hyphenate

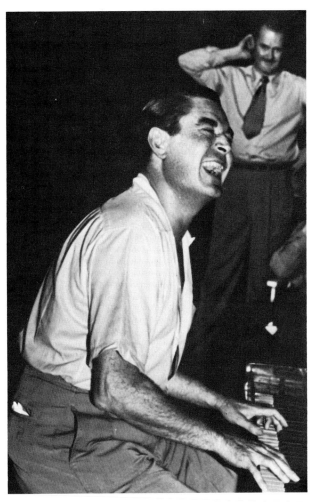

Besides producing, directing, and writing, the versatile McCarey could write lyrics.

McCarey at the 25th annual Academy Awards ceremony in New York

job title, since he also produced *Going My Way*, which was named Best Picture of 1944. The talented comedy director followed the dictum of his friend, Frank Capra: "One man, one film." Altogether, Leo McCarey was nominated three times as a writer and three times as a director. His versatility did not stop there: In 1957 he was nominated as a lyricist for *An Affair to Remember*.

François Truffaut has called him "great," but McCarey enjoyed less esteem among American critics. They found his 1940s works, particularly, to be too sentimental.

McCarey's career started in the silent days, when he wrote and directed some of the Laurel and Hardy shorts. Sometimes the writing and directing went on simultaneously, he recalled: "Those were the days at Roach [studios] when some guy would come in and say, 'Listen—Laurel and Hardy in a cobbler's shop.' I'd say, 'Yes? Then what?' and the guy would say, 'That's it—take over.'"

It is little wonder that he learned to do it all.

1927-28

(Adaptation)

Benjamin Glazer for *Seventh Heaven*, Fox

(Original Story)

Ben Hecht for *Underworld*, Paramount

(Title Writing—not given after this year)

Joseph Farnham for *The Fair Co-ed*, Metro-Goldwyn-Mayer
Joseph Farnham for *Laugh, Clown, Laugh*, MGM
Joseph Farnham for *Telling the World*, MGM

1928-29

Hans Kraly for *The Patriot*, Paramount

1929-30

Frances Marion for *The Big House*, MGM

Veteran novelist Frances Marvin won Oscars for writing *The Big House* (1930) and *The Champ* (1931).

1930-31

(Adaptation)

Howard Estabrook for *Cimarron*, RKO Radio

(Original Story)

John Monk Saunders for the *The Dawn Patrol*, Warner Bros.-First Natl.

1931-32

(Adaptation)

Edwin Burke for *Bad Girl*, Fox

(Original Story)

Frances Marion for *The Champ*, MGM

1932-33

(Adaptation)

Victor Heerman and **Sarah Y. Mason** for *Little Women*, RKO Radio

(Original Story)

Robert Lord for *One Way Passage*, Warner Bros.

1934

(Adaptation)

Robert Riskin for *It Happened One Night*, Columbia

(Original Story)

Arthur Caesar for *Manhattan Melodrama*, MGM

1935

(Original Story)

Ben Hecht and **Charles MacArthur** for *The Scoundrel*, Paramount

(Screenplay)

Dudley Nichols for *The Informer*, RKO Radio

1936

(Original Story)

Pierre Collings and **Sheridan Gibney** for *The Story of Louis Pasteur*, Warner Bros.

(Screenplay)

Pierre Collings and **Sheridan Gibney** for *The Story of Louis Pasteur*, Warner Bros.

1937

(Original Story)

William A Wellman and **Robert Carson** for *A Star Is Born*, UA

(Screenplay)

Heinz Herald, **Geza Herczeg**, and **Norman Reilly Raine** for *The Life of Emile Zola*, Warner Bros.

1938

(Adaptation)

Ian Dalrymple, **Cecil Lewis**, and **W. P. Lipscomb** for *Pygmalion*, MGM (British)

(Original Story)

Eleanore Griffin and **Dore Schary** for *Boys Town*, MGM

(Screenplay)

George Bernard Shaw for *Pygmalion*, MGM (British)

1939

(Original Story)

Lewis R. Foster for *Mr. Smith Goes to Washington*, Columbia

Lewis Foster (right) received the 1939 Original Story Writing award from author Sinclair Lewis for *Mr. Smith Goes to Washington*.

(Screenplay)

Sidney Howard for *Gone with the Wind*, MGM

1940

(Original Story)

Benjamin Glazer and **John S. Toldy** for *Arise, My Love*, Paramount

Best Writing

Sidney Howard's screenplay of Margaret Mitchell's *Gone with the Wind* brought him an Oscar for writing in 1939.

(Original Screenplay)

Preston Sturges for *The Great McGinty*, Paramount

(Screenplay)

Donald Ogden Stewart for *The Philadelphia Story*, MGM

1941

(Original Story)

Harry Segall for *Here Comes Mr. Jordan*, Columbia

(Original Screenplay)

Herman J. Mankiewicz and **Orson Welles** for *Citizen Kane*, RKO Radio

(Screenplay)

Sidney Buchman and **Seton I. Miller** for *Here Comes Mr. Jordan*, Columbia

1942

(Original Story)

Emeric Pressburger for *The Invaders*, Columbia (British)

(Original Screenplay)

Michael Kanin and **Ring Lardner, Jr.,** for *Woman of the Year*, MGM

(Screenplay)

George Froeschel, **James Hilton**, **Claudine West**, and **Arthur Wimperis** for *Mrs. Miniver*, MGM

1943

(Original Story)

William Saroyan for *The Human Comedy*, MGM

(Original Screenplay)

Norman Krasna for *Princess O'Rourke*, Warner Bros.

(Screenplay)

Julius J. Epstein, **Philip G. Epstein**, and **Howard Koch** for *Casablanca*, Warner Bros.

1944

(Original Story)

Leo McCarey for *Going My Way*, Paramount

(Original Screenplay)

Lamar Trotti for *Wilson*, 20th C.-Fox

(Screenplay)

Frank Butler and **Frank Cavett** for *Going My Way*, Paramount

Ring Lardner, Jr., took home an Oscar in 1942 for co-writing the original story, *Woman of the Year*. Lardner won again in 1970 for his screenplay, *M*A*S*H.*

1945

(Original Story)

Charles G. Booth for *The House on 92nd Street*, 20th C.-Fox

(Original Screenplay)

Richard Schweizer for *Marie-Louise*, Praesens Films (Swiss)

(Screenplay)

Charles Brackett and **Billy Wilder** for *The Lost Weekend*, Paramount

1946

(Original Story)

Clarence Dane for *Vacation from Marriage*, MGM (British)

(Original Screenplay)

Muriel Box and **Sydney Box** for *The Seventh Veil*, Universal (British)

(Screenplay)

Robert E. Sherwood for *The Best Years of Our Lives*, RKO Radio

1947

(Original Story)

Valentine Davies for *Miracle on 34th Street*, 20th C.-Fox

(Original Screenplay)

Sidney Sheldon for *The Bachelor and the Bobby-Soxer*, RKO Radio

(Screenplay)

George Seaton for *Miracle on 34th Street*, 20th C.-Fox

1948

(Motion Picture Story)

Richard Schweizer and **David Wechsler** for *The Search*, Praesens Films, MGM (Swiss)

(Screenplay)

John Huston for *The Treasure of the Sierra Madre*, Warner Bros.

1949

(Motion Picture Story)

Douglas Morrow for *The Stratton Story*, MGM

(Screenplay)

Joseph L. Mankiewicz for *A Letter to Three Wives*, 20th C.-Fox

(Story and Screenplay)

Robert Pirosh for *Battleground*, MGM

1950

(Motion Picture Story)

Edna Anhalt and **Edward Anhalt** for *Panic in the Streets*, 20th C.-Fox

(Screenplay)

Joseph L. Mankiewicz for *All about Eve*, 20th C.-Fox

(Story and Screenplay)

Charles Brackett, Billy Wilder, and **D. M. Marshman, Jr.,** for *Sunset Boulevard*, Paramount

(Story and Screenplay)

Alan Jay Lerner for *An American in Paris*, MGM

1952

(Motion Picture Story)

Frederic M. Frank, Theodore St. John, and **Frank Cavett** for *The Greatest Show on Earth*, Paramount

(Screenplay)

Charles Schnee for *The Bad and the Beautiful*, MGM

(Story and Screenplay)

T. E. B. Clarke for *The Lavender Hill Mob*, U-I (British)

1953

(Motion Picture Story)

Ian McLellan Hunter for *Roman Holiday*, Paramount

1954

(Motion Picture Story)

Philip Yordan for *Broken Lance*, 20th C.-Fox

(Screenplay)

George Seaton for *The Country Girl*, Paramount

(Story and Screenplay)

Budd Schulberg for *On the Waterfront*, Columbia

1955

(Motion Picture Story)

Daniel Fuchs for *Love Me or Leave Me*, MGM

(Best Screenplay)

Paddy Chayefsky for *Marty*, UA

A young Paddy Chayefsky received a kiss from actress Claudette Colbert after receiving an Oscar for writing *Marty* (1955). The screenwriter went on to win Oscars for two more screenplays, *The Hospital* (1971) and *Network* (1976).

Director-writer Billy Wilder (right) co-wrote and directed *Sunset Boulevard* (1950), which starred Gloria Swanson and producer Cecil B. De Mille (left) as himself. Wilder has won an Oscar for co-writing three screenplays: *The Lost Weekend* (1945) and *The Apartment* (1960) as well as *Sunset Boulevard.*

1951

(Motion Picture Story)

Paul Dehn and **James Bernard** for *Seven Days to Noon*, Mayer-Kingsley-Distinguished Films (British)

(Screenplay)

Michael Wilson and **Harry Brown** for *A Place in the Sun*, Paramount

(Screenplay)

Daniel Taradash for *From Here to Eternity*, Columbia

(Story and Screenplay)

Charles Brackett, Walter Reisch, and **Richard Breen** for *Titanic*, 20th C.-Fox

(Story and Screenplay)

William Ludwig and **Sonya Levien** for *Interrupted Melody*, MGM

1956

(Motion Picture Story)

Robert Rich (a.k.a. Dalton Trumbo) for *The Brave One*, RKO Radio

(Best Screenplay—adapted)

James Poe, **John Farrow**, and **S. J. Perelman** for *Around the World in 80 Days*, UA

(Best Screenplay—original)

Albert Lamorisse for *The Red Balloon*, Lopert Films Dist. Corp. (French)

1957

(Best Screenplay—based on material from another medium)

Pierre Boulle for *The Bridge on the River Kwai*, Columbia

(Best Story and Screenplay—written directly for the screen)

George Wells for *Designing Woman*, MGM

1958

(Best Screenplay—based on material from another medium)

Alan Jay Lerner for *Gigi*, MGM

(Best Story and Screenplay—written directly for the screen)

Nathan E. Douglas and **Harold Jacob Smith** for *The Defiant Ones*, UA

1959

(Best Screenplay—based on material from another medium)

Neil Paterson for *Room at the Top*, Continental Dist., Inc. (British)

(Best Story and Screenplay—written directly for the screen)

Russel Rouse and **Clarence Greene** (Story); **Stanley Shapiro** and **Maurice Richlin** (Screenplay) for *Pillow Talk*, U-I

1960

(Best Screenplay—based on material from another medium)

Richard Brooks for *Elmer Gantry*, UA

(Best Story and Screenplay—written directly for the screen)

Billy Wilder and **I. A. L. Diamond** for *The Apartment*, UA

1961

(Best Screenplay—based on material from another medium)

Abby Mann for *Judgment at Nuremburg*, UA

(Best Story and Screenplay—written directly for the screen)

William Inge for *Splendor in the Grass*, Warner Bros.

1962

(Best Screenplay—based on material from another medium)

Horton Foote for *To Kill a Mockingbird*, U-I

(Best Story and Screenplay—written directly for the screen)

Ennio De Concini, **Alfredo Giannetti**, and **Pietro Germi** for *Divorce—Italian Style*, Embassy Pictures

1963

(Best Screenplay—based on material from another medium)

John Osborne for *Tom Jones*, UA

(Best Story and Screenplay—written directly for the screen)

James R. Webb for *How the West Was Won*, MGM-Cinerama

1964

(Best Screenplay—based on material from another medium)

Edward Anhalt for *Becket*, Paramount

(Best Story and Screenplay—written directly for the screen)

S. H. Barnett (Story); **Peter Stone** and **Frank Tarloff** (Screenplay) for *Father Goose*, Universal

1965

(Best Screenplay—based on material from another medium)

Robert Bolt for *Doctor Zhivago*, MGM

(Best Story and Screenplay—written directly for the screen)

Frederic Raphael for *Darling*, Embassy

1966

(Best Screenplay—based on material from another medium)

Robert Bolt for *A Man for all Seasons*, Columbia

(Best Story and Screenplay—written directly for the screen)

Claude Lelouch (Story); **Pierre Uytterhoeven** and **Claude Lelouch** (Screenplay) for *A Man and a Woman*, Allied Artists

1967

(Best Screenplay—based on material from another medium)

Stirling Silliphant for *In the Heat of the Night*, UA

(Best Story and Screenplay—written directly for the screen)

William Rose for *Guess Who's Coming to Dinner*, Columbia

1968

(Best Screenplay—based on material from another medium)

James Goldman for *A Lion in Winter*, Avco Embassy

(Best Story and Screenplay—written directly for the screen)

Mel Brooks for *The Producers*, Avco Embassy

1969

(Best Screenplay—based on material from another medium)

Waldo Salt for *Midnight Cowboy*, UA

(Best Story and Screenplay—based on material not previously published or produced)

William Goldman for *Butch Cassidy and the Sundance Kid*, 20th C.-Fox

1970

(Best Screenplay—based on material from another medium)

Ring Lardner, Jr., for *M*A*S*H*, 20th C.-Fox

(Best Story and Screenplay—based on factual material or material not previously published or produced)

Francis Ford Coppola and **Edmund H. North** for *Patton*, 20th C.-Fox

1971

(Best Screenplay—based on material from another medium)

Ernest Tidyman for *The French Connection*, 20th C.-Fox

(Best Story and Screenplay—based on factual material or material not previously published or produced)

Paddy Chayefsky for *The Hospital*, UA

1972

(Best Screenplay—based on material from another medium)

Mario Puzo and **Francis Ford Coppola** for *The Godfather*, Paramount

(Best Story and Screenplay—based on factual material or material not previously published or produced)

Jeremy Larner for *The Candidate*, Warner Bros.

1973

(Best Screenplay—based on material from another medium)

William Peter Blatty for *The Exorcist*, Warner Bros.

(Best Story and Screenplay—based on factual or previously unpublished or produced material)

David S. Ward for *The Sting*, Universal

1974

(Best Original Screenplay)

Robert Towne for *Chinatown*, Paramount

(Best Screenplay—adapted from other material)

Francis Ford Coppola and **Mario Puzo** for *The Godfather Part II*, Paramount

1975

(Best Original Screenplay)

Frank Pierson for *Dog Day Afternoon*, Warner Bros.

(Best Screenplay—adapted from other material)

Lawrence Hauben and **Bo Goldman** for *One Flew over the Cuckoo's Nest*, UA

1976

(Best Screenplay—written directly for the screen)

Paddy Chayefsky for *Network*, MGM

(Best Screenplay—based on material from another medium)

William Goldman for *All the President's Men*, Warner Bros.

1977

(Best Original Screenplay)

Woody Allen and **Marshall Brickman** for *Annie Hall*, UA

(Best Screenplay—based on material from another medium)

Alvin Sargent for *Julia*, 20th C.-Fox

1978

(Best Screenplay—written directly for the screen)

Waldo Salt and **Robert C. Jones** for *Coming Home*, UA

(Best Screenplay—based on material from another medium)

Oliver Stone for *Midnight Express*, Columbia (British)

At the 1976 Awards show Norman Mailer (right) presented William Goldman with an Oscar for Best Screenplay for *All the President's Men*. Goldman had also won a writing Oscar for the 1969 film, *Butch Cassidy and the Sundance Kid*.

1979

(Best Screenplay—written directly for the screen)

Steve Tesich for *Breaking Away*, 20th C.-Fox

(Best Screenplay—based on material from another medium)

Robert Benton for *Kramer vs. Kramer*, Columbia

1980

(Best Original Screenplay)

Bo Goldman for *Melvin and Howard*

(Best Adapted Screenplay)

Alvin Sargent for *Ordinary People*, Paramount

Ernest Thompson successfully reworked his play, *On Golden Pond*, to win the 1982 Best Screenplay award.

1981

(Best Original Screenplay)

Colin Welland for *Chariots of Fire*, Warner Bros.

(Best Adapted Screenplay)

Ernest Thompson for *On Golden Pond*, Universal

1982

(Best Original Screenplay)

John Briley for *Gandhi*, Columbia

(Best Adapted Screenplay)

Constantin Costa-Gavras and **Donald Stewart** for *Missing*, Universal

Producer-director-writer Preston Sturges' only Oscar was for the original screenplay of *The Great McGinty* (1940).

CHAPTER 9

Best Music Awards

Writing film music requires "a stop-watch, a mathematical mind, and quarts of blood," as composer Johnny Green, a four-time Oscar winner, put it.

The Academy's winning scores are all the more remarkable as musical compositions because their creators faced such tight constraints. The medium has proved challenging to some composers well-known for their serious work on the concert stage. Two examples are Aaron Copland (Oscar winner for *The Heiress*, 1949) and Leonard Bernstein (nominee for *On the Waterfront*, 1954). But most of the winning composers have worked with little recognition from the public and often even less appreciation for what they do.

A musical soundtrack, first of all, must fit its picture. And while it is being squeezed into what Green has called a "cinematic straitjacket," the music is also expected to establish atmosphere and mood, heighten suspense, accentuate climaxes, and even add significance to characters. Though audiences are often unaware of it, music can pack much of a movie's psychological punch.

Movie composers had already discovered the secret to accomplishing these tasks in 1934, when the Music Award for Scoring was established (along with the Best Song award). From Wagner's dramatic operas they borrowed the idea of *leitmotif*—the musical theme or 'label' that could be associated with a person, place, or thing. As a plot developed, these themes accumulated new meanings and memories. By the end of a movie, they could suggest ideas on their own, even when the visuals seemed to be saying something else.

Early use of themes was not subtle. The 1935 Oscar winner *The Informer*, scored by Max Steiner, was considered a landmark in its day. But its musical themes were matched literally to the visual shots.

Dimitri Tiomkin's score for *The High and the Mighty* (1954) brought him an Oscar and a reason to smile.

Four-time Oscar winner Johnny Green

Andre Previn, well-known for his serious work on the concert stage, won Oscars for composing the musical scores to *Gigi* (1958) and *Irma La Douce* (1963).

Musician Harry Warren (left) and lyricist Mack Gordon wrote the beloved song, "I've Got a Gal in Kalamazoo," for the film *Orchestra Wires* (1942). That song was nominated for an Oscar, and the song "You'll Never Know" (from *Hello Frisco, Hello*) earned the songwriting team an Oscar in 1943.

"A blind man could have sat in the theater and known when Gypo [the character played by Victor McLaglen] was on the screen," Steiner has acknowledged.

As themes came to be used more poetically, the music also broke its lockstep synchronization with action. Composers became more at ease with psychological themes. Miklos Rozsa's tension-filled score for *Spellbound* (the 1945 Oscar winner) reflected the turmoil of a troubled mind. Hugo Friedhofer's winning effort for *The Best Years of Our Lives* (1946) used themes that at once conveyed the

pride and melancholy of the characters' mixed feelings.

A change came in 1952 when *High Noon*, a serious western, won both the Music Scoring and the Best Song awards. Before that, almost every Best Song had occurred in a musical, and the characters had sung it on camera. In *High Noon*, Dimitri Tiomkin and Ned Washington's "Do Not Forsake Me, Oh My Darlin'" was a voice-over, entirely separable from the film, and it was one of the first such songs to achieve great popularity.

The "song craze," as purists called it,

Noted songwriter Irving Berlin penned "White Christmas" for *Holiday Inn.* The song was voted 1942's best.

Lyricist Johnny Mercer (left) and musician Henry Mancini won a 1962 Oscar for their song, "Days of Wine and Roses," from the movie of the same name. The year before, the songwriting duo had won an Oscar for "Moon River" from *Breakfast at Tiffany's.*

Star Wars android C3PO visited composer John Williams and the Boston Pops Orchestra in Boston's Symphony Hall. Williams won an Oscar for composing the rousing score to the space adventure story *Star Wars* (1977).

flourished in the 1960s and continues today. Henry Mancini and Johnny Mercer won back-to-back song Oscars in 1961 and 1962 for *Breakfast at Tiffany's* ("Moon River") and *Days of Wine and Roses* (the title song). The 1969 winner was another voice-over that became a radio hit, "Raindrops Keep Fallin' on My Head," written by Burt Bacharach and Hal David for *Butch Cassidy and the Sundance Kid.*

Recently, the growing importance of soundtrack-album sales has called for film music that is listenable as well as dramatic. Winning scores in 1977 (*Star Wars* by John Williams) and 1981 (*Chariots of Fire* by Vangelis) became top sellers in the recording industry.

"I think there's a tendency to pooh-pooh film music," said Johnny Green, who won Oscars for *Easter Parade* (1948), *An American in Paris* (1951), *West Side Story* (1961), and *Oliver!* (1968). "This is because of the few obvious clichés and the few gaucheries that come quickly to eye and ear. Instead, we should think of the vast quantity of film music that does the job it is supposed to do — and does it brilliantly."

Alfred Newman was already an accomplished Broadway and symphony-hall conductor when he moved to Hollywood in 1930 at the age of 29.

Neither Betty Grable nor Dan Dailey won awards for their performances in *Mother Wore Tights,* but Alfred Newman's score earned the composer a 1947 Academy Award.

*A*lfred Newman's extraordinary musical talent was apparent from childhood. He gave his first public piano performance at age eight, and he was conducting orchestras as a teenager. By the time he went to Hollywood in 1930 at age 29, he was a thoroughly accomplished Broadway and symphony-hall conductor.

During the next four decades—much of it at 20th Century-Fox where he served several years as musical director—Newman composed or collaborated on the scores of 200 films. He won nine Oscars and 33 nominations. (More than five nominations were permitted in the scoring categories from 1937 to 1946; this made it possible for Newman to receive, for example, four nominations for 1939 alone.)

Most of his awards were for musicals: *Alexander's Ragtime Band* (1938); *Tin Pan Alley* (1940); *Mother Wore Tights* (1947); *With a Song in My Heart* (1952); *Call Me Madam* (1953); *The King and I* (1956); and *Camelot* (1967).

But Newman was known for his versatility. He won for two dramatic films, *The Song of Bernadette* (1943) and *Love Is a Many-*

Leading Scorer

Co-composers Alfred Newman and Ken Darby won Oscars for the score of *The King and I* (1956).

Newman, who served for many years as 20th Century–Fox's musical director, composed or collaborated on the scores of 200 films.

Splendored Thing (1955), and he received nominations for such diverse films as the early disaster movie *Hurricane* (1937), the tempestuous romance *Wuthering Heights* (1939), the biography *Wilson* (1944), and the biblical epic *David and Bathsheba* (1951).

Newman set trends with new ways of orchestrating. He loved to experiment with microphone placement, trying to emphasize certain instruments in ways that would not be possible in the concert hall.

Newman rejected sound-tracks that repeated literally the messages of the pictures, as early film scores often did. "Whenever a man plunged through a manhole," he said, "the movie music would follow him right into the bass clef. Or, should a girl run upstairs, a light little upward run would run up the flute with her."

As important as he was in providing and leading others to provide freer, more inspired music, he remained modest about his craft. "If I want to write 'great music,'" he once said, "I've no right to be here. Good picture music must always be inspired by the picture of which it is a part, not by the desire of the composer to 'express himself.'"

The Academy, however, found his work expressive to the end. His music for *Airport*, the last film on which he worked, received a nomination as the Best Original Score of 1970. He died that same year. Alfred Newman's talent was inherited by his son, popular singer/composer Randy Newman.

1934

(Best Score)

One Night of Love, Columbia Studio Music Department: **Louis Silvers**, Head. Thematic Music by **Victor Schertzinger** and **Gus Kahn**

(Best Song)

"**The Continental**" from *The Gay Divorcee*, RKO Radio: Music by **Con Conrad**; lyrics by **Herb Magidson**

Fred Astaire and Ginger Rogers danced "The Continental" in *The Gay Divorcee* (1934). Songwriters Con Conrad and Herb Magidson received Oscars for the song.

1935

(Best Score)

The Informer, RKO Radio Studio Music Department: **Max Steiner**, Head. Score by **Max Steiner**

(Best Song)

"**Lullaby of Broadway**" from *Gold Diggers of 1935*, Warner Brothers: Music by **Harry Warren**; lyrics by **Al Dubin**

1936

(Best Score)

Anthony Adverse, Warner Bros. Studio Music Department: **Leo Forbstein**, Head. Score by **Erich Wolfgang Korngold**

Two-time Oscar winning composer Erich Wolfgang Korngold at his piano

(Best Song)

"**The Way You Look Tonight**" from *Swing Time*, RKO Radio: Music by **Jerome Kern**; lyrics by **Dorothy Fields**

1937

(Best Score)

One Hundred Men and a Girl, Universal Studio Music Department: **Charles Previn**, Head

(Best Song)

"**Sweet Leilani**" from *Waikiki Wedding*, Parmount: Music and lyrics by **Harry Owens**

1938

(Best Score)

Alexander's Ragtime Band, 20th Century-Fox: **Alfred Newman**

(Original Score)

The Adventures of Robin Hood, Warner Bros.: **Erich Wolfgang Korngold**

(Best Song)

"**Thanks for the Memory**" from *Big Broadcast of 1938*, Paramount: Music by **Ralph Rainger**; lyrics by **Leo Robin**

1939

(Best Score)

Stagecoach, United Artists: **Richard Hageman, Frank Harling, John Leipold**, and **Leo Shuken**

(Original Score)

The Wizard of Oz, MGM: **Herbert Stothart**

(Best Song)

"*Over the Rainbow*" from *The Wizard of Oz*, MGM: Music by **Harold Arlen**; lyrics by **E. Y. Harburg**

Harold Arlen's "Somewhere over the Rainbow" from *The Wizard of Oz* (1939) captured millions of hearts as well as an Academy Award for Best Song.

1940

(Best Score)

Tin Pan Alley, 20th C.-Fox: **Alfred Newman**

(Original Score)

Pinocchio, Disney-RKO Radio: **Leigh Harline, Paul J. Smith**, and **Ned Washington**

(Best Song)

"**When You Wish upon a Star**" from *Pinocchio*, Disney-RKO Radio: Music by **Leigh Harline**; lyrics by **Ned Washington**

Music:
Best Scoring and Best Song

1941

(Scoring of a Dramatic Picture)

All that Money Can Buy, RKO Radio: **Bernard Herrmann**

(Scoring of a Musical Picture)

Dumbo, Disney-RKO Radio: **Frank Churchill** and **Oliver Wallace**

(Best Song)

"**The Last Time I Saw Paris**" from *Lady Be Good*, MGM: Music by **Jerome Kern**; lyrics by **Oscar Hammerstein II**

1942

(Scoring of a Dramatic or Comedy Picture)

Now, Voyager, Warner Bros.: **Max Steiner**

(Scoring of a Musical Picture)

Yankee Doodle Dandy, Warner Bros.: **Ray Heindorf** and **Heinz Roemheld**

(Best Song)

"**White Christmas**" from *Holiday Inn*, Paramount: Music and lyrics by **Irving Berlin**

1943

(Scoring of a Dramatic or Comedy Picture)

The Song of Bernadette, 20th C.-Fox: **Alfred Newman**

(Scoring of a Musical Picture)

This Is the Army, Warner Bros.: **Ray Heindorf**

(Best Song)

"**You'll Never Know**" from *Hello, Frisco, Hello*, 20th C.-Fox: Music by **Harry Warren**; lyrics by **Mack Gordon**

1944

(Scoring of a Dramatic or Comedy Picture)

Since You Went Away, UA: **Max Steiner**

(Scoring of a Musical Picture)

Cover Girl, Columbia: **Carmen Dragon** and **Morris Stoloff**

(Best Song)

"**Swinging on a Star**" from *Going My Way*, Paramount: Music by **James Van Heusen**; lyrics by **Johnny Burke**

1945

(Scoring of a Dramatic or Comedy Picture)

Spellbound, Selznick, UA: **Miklos Rozsa**

(Scoring of a Musical Picture)

Anchors Aweigh, MGM: **George Stoll**

(Best Song)

"**It Might as Well Be Spring**" from *State Fair*, 20th C.-Fox: Music by **Richard Rodgers**; lyrics by **Oscar Hammerstein II**

1946

(Scoring of a Dramatic or Comedy Picture)

The Best Years of Our Lives, Goldwyn-RKO Radio: **Hugo Friedhofer**

(Scoring of a Musical Picture)

The Jolson Story, Columbia: **Morris Stoloff**

(Best Song)

"**On the Atchinson, Topeka and Santa Fe**" from *The Harvey Girls*, MGM: Music by **Harry Warren**; lyrics by **Johnny Mercer**

1947

(Scoring of a Dramatic or Comedy Picture)

A Double Life, Universal-International: **Miklos Rozsa**

(Scoring of a Musical Picture)

Mother Wore Tights, 20th C.-Fox: **Alfred Newman**

(Best Song)

"**Zip-a-Dee-Doo-Dah**" from *Song of the South*, Disney-RKO Radio: Music by **Allie Wrubel**; lyrics by **Ray Gilbert**

1948

(Scoring of a Dramatic or Comedy Picture)

The Red Shoes, Rank-Archers-Eagle-Lion (British): **Brian Easdale**

(Scoring of a Musical Picture)

Easter Parade, MGM: **Johnny Green** and **Roger Edens**

(Best Song)

"**Buttons and Bows**" from *The Paleface*, Paramount: Music and lyrics by **Jay Livingston** and **Ray Evans**

1949

(Scoring of a Dramatic or Comedy Picture)

The Heiress, Paramount: **Aaron Copland**

(Best Song)

"**Baby It's Cold Outside**" from *Neptune's Daughter*, MGM: Music and lyrics by **Frank Loesser**

1950

(Scoring of a Dramatic or Comedy Picture)

Sunset Boulevard, Paramount: **Franz Waxman**

(Scoring of a Musical Picture)

Annie Get Your Gun, MGM: **Adolph Deutsch** and **Roger Edens**

(Best Song)

"**Mona Lisa**" from *Captain Carey*, Paramount: Music and lyrics by **Ray Evans** and **Jay Livingston**

1951

(Scoring of a Dramatic or Comedy Picture)

A Place in the Sun, Paramount: **Franz Waxman**

(Scoring of a Musical Picture)

An American in Paris, MGM: **Johnny Green** and **Saul Chaplin**

(Best Song)

"**In the Cool, Cool, Cool of the Evening**" from *Here Comes the Groom*: Music by **Hoagy Carmichael**; lyrics by **Johnny Mercer**

1952

(Scoring of a Dramatic or Comedy Picture)

High Noon, UA: **Dimitri Tiomkin**

(Scoring of a Musical Picture)

With a Song in My Heart, 20th C.-Fox: **Alfred Newman**

(Best Song)

"**High Noon (Do Not Forsake Me, Oh My Darlin')**" from *High Noon*: Music by **Dimitri Tiomkin**; lyrics by **Ned Washington**

1953

(Scoring of a Dramatic or Comedy Picture)

Lili, MGM: **Bronislau Kaper**

(Scoring of a Musical Picture)

Call Me Madam, 20th C.-Fox: **Alfred Newman**

(Best Song)

"Secret Love" from Calamity Jane, Warner Bros.: Music by **Sammy Fain**; lyrics by **Paul Francis Webster**

1954

(Scoring of a Dramatic or Comedy Picture)

The High and the Mighty, Warner Bros.: **Dimitri Tiomkin**

(Scoring of a Musical Picture)

Seven Brides for Seven Brothers, MGM: **Adolph Deutsch** and **Saul Chaplin**

(Best Song)

"**Three Coins in the Fountain**" from *Three Coins in the Fountain*: Music by **Jule Styne**; lyrics by **Sammy Cahn**

1955

(Scoring of a Dramatic or Comedy Picture)

Love Is a Many-Splendored Thing, 20th C.-Fox: **Alfred Newman**

(Scoring of a Musical Picture)

Oklahoma!, Rogers & Hammerstein Pictures, Inc.: **Robert Russell Bennett, Jay Blackton,** and **Adolph Deutsch**

(Best Song)

"**Love Is a Many-Splendored Thing**" from *Love Is a Many-Splendored Thing,* 20th C.-Fox: Music by

Sammy Fain; lyrics by **Paul Francis Webster**

1956

(Scoring of a Dramatic or Comedy Picture)

Around the World in 80 Days, UA: **Victor Young**

(Scoring of a Musical Picture)

The King and I, 20th C.-Fox: **Alfred Newman** and **Ken Darby**

(Best Song)

"**Whatever Will Be, Will Be (Que Sera, Sera)**" from *The Man Who Knew Too Much*, Paramount: Music and lyrics by **Jay Livingston** and **Ray Evans**

1957

(Best Music Scoring)

The Bridge on the River Kwai, Columbia: **Malcolm Arnold**

(Best Song)

"All the Way" from *The Joker Is Wild*: Music by **James Van Heusen**; lyrics by **Sammy Cahn**

1958

(Scoring of a Dramatic or Comedy Picture)

The Old Man and the Sea, Warner Bros.: **Dimitri Tiomkin**

(Scoring of a Musical Picture)

Gigi, MGM: **André Previn**

(Best Song)

"**Gigi**" from *Gigi*, MGM: Music by **Frederick Loewe**; lyrics by **Alan Jay Lerner**

1959

(Scoring of a Dramatic or Comedy Picture)

Ben Hur, MGM, **Miklos Rozsa**

(Scoring of a Musical Picture)

Porgy and Bess, Goldwyn-Columbia: **André Previn** and **Ken Darby**

(Best Song)

"High Hopes" from *A Hole in the Head*, UA: Music by **James Van Heusen**; lyrics by **Sammy Cahn**

James Van Heusen (left) and Sammy Cahn collected their third Oscar for Best Song, "High Hopes" from *A Hole in the Head* (1959).

1960

(Scoring of a Dramatic or Comedy Picture)

Exodus, UA: **Ernest Gold**

(Scoring of a Musical Picture)

Song without End (the Story of Franz Liszt), Columbia: **Morris Stoloff** and **Harry Sukman**

(Best Song)

"**Never on Sunday**" from *Never on Sunday*, Lopert Picture Corp. (Greek): Music and lyrics by **Manos Hadjidakis**

1961

(Scoring of a Dramatic or Comedy Picture)

Breakfast at Tiffany's, Paramount: **Henry Mancini**

(Scoring of a Musical Picture)

West Side Story, UA: **Saul Chaplin, Johnny Green, Sid Ramin,** and **Irwin Kostal**

(Best Song)

"**Moon River**" from *Breakfast at Tiffany's,* Paramount. Music by **Henry Mancini**; lyrics by **Johnny Mercer**

1962

(Music Score—substantially original)

Lawrence of Arabia, Columbia: **Maurice Jarre**

(Scoring of Music—adaptation or treatment)

The Music Man, Warner Bros.: **Ray Heindorf**

Maurice Jarre won his second Oscar for the original score of *Doctor Zhivago* in 1965. His first was for the score of *Lawrence of Arabia* in 1962.

(Best Song)

"Days of Wine and Roses" from *Days of Wine and Roses*, Warner Bros.: Music by **Henry Mancini**; lyrics by **Johnny Mercer**

1963

(Music Score—substantially original)

Tom Jones, UA-Lopert Pictures: **John Addison**

(Scoring of Music—adaptation or treatment)

Irma La Douce, UA: **André Previn**

(Best Song)

"Call Me Irresponsible" from *Papa's Delicate Condition*, Paramount: Music by **James Van Heusen**; lyrics by **Sammy Cahn**

1964

(Music Score—substantially original)

Mary Poppins, Walt Disney Prods.: **Richard M. Sherman** and **Robert B. Sherman**

(Scoring of Music—adaptation or treatment)

My Fair Lady, Warner Bros.: **André Previn**

(Best Song)

"Chim Chim Cher-ee" from *Mary Poppins*, Walt Disney Prods.: Music and lyrics by **Richard M. Sherman** and **Robert B. Sherman**

1965

(Music Score—substantially original)

Doctor Zhivago, MGM: **Maurice Jarre**

(Scoring of Music—adaptation or treatment)

The Sound of Music, 20th C.-Fox: **Irwin Kostal**

(Best Song)

"The Shadow of Your Smile" from *The Sandpiper*, MGM: Music by **Johnny Mandel**; lyrics by **Paul Francis Webster**

1966

(Original Music Score)

Born Free, Columbia: **John Barry**

(Scoring of Music—adaptation or treatment)

A Funny Thing Happened on the Way to the Forum, UA: **Ken Thorne**

(Best Song)

"Born Free" from *Born Free*, Columbia: Music by **John Barry**; lyrics by **Don Black**

1967

(Original Music Score)

Thoroughly Modern Millie, Universal: **Elmer Bernstein**

(Scoring of Music—adaptation or treatment)

Camelot, Warner Bros.-Seven Arts: **Alfred Newman** and **Ken Darby**

(Best Song)

"Talk to the Animals" from *Doctor Dolittle*, 20th C.-Fox: Music and lyrics by **Leslie Bricusse**

1968

(Best Original Score—for a non-musical)

The Lion in Winter, Avco Embassy: **John Barry**

(Best Score of a Musical Picture—original or adaptation)

Oliver!, Columbia: Adapted by **John Green**

(Best Song)

"The Windmills of Your Mind" from *The Thomas Crown Affair*, UA: Music by **Michel Legrand**; lyrics by **Alan** and **Marilyn Bergman**

1969

(Best Original Score—for a non-musical)

Butch Cassidy and the Sundance Kid, 20th C.-Fox: **Burt Bacharach**

(Best Score of a Musical Picture—original or adaptation)

Hello Dolly!, 20th C.-Fox: Adapted by **Lennie Hayton** and **Lionel Newman**

(Best Song)

"Raindrops Keep Fallin' on My Head" from *Butch Cassidy and the Sundance Kid*, 20th C.-Fox: Music by **Burt Bacharach**; lyrics by **Hal David**

1970

(Best Original Score)

Love Story, Paramount: **Francis Lai**

(Best Original Song Score)

Let It Be, UA: Music and lyrics by **The Beatles**

(Best Song)

"**For All We Know**" from *Lovers and Other Strangers*, Cinerama: Music by **Fred Karlin**; lyrics by **Robb Royer** and **James Griffin** (a.k.a. **Robb Wilson** and **Arthur James**)

1971

(Best Original Dramatic Score)

Summer of '42, Warner Bros.: **Michel Legrand**

(Best Scoring: Adaptation and Original Song Score)

Fiddler on the Roof, UA: Adapted by **John Williams**

(Best Song)

"**Theme from Shaft**" from *Shaft*, MGM: Music and lyrics by **Isaac Hayes**

1972

(Best Original Dramatic Score)

Limelight, Columbia: **Charles Chaplin**, **Raymond Rasch**, and **Larry Russell**

(Best Scoring: Adaptation and Original Song Score)

Cabaret, Allied Artists: Adapted by **Ralph Burns**

(Best Song)

"**The Morning After**" from *The Poseidon Adventure*, 20th C.-Fox: Music and lyrics by **Al Kasha** and **Joel Hirschhorn**

1973

(Best Original Dramatic Score)

The Way We Were, Columbia: **Marvin Hamlisch**

(Best Scoring: Original Song Score and/or Adaptation)

The Sting, Universal: Adapted by **Marvin Hamlisch**

(Best Song)

"**The Way We Were**" from *The Way We Were*, Columbia: Music by **Marvin Hamlisch**; lyrics by **Alan** and **Marilyn Bergman**

1974

(Best Original Dramatic Score)

The Godfather Part II, Paramount: **Nino Rota** and **Carmine Coppola**

(Best Scoring: Original Song Score and/or Adaptation)

The Great Gatsby, Paramount: Adapted by **Nelson Riddle**

(Best Song)

"**We May Never Love Like This Again**" from *The Towering Inferno*, 20th C.-Fox-Warner Bros.: Music and lyrics by **Al Kasha** and **Joel Hirschhorn**

1975

(Best Original Score)

Jaws, Universal: **John Williams**

(Best Scoring: Original Song Score and/or Adaptation)

Barry Lyndon, Warner Bros.: Adapted by **Leonard Roseman**

(Best Original Song)

"**I'm Easy**" from *Nashville*, Paramount: Music and lyrics by **Keith Carradine**

1976

(Best Original Score)

The Omen, 20th C.-Fox: **Jerry Goldsmith**

(Best Original Song Score and Its Adaptation or Best Adaptation Score)

Bound for Glory, UA: Adapted by **Leonard Rosenman**

(Best Original Song)

"**Evergreen**" from *A Star Is Born*, Warner Bros.: Music by **Barbra Streisand**; lyrics by **Paul Williams**

1977

(Best Original Score)

Star Wars, 20th C.-Fox: **John Williams**

(Best Original Song Score and Its Adaptation or Best Adaptation Score)

A Little Night Music, New World Pictures: Adapted by **Jonathan Tunick**

(Best Song)

"**You Light Up My Life**" from *You Light Up My Life*, Columbia: Music and lyrics by **Joseph Brooks**

1978

(Best Original Score)

Midnight Express, Columbia (British): **Giorgio Moroder**

Isaac Hayes' "Theme from Shaft" was the Best Song of 1971.

Barbra Streisand and Paul Williams' first collaboration, "Evergreen" from *A Star Is Born*, brought them Oscars for the Best Song of 1976.

(Best Adaptation Score)

***The Buddy Holly Story:* Joe Renzetti**

(Best Original Song)

"Last Dance" from *Thank God It's Friday:* Music and lyrics by **Paul Jabara**

1979

(Best Original Score)

***A Little Romance*: Georges Delerue**

(Best Adaptation Score)

***All That Jazz*, 20th C.-Fox: Ralph Burns**

(Best Original Song)

"It Goes Like It Goes" from *Norma Rae*, 20th C.-Fox: Music by **David Shire**; lyrics by **Norman Gimbel**

1980

(Best Original Score)

***Fame*: Michael Gore**

(Best Original Song)

"Fame" from *Fame:* Music by **Michael Gore**; lyrics by **Dean Pitchford**

1981

(Best Original Score)

***Chariots of Fire*, Warner Bros.: Vangelis**

(Best Original Song)

"Arthur's Theme (Best that You Can Do)" from *Arthur:* Music and lyrics by **Burt Bacharach, Carole Bayer Sager, Christopher Cross, and Peter Allen**

1982

(Best Original Score)

***E.T.—the Extra-Terrestrial*, Universal: John Williams**

(Best Adaptation Score or Original Score and Its Adaptation)

***Victor/Victoria:* Song score by Henry Mancini and Leslie Bricusse; adapted by Henry Mancini**

(Best Original Song)

"Up Where We Belong," from *An Officer and a Gentleman*: Music by **Jack Nitzsche** and **Buffy St. Marie**; lyrics by **Will Jennings**

CHAPTER 10

Behind-
the-Scenes
Awards

No single individual can make a theatrical movie. Filmmaking is a collaborative art that depends upon effective teamwork among a large number of specialists behind the scenes. The limelight, of course, falls mostly upon the performers and a few directors. But the Academy Awards have fittingly spread that light so that some of it also shines on art directors, cinematographers, costume designers, film editors, sound engineers, and special-effects engineers.

Two of the backstage awards categories—Cinematography and Art Direction/Set Decoration—date from the first year of the Oscars. The Sound awards began in the third year, the Film Editing awards in the seventh, the Special Effects awards in the 12th, and the Costume Design awards in the 21st. The Makeup award began in 1981. In various years before 1967, the Cinematography, Art Direction/Set Decoration, and Costume Design categories included separate awards for black-and-white and color films.

Most of the individual winners in these categories—including some who have been honored or nominated several times—remain little known among audiences. Sound man Douglas Shearer, who has won five Oscars for Sound Recording and two for Special Sound Effects, is hardly a household name. The same can be said for A. Arnold Gillespie and L. B. Abbott, special-effects engineers who have won four Oscars each. Costume designers Edith Head (eight Oscars) and Irene Sharaff (five), cinematographer Joseph Ruttenberg (three), film editor Daniel Mandell (three), and set decorator Edwin B. Willis (eight) are known to few who are not movie buffs or industry insiders.

These behind-the-scenes winners and their colleagues deserve more glory, and the Academy attempts to provide it. They are responsible for an obvious charac-

Cinematographer and cameraman Gregg Toland was the vision behind some of Hollywood's greatest films, including *Les Miserables* (1935), *Wuthering Heights* (1939), and *Citizen Kane* (1941).

Ben Hur's 11 Oscars included many behind-the-scenes awards—Best Color Cinematography, Best Art Direction/Set Decoration, Best Sound, Best Film Editing, Best Costume Design, and Best Special Effects.

The Song of Bernadette was an Academy favorite in 1943, winning Oscars in the Actress, Cinematography, Interior Decoration, and Music categories.

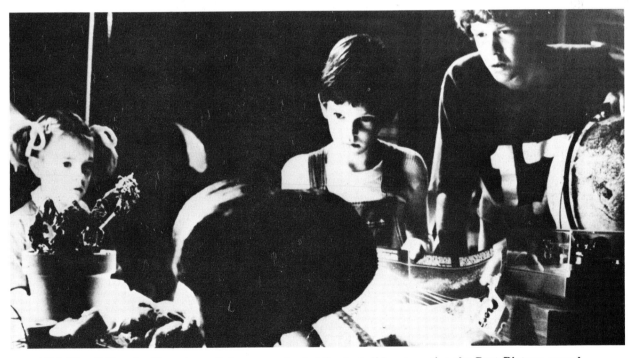

The 1982 film *E.T.—the Extraterrestial* was nominated for but did not receive the Best Picture award. However, the movie did win awards for visual and sound effects. *E.T.*'s young cast included (from left to right) Drew Barrymore, Henry Thomas, and Robert MacNaughton.

teristic of American movies that American audiences often take for granted: their technical excellence. More than that, these people can affect the way a movie looks and sounds—often more directly than the people whose names are above the title. The craftsmen can contribute to a movie's mood or atmosphere and underline details of meaning. Collectively, their actions can determine a movie's success or failure.

One of the earliest Hollywood disaster films, *The Rains Came,* won the first Special Effects award in 1939. Its cast included Brenda Joyce, George Brenda, and Myrna Loy.

The 1974 disaster film, *The Towering Inferno,* won the Special Effects award as well as the Cinematography, Film Editing, and Best Song awards.

*F*rom the day in 1902 when Georges Melies used a cardboard moon as the destination of a studio rocket ship in *A Trip to the Moon,* the movies have used special effects to simulate scenes that would be too difficult (if not impossible), too expensive, or too dangerous to shoot in reality. Special effects have been recognized with regular Academy Awards since 1939. In 1963 the award was split into two categories, Special Visual Effects and Sound Effects.

The first winner of the Special Effects Oscar was *The Rains Came* (1939), a vintage disaster film that pitted Myrna Loy and Tyrone Power against torrents of sprinkler rain and a camera-shaking earthquake.

Such essentially mechanical effects have remained staples of special-effects craftsmen. Performers "fly" on invisible wires (as in *Mary Poppins,* the 1964 Oscar winner), get "killed" by explosive powders (*The Longest Day,* 1962) and fall through breaking "glass" (*The Towering Inferno,* 1974).

But over the years, effects shops have also perfected more sophisticated techniques. Their repertoire now includes

More Special Every Year

A collaboration between Stanley Kubrick and Arthur C. Clarke, *2001: A Space Odyssey* (1968) was considered by many to be years ahead of its time.

Like *Star Wars* (1977), the sequel *The Empire Strikes Back* (1980) used computerized cameras to achieve dazzling visual effects.

miniatures, composite photography, opticals, full-scale mechanical models, electronically controlled animation, computer graphics, and lasers.

A creative explosion of new techniques began with the 1968 winner of the Special Visual Effects award, *2001: A Space Odyssey*. The film opens with front-projection scenes of a prehistoric landscape and closes with a depiction of a mysterious time-space warp. One often-copied effect was the "stargate corridor." The camera slowly exposed a single frame as it dollied toward lights behind a windowed screen. When the frame was replicated many times and projected, it yielded both a dazzling light show and the illusion of high-speed travel through trackless space.

Douglas Trumbull has been recognized as the creator of the stargate corridor effect and others in *2001* (although the award officially went to the film's director, Stanley Kubrick). Trumbull later worked on a 1979 nominee, *Star Trek: The Motion Picture*. His protégé, John Dykstra, contributed to the 1977 winner, *Star Wars*, and won a technical award the same year for his Dykstraflex camera. Computer controls on this camera made possible precise matching of multiple images in the climactic battle scene of *Star Wars*. Similar devices were used in *The Black Hole* (a 1979 nominee) and *The Empire Strikes Back* (the 1980 winner).

In recent nominated and winning movies—including *Star Wars* and *The Black Hole*—computer graphics have played a part. Once an object's dimensions and colors are programmed, the computer can calculate any camera angle or perspective; objects can be flipped, moved, or reshaped far more easily than with conventional animation. The computer has opened a new age of motion picture special effects.

Edith Head is shown holding one of her eight Oscars, this one for the Costume Design of the black-and-white film, *Sabrina* (1954). With her is Machiko Nagata, producer of *Gate of Hell*, a Japanese film that won the color film Costume Design award.

Hedy Lamarr wore a costume in *Samson and Delilah* (1950) designed by Oscar winners Edith Head, Dorothy Jeakins, Elois Jenssen, Gile Steele, and Gwen Wakeling.

*T*he Academy Award for Costume Design was first given in 1948, and in every one of the first 19 years, until 1966, Edith Head received at least one nomination. In nine of those years she was nominated twice, and in 1963, three times. Altogether, she received eight Oscars and 33 nominations.

The designer's work is most apparent in sumptuous spectacles such as Cecil B. De Mille's *Samson and Delilah* (1950), and Head won the Oscar for her fabulous fashions in that film. But she also won for dressing people in black and white films in more contemporary settings, such as *A Place in the Sun* (1951) and *The Facts of Life* (1960). She has been called a "journalistic" designer for the observant, realistic details she incorporates in her work.

One of the few Hollywood designers to work on both men's and women's wardrobes, she has won Oscars for her costume creations for Montgomery Clift and Olivia De Havilland (*The Heiress*, 1950); Bette Davis and George Sanders (*All About Eve*, 1950); Audrey Hepburn and Gregory Peck (*Roman Holiday*, 1953); Humphrey Bogart

Mistress of Seamstresses

and Audrey Hepburn again (*Sabrina*, 1954); and Paul Newman and Robert Redford (*The Sting*, 1973).

When she received her Oscar for *The Sting*, she commented that it seemed superfluous to get an award for an assignment "to dress the two most handsome men in the world." Typically, she was modest about her achievements. "I never got a call from the front office," she once said. "We did what we were hired to do. We were professionals, and if we did what we were supposed to do, why should anyone say anything?"

Regarding the importance of costumes, however, she spoke assertively. In her autobiography, *The Dress Doctor*, she wrote: "Clothes have to do with happiness, with poise, with how you *feel*. You never forget the dress or suit in which you looked well, felt right, and lived wonderful moments—the 'Alice Blue Gown.' Grace Kelly felt drab, dull and downbeat in her *Country Girl* sweater; the clothes depressed her. Anna Magnani felt slovenly and miserable in her sack slip. From Charles Laughton to Yul Brynner, costume has helped immeasurably with every role an actor has to play."

Edith Head's Oscar-winning costumes in *Roman Holiday* helped Audrey Hepburn win the 1953 Best Actress award.

"One of the most handsome men in the world," Robert Redford, was costumed by Edith Head for *The Sting* (1973).

Already a 15-year veteran of films at the age of 30, cinematographer Gregg Toland (right) is shown contemplating the camera's angle on the set at the Samuel Goldwyn Studios.

A recipient of 18 nominations, cinematographer Leon Shamroy won four Oscars for his work.

*C*inematography requires painting with light, and that is just as hard as it sounds. It is an elusive and varied art.

Directors of photography routinely have to capture such effects as sunlight streaming into a coffee shop or rain sweeping a street. The films that have won the Cinematography Oscar involve more complex assignments: fog-shrouded landscapes (*Wuthering Heights*, 1939, cinematographer Greg Toland); combat conditions (*Battleground*, 1949, Paul C. Vogel); or dimly lit interiors (*The Hustler*, 1961, Eugen Shuftan). Each cameraman handles each shot in his own style and may put a stamp of visual authorship on a film that rivals a director's.

Great achievements were possible in the silent days, even though there were no exposure meters and other equipment was primitive by today's standards. The first Academy Award for Cinematography went to Charles Rosher and Karl Struss for the silent *Sunrise* (1927–28). In one shot they simulated steadily brightening sunlight by removing layers of gauze from the front of the lens.

Some of the great changes in movie technology since then initially caused headaches for cameramen. Sound required blimping devices to keep the camera's whirring out of

The Cameraman's Art

Cameraman James Wong Howe is shown here with an Oscar for *The Rose Tattoo* (1955). He also won an Oscar for *Hud* in 1963.

Victor Milner, the cinematographer of *Cleopatra* (starring Claudette Colbert and Henry Wilcoxon), won the Best Cinematography award for 1934.

the microphones. Unhappily, the bulky soundproofing also tended to immobilize the camera. Color meant more light was needed for an exposure, making it harder to achieve a natural look with directional light and shadows. Wide-screen processes, introduced in the 1950s, brought problems of focus and distortion.

Cameramen solved these problems and took on new challenges. More sensitive film stock inspired more location shooting and night photography. (Formerly many night shots were faked in daylight by using filters.) A cameraman had to experiment—under difficult conditions.

Some winning cameramen maintained stylishly distinctive approaches: Robert Krasker used expressionistic tilts and shadows in *The Third Man* (1950); Haskell Wexler simulated a documentary look in *Bound for Glory* (1976); and Geoffrey Unsworth and Ghislain Cloquet achieved glowing lyricism in *Tess* (1980).

A number of others insisted less was best. "To light economically is a rarity in this business," said Leon Shamroy, Cinematography award winner for *The Black Swan* (1942), *Wilson* (1944), *Leave Her to Heaven* (1945), and *Cleopatra* (1963). "I'd always say, 'God was a great photographer. He'd gotten only one light.' " Likewise, James Wong Howe (*The Rose Tattoo,* 1955, and *Hud,* 1963) attempted "to make all sources of light absolutely naturalistic." Lee Garmes, honored for *Shanghai Express* (1932), put it this way: "I don't like photography to *steal* a scene."

1927-28

Charles Rosher and **Karl Struss** for *Sunrise*, Fox

1928-29

Clyde De Vinna for *White Shadows in the South Seas*, Metro-Goldwyn-Mayer

1929-30

Joseph T. Rucker and **Willard Van Der Veer** for *With Byrd at the South Pole*, Paramount

1930-31

Floyd Crosby for *Tabu*, Paramount

1931-32

Lee Garmes for *Shanghai Express*, Paramount

1932-33

Charles Bryant Lang, Jr., for *A Farewell to Arms*, Paramount

1934

Victor Milner for *Cleopatra*, Paramount

1935

Hal Mohr for *A Midsummer Night's Dream*, Warner Brothers

1936

Gaetano Gaudio for *Anthony Adverse*, Warner Bros.

1937

Karl Freund for *The Good Earth*, MGM

1938

Joseph Ruttenberg for *The Great Waltz*, MGM

1939

(Black and White)

Gregg Toland for *Wuthering Heights*, UA

(Color)

Ernest Haller and **Ray Rennahan** for *Gone with the Wind*, MGM

1940

(Black and White)

George Barnes for *Rebecca*, UA

(Color)

George Perinal for *Thief of Bagdad*, UA (British)

1941

(Black and White)

Arthur Miller for *How Green Was My Valley*, 20th Century-Fox

(Color)

Ernest Palmer and **Ray Rennahan** for *Blood and Sand*, 20th C.-Fox

1942

(Black and White)

Joseph Ruttenberg for *Mrs. Miniver*, MGM

(Color)

Leon Shamroy for *The Black Swan*, 20th C.-Fox

1943

(Black and White)

Arthur Miller for *The Song of Bernadette*, 20th C.-Fox

(Color)

Hal Mohr and **W. Howard Greene** for *Phantom of the Opera*, Universal

1944

(Black and White)

Joseph LaShelle for *Laura*, 20th C.-Fox

(Color)

Leon Shamroy for *Wilson*, 20th C.-Fox

1945

(Black and White)

Harry Stradling for *The Picture of Dorian Gray*, MGM

(Color)

Leon Shamroy for *Leave Her to Heaven*, 20th C.-Fox

1946

(Black and White)

Arthur Miller for *Anna and the King of Siam*, 20th C.-Fox

(Color)

Charles Rosher, Leonard Smith and **Arthur Arling** for *The Yearling*, MGM

1947

(Black and White)

Guy Green for *Great Expectations*, Universal-International (British)

(Color)

Jack Cardiff for *Black Narcissus*, U-I (British)

1948

(Black and White)

William Daniels for *The Naked City*, U-I

(Color)

Joseph Valentine, William V. Skall and **Winton Hoch** for *Joan of Arc*, RKO Radio

1949

(Black and White)

Paul C. Vogel for *Battleground*, MGM

(Color)

Winton Hoch for *She Wore a Yellow Ribbon*, RKO Radio

1950

(Black and White)

Robert Krasker for *The Third Man*, SRO (British)

(Color)

Robert Surtees for *King Solomon's Mines*, MGM

1951

(Black and White)

William C. Mellor for *A Place in the Sun*, Paramount

Best Cinematography

(Color)

Alfred Gilks for *An American in Paris*, MGM; ballet photographed by John Alton

1952

(Black and White)

Robert Surtees for *The Bad and the Beautiful*, MGM

(Color)

Winton Hoch and **Archie Stout** for *The Quiet Man*, Republic

1953

(Black and White)

Burnett Guffy for *From Here to Eternity*, Columbia

(Color)

Loyal Griggs for *Shane*, Paramount

1954

(Black and White)

Boris Kaufman for *On the Waterfront*, Columbia

(Color)

Milton Krasner for *Three Coins in the Fountain*, 20th C.-Fox

1955

(Black and White)

James Wong Howe for *The Rose Tattoo*, Paramount

(Color)

Robert Burks for *To Catch a Thief*, Paramount

1956

(Black and White)

Joseph Ruttenberg for *Somebody Up There Likes Me*, MGM

(Color)

Lionel Linden for *Around the World in 80 Days*, UA

1957

Jack Hildyard for *The Bridge on the River Kwai*, Columbia

1958

(Black and White)

Sam Leavitt for *The Defiant Ones*, UA

(Color)

Joseph Ruttenberg for *Gigi*, MGM

1959

(Black and White)

William C. Mellor for *The Diary of Anne Frank*, 20th C.-Fox

(Color)

Robert Surtees for *Ben Hur*, MGM

1960

(Black and White)

Freddie Francis for *Sons and Lovers*, 20th C.-Fox

(Color)

Russell Metty for *Spartacus*, U-I

1961

(Black and White)

Eugen Shuftan for *The Hustler*, 20th C.-Fox

(Color)

Daniel L. Fapp for *West Side Story*, UA

1962

(Black and White)

Jean Bourgoin and **Walter Wottitz** for *The Longest Day*, 20th C.-Fox

(Color)

Fred A. Young for *Lawrence of Arabia*, Columbia

1963

(Black and White)

James Wong Howe for *Hud*, Paramount

(Color)

Leon Shamroy for *Cleopatra*, 20th C.-Fox

1964

(Black and White)

Walter Lassally for *Zorba the Greek*, Intl. Classics

(Color)

Harry Stradling for *My Fair Lady*, Warner Bros.

1965

(Black and White)

Ernest Laszlo for *Ship of Fools*, Columbia

(Color)

Freddie Young for *Doctor Zhivago*, MGM

1966

(Black and White)

Haskell Wexler for *Who's Afraid of Virginia Woolf?*, Warner Bros.

(Color)

Ted Moore for *A Man for All Seasons*, Columbia

1967

Burnett Guffy for *Bonnie and Clyde*, Warner Bros.-Seven Arts

1968

Pasqualino De Santis for *Romeo and Juliet*, Paramount

1969

Conrad Hall for *Butch Cassidy and the Sundance Kid*, 20th C.-Fox

1970

Freddie Young for *Ryan's Daughter*, MGM

1971

Oswald Morris for *Fiddler on the Roof*, UA

1972

Geoffrey Unsworth for *Cabaret*, Allied Artists

Dustin Hoffman (right) and Katharine Ross presented cinematographer Burnett Guffey with the 1967 award for Cinematography of *Bonnie and Clyde*.

1973

Sven Nykvist for *Cries and Whispers*, New World Pictures

1974

Fred Koenekamp and **Joseph Biroc** for *The Towering Inferno*, 20th C.-Fox-Warner Bros.

1975

John Alcott for *Barry Lyndon*, Warner Bros.

1976

Haskell Wexler for *Bound for Glory*, UA

1977

Vilmos Zsigmond for *Close Encounters of the Third Kind*, Columbia

1978

Nestor Alemendros for *Days of Heaven*

1979

Vittorio Storaro for *Apocalypse Now*, UA

1980

Geoffrey Unsworth and **Ghislain Cloquet** for *Tess*, Columbia

1981

Vittorio Storaro for *Reds*, Paramount

1982

Billy Williams and **Ronnie Taylor** for *Gandhi*, Columbia

In 1965 Rod Taylor and Doris Day helped cinematographer Leon Shamroy (right) celebrate his 27th year with 20th Century-Fox. The cameraman was nominated 16 times and won four Oscars for his work.

1927-28

William Cameron Menzies for *The Dove*, United Artists
William Cameron Menzies for *The Tempest*, UA

1928-29

Cedric Gibbons for *The Bridge of San Luis Rey*, Metro-Goldwyn-Mayer

1929-30

Herman Rosse for *King of Jazz*, Universal

1930-31

Max Ree for *Cimarron*, RKO Radio

1931-32

Gordon Wiles for *Transatlantic*, Fox

1932-33

William S. Darling for *Cavalcade*, Fox

1934

Cedric Gibbons and **Frederic Hope** for *The Merry Widow*, MGM

1935

Richard Day for *The Dark Angel*, UA

1936

Richard Day for *Dodsworth*, Goldwyn-UA

1937

Stephen Goosson for *Lost Horizon*, Columbia

1938

Carl J. Weyl for *Adventures of Robin Hood*, Warner Bros.

1939

Lyle Wheeler for *Gone with the Wind*, MGM

1940

(Black and White)

Cedric Gibbons and **Paul Groesse** for *Pride and Prejudice*, MGM

(Color)

Vincent Korda for *Thief of Bagdad*, UA

1941

(Black and White)

Richard Day and **Nathan Juran** for *How Green Was My Valley*, 20th CenturyFox. Interior Decoration, **Thomas Little**

(Color)

Cedric Gibbons and **Urie McCleary** for *Blossoms in the Dust*, MGM. Interior Decoration, **Edwin B. Willis**

1942

(Black and White)

Richard Day and **Joseph Wright** for *This Above All*, 20th C.-Fox. Interior Decoration, **Thomas Little**

(Color)

Richard Day and **Joseph Wright** for *My Gal Sal*, 20th C.-Fox. Interior Decoration, **Thomas Little**

1943

(Black and White)

James Basevi and **William Darling** for *The Song of Bernadette*, 20th C.-Fox. Interior Decoration, **Thomas Little**

(Color)

Alexander Golitzen and **John B. Goodman** for *Phantom of the Opera*, Universal. Interior Decoration, **Russell Gausman** and **Ira S. Webb**

1944

(Black and White)

Cedric Gibbons and **William Ferrari** for *Gaslight*, MGM. Interior Decoration, **Edwin B. Willis** and **Paul Huldschinsky**

(Color)

Wiard Ihnen for *Wilson*, 20th C.-Fox. Interior Decoration, **Thomas Little**

1945

(Black and White)

Wiard Ihnen for *Blood on the Sun*, UA. Interior Decoration, **A. Roland Fields**

(Color)

Hans Dreier and **Ernst Fegte** for *Frenchman's Creek*, Paramount. Interior Decoration, **Sam Comer**

1946

(Black and White)

Lyle Wheeler and **William Darling** for *Anna and the King of Siam*, 20th C.-Fox. Interior Decoration, **Thomas Little** and **Frank E. Hughes**

(Color)

Cedric Gibbons and **Paul Groesse** for *The Yearling*, MGM. Interior Decoration, **Edwin B. Willis**

1947

(Black and White)

John Bryan for *Great Expectations*, Universal-International (British). Set Decoration, **Wilfred Shingleton**

(Color)

Alfred Junge for *Black Narcissus*, U-I (British). Set Decoration, **Alfred Junge**

1948

(Black and White)

Roger K. Furse for *Hamlet*, U-I (British). Set Decoration, **Carmen Dillon**

(Color)

Hein Heckroth for *The Red Shoes*, Eagle-Lion (British). Set Decoration, **Arthur Lawson**

1949

(Black and White)

John Meehan and **Harry Horner** for *The Heiress*, Paramount. Set Decoration, **Emile Kuri**

Best Art Direction/Set Direction

(Color)

Cedric Gibbons and **Paul Groesse** for *Little Women*, MGM. Set Decoration, **Edwin B. Willis** and **Jack D. Moore**

1950

(Black and White)

Hans Dreier and **John Meehan** for *Sunset Boulevard*, Paramount. Set Decoration, **Sam Comer** and **Ray Moyer**

(Color)

Hans Dreier and **Walter Tyler** for *Samson and Delilah*, Paramount. Set Decoration, **Sam Comer** and **Ray Moyer**

1951

(Black and White)

Richard Day for *A Streetcar Named Desire*, Warner Bros. Set Decoration, **George James Hopkins**

(Color)

Cedric Gibbons and **Preston Ames** for *An American in Paris*, MGM. Set Decoration, **Edwin B. Willis** and **Keogh Gleason**

1952

(Black and White)

Cedric Gibbons and **Edward Carfagno** for *The Bad and the Beautiful*, MGM. Set Decoration, **Edwin B. Willis** and **Keogh Gleason**

(Color)

Paul Sheriff for *Moulin Rouge*, Romulus Films, UA. Set Decoration, **Marcel Vertes**

1953

(Black and White)

Cedric Gibbons and **Edward Carfagno** for *Julius Caesar*, MGM. Set Decoration, **Edwin B. Willis** and **Hugh Hunt**

(Color)

Lyle Wheeler and **George W. Davis** for *The Robe*, 20th C.-Fox. Set Decoration, **Walter M. Scott** and **Paul S. Fox**

1954

(Black and White)

Richard Day for *On the Waterfront*, Columbia

Writer Bud Schulberg and director Elia Kazan (left) won 1954 Oscars for *On the Waterfront*, as did behind-the-scenes workers Boris Kaufman (Cinematography) and Richard Day (Art Direction).

(Color)

John Meehan for *20,000 Leagues under the Sea*, Walt Disney. Set Decoration, **Emile Kuri**

1955

(Black and White)

Hal Pereira and **Tambi Larsen** for *The Rose Tattoo*, Paramount. Set Decoration, **Sam Comer** and **Arthur Krams**

(Color)

William and **Jo Mielziner** for *Picnic*, Columbia. Set Decoration, **Robert Priestley**

1956

(Black and White)

Cedric Gibbons and **Malcolm F. Brown** for *Somebody Up There Likes Me*, MGM. Set Decoration, **Edwin B. Willis** and **Keogh Gleason**

(Color)

Lyle R. Wheeler and **John DeCuir** for *The King and I*, 20th C.-Fox. Set Decoration, **Walter M. Scott** and **Paul S. Fox**

1957

Ted Haworth for *Sayonara*, Warner Bros. Set Decoration, **Robert Priestley**

1958

William A. Horning and **Preston Ames** for *Gigi*, MGM. Set Decoration, **Henry Grace** and **Keogh Gleason**

1959

(Black and White)

Lyle R. Wheeler and **George M. Davis** for *The Diary of Anne Frank*, 20th C.-Fox. Set Decoration, **Walter M. Scott** and **Stuart A. Reiss**

(Color)

William A. Horning and **Edward Carfagno** for *Ben-Hur*, MGM. Set Decoration, **Hugh Hunt**

1960

(Black and White)

Alexander Trauner for *The Apartment*, UA. Set Decoration, **Edward G. Boyle**

(Color)

Alexander Golitzen and **Eric Orbom** for *Spartacus*, U-I. Set Decoration, **Russell A. Gausman** and **Julia Heron**

1961

(Black and White)

Harry Horner for *The Hustler*, 20th C.-Fox. Set Decoration, **Gene Callahan**

(Color)

Boris Leven for *West Side Story*, UA. Set Decoration, **Victor A. Gangelin**

1962

(Black and White)

Alexander Golitzen and **Henry Bumstead** for *To Kill a Mockingbird*, U-I. Set Decoration, **Oliver Emert**

(Color)

John Box and **John Stoll** for *Lawrence of Arabia*, Columbia. Set Decoration, **Dario Simoni**

1963

(Black and White)

Gene Callahan for *America, America*, Warner Bros.

(Color)

John DeCuir, Jack Martin Smith, Hilyard Brown, Herman Blumenthal, Elven Webb, Maurice Pelling and **Boris Juraga** for *Cleopatra*, 20th C.-Fox. Set Decoration, **Walter M. Scott, Paul S. Fox** and **Ray Moyer**

1964

(Black and White)

Vassilis Fotopoulos for *Zorba the Greek*, Intl. Classics

(Color)

Gene Allen and **Cecil Beaton** for *My Fair Lady*, Warner Bros. Set Decoration, **George James Hopkins**

1965

(Black and White)

Robert Clatworthy for *Ship of Fools*, Columbia. Set Decoration, **Joseph Kish**

(Color)

John Box and **Terry Marsh** for *Dr. Zhivago*, MGM. Set Decoration, **Dario Simoni**

1966

(Black and White)

Richard Sylbert for *Who's Afraid of Virginia Woolf?*, Warner Bros. Set Decoration, **George James Hopkins**

(Color)

Jack Martin Smith and **Dale Hennesy** for *Fantastic Voyage*, 20th C.-Fox. Set Decoration, **Walter M. Scott** and **Stuart A. Reiss**

1967

John Truscott and **Edward Carrere** for *Camelot*, Warner Bros. Set Decoration, **John W. Brown**

1968

John Box and **Terence Marsh** for *Oliver!*, Columbia. Set Decoration, **Vernon Dixon** and **Ken Muggleston**

1969

John De Cuir, Jack Martin Smith and **Herman Blumenthal** for *Hello Dolly!*, 20th C.-Fox. Set Decoration, **Walter M. Scott, George James Hopkins**, and **Raphael Bretton**

1970

Urie McCleary and **Gil Parrondo** for *Patton*, 20th C.-Fox. Set Decoration, **Antonio Mateos** and **Pierre-Louis Thevenet**

1971

John Box, Ernest Archer, Jack Maxsted, and **Gil Parrondo** for *Nicholas and Alexandra*, Columbia. Set Decoration, **Vernon Dixon**

King Arthur's court was recreated in Hollywood for the filming of *Camelot,* **which won 1967 Oscars for Art Direction, Score, and Costume Design.**

1972

Rolf Zehetbauer and **Jurgen Kiebach** for *Cabaret*, Allied Artists. Set Decoration, **Herbert Strabel**

1973

Henry Bumstead for *The Sting*, Universal. Set Decoration, **James Payne**

1974

Dean Tavoularis and **Angelo Graham** for *The Godfather Part II*, Paramount. Set Decoration, **George R. Nelson**

1975

Ken Adam and **Roy Walker** for *Barry Lyndon*, Warner Bros. Set Decoration, **Vernon Dixon**

1976

George Jenkins for *All the President's Men*, Warner Bros. Set Decoration, **George Gaines**

1977

John Barry, Norman Reynolds, and **Leslie Dilley** for *Star Wars*, 20th C.-Fox. Set Decoration, **Roger Christian**

1978

Paul Sybert and **Edwin O'Donovan** for *Heaven Can Wait*, Paramount. Set Decoration, **George Gaines**

1979

Philip Rosenberg and **Tony Walton** for *All That Jazz*, 20th C.-Fox. Set Decoration, **Edward Stewart** and **Gary Brink**

1980

Pierre Guffroy and **Jack Stephens** for *Tess*, Columbia.

1981

Norman Reynolds and **Leslie Dilley** for *Raiders of the Lost Ark*, Paramount. Set Direction, **Michael Ford**

1982

Stuart Craig and **Bob Laing** for *Gandhi*, Columbia. Set Direction, **Michael Seirton**

1929-30

Douglas Shearer for *The Big House*, Metro-Goldwyn-Mayer

1930-31

Paramount Studio Sound Department

1931-32

Paramount Studio Sound Department

1932-33

Harold C. Lewis for *A Farewell to Arms*, Paramount

1934

Paul Neal for *One Night of Love*, Columbia

1935

Douglas Shearer for *Naughty Marietta*, MGM

1936

Douglas Shearer for *San Francisco*, MGM

1937

Thomas Moulton for *The Hurricane*, Samuel Goldwyn Studios-United Artists

1938

Thomas Moulton for *The Cowboy and the Lady*, Goldwyn-UA

1939

Bernard B. Brown for *When Tomorrow Comes*, Universal

1940

Douglas Shearer for *Strike Up the Band*, MGM

1941

Jack Whitney, General Service, for *That Hamilton Woman*, UA

1942

Nathan Levinson for *Yankee Doodle Dandy*, Warner Brothers

1943

Stephen Dunn for *This Land Is Mine*, RKO Radio

Yankee Doodle Dandy's three Oscars in 1942 included the award for Best Sound Recording.

1944

E. H. Hansen for *Wilson*, 20th Century-Fox

1945

Stephen Dunn for *The Bells of St. Mary's*, RKO Radio

1946

John Livadary for *The Jolson Story*, Columbia

1947

Goldwyn Sound Department for *The Bishop's Wife*, Goldwyn-RKO Radio

1948

20th C.-Fox Sound Department for *The Snake Pit*, 20th C.-Fox

1949

20th C.-Fox Sound Department for *Twelve O'Clock High*, 20th C.-Fox

1950

20th C.-Fox Sound Department for *All about Eve*, 20th C.-Fox

1951

Douglas Shearer, Sound Director, for *the Great Caruso*, MGM

1952

London Film Sound Department for *Breaking the Sound Barrier*, London Films-UA (British)

1953

John P. Livadary, Sound Director, for *From Here to Eternity*, Columbia

1954

Leslie I. Carey, Sound Director, for *The Glenn Miller Story*, Universal-International

1955

Fred Hynes, Sound Director, for *Oklahoma!*, Todd-AO

1956

Carl Faulkner, Sound Director, for *The King and I*, 20th C.-Fox

1957

George Groves, Sound Director, for *Sayonara*, Warner Bros.

1958

Fred Hynes, Sound Director, for *South Pacific*, Todd-AO

Best Sound

1959

Franklin E. Milton, Sound Director, for *Ben-Hur*, MGM

1960

Gordon E. Sawyer, Goldwyn Studio Sound Director, and **Fred Hynes**, Todd A-O Sound Director, for *The Alamo*, Goldwyn-Todd-AO

1961

Fred Hynes, Todd-AO Sound Director, and **Gordon E. Sawyer**, Goldwyn Studio Sound Director, for *West Side Story*, Goldwyn-Todd-AO

1962

John Cox, Sound Director, for *Lawrence of Arabia*, Shepperton Studio

1963

Franklin E. Milton, Sound Director, for *How the West Was Won*, MGM

1964

George R. Groves, Sound Director, for *My Fair Lady*, Warner Bros.

1965

James P. Corcoran, 20th C.-Fox Studio Sound Director, and **Fred Hynes**, Todd-AO Sound Director, for *The Sound of Music*, 20th C.-Fox-Todd-AO

1966

Franklin E. Milton, Sound Director, for *Grand Prix*, MGM

1967

Samuel Goldwyn Studio Sound Department for *In the Heat of the Night*, Goldwyn

1968

Shepperton Studio Sound Department for *Oliver!*, Shepperton

1969

Jack Solomon and **Murray Spivack** for *Hello, Dolly!*, 20th C.-Fox

1970

Douglas Williams and **Don Bassman** for *Patton*, 20th C.-Fox

1971

Gordon K. McCallum and **David Hildyard** for *Fiddler on the Roof*, UA

1972

Robert Knudson and **David Hildyard** for *Cabaret*, Allied Artists

1973

Robert Knudson and **Chris Newman** for *The Exorcist*, Warner Bros.

1974

Ronald Pierce and **Melvin Metcalfe, Sr.**, for *Earthquake*, Universal

1975

Robert L. Hoyt, Roger Heman, Earl Madery, and **John Carter** for *Jaws*, Universal

1976

Arthur Piantadosi, Les Fresholtz, Dick Alexander and **Jim Webb** for *All the President's Men*, Warner Bros.

1977

Don MacDougall, Ray West, Bob Minkler, and **Derek Ball** for *Star Wars*, 20th C.-Fox

1978

Richard Portman, William McCaughey, Aaron Rochin, and **Darin Knight** for *The Deer Hunter*, Universal

1979

Walter Murch, Mark Berger, Richard Beggs, and **Nat Boxer** for *Apocalypse Now*, UA

1980

Bill Varney, Steve Maslow, Gregg Landaker, and **Peter Sutton** for *The Empire Strikes Back*, 20th C.-Fox

1981

Bill Varney, Steve Maslow, Greg Landaker, and **Roy Charman** for *Raiders of the Lost Ark*, Paramount

1982

Russ Knudson, Robert Glass, Don Digirolamo, and **Gene Cantamessa** for *E. T.—the Extra-Terrestrial*, Universal

1934

Conrad Nervig for *Eskimo*, Metro-Goldwyn-Mayer

1935

Ralph Dawson for *A Midsummer Night's Dream*, Warner Bros.

1936

Ralph Dawson for *Anthony Adverse*, Warner Bros.

1937

Gene Havlick and **Gene Milford** for *Lost Horizon*, Columbia

1938

Ralph Dawson for *The Adventures of Robin Hood*, Warner Bros.

1939

Hal C. Kern and **James E. Newcom** for *Gone with the Wind*, MGM

1940

Anne Bauchens for *North West Mounted Police*, Paramount

1941

William Holmes for *Sergeant York*, Warner Bros.

1942

Daniel Mandell for *The Pride of the Yankees*, RKO Radio

1943

George Amy for *Air Force*, Warner Bros.

1944

Barbara McLean for *Wilson*, 20th Century Fox

1945

Robert J. Kern for *National Velvet*, MGM

1946

Daniel Mandell for *The Best Years of Our Lives*, RKO Radio

1947

Francis Lyon and **Robert Parrish** for *Body and Soul*, UA

1948

Paul Weatherwax for *The Naked City*, Universal-International

1949

Harry Gerstad for *Champion*, UA

1950

Ralph E. Winters and **Conrad A. Nervig** for *King Solomon's Mines*, MGM

1951

William Hornbeck for *A Place in the Sun*, Paramount

1952

Elmo Williams and **Harry Gerstad** for *High Noon*, UA

1953

William Lyon for *From Here to Eternity*, Columbia

1954

Gene Milford for *On the Waterfront*, Columbia

1955

Charles Nelson and **William Lyon** for *Picnic*, Columbia

1956

Gene Ruggiero and **Paul Weatherwax** for *Around the World in 80 Days*, UA

1957

Peter Taylor for *The Bridge on the River Kwai*, Columbia

1958

Adrienne Fazan for *Gigi*, MGM

1959

Ralph E. Winters and **John D. Dunning** for *Ben Hur*, MGM

1960

Daniel Mandell for *The Apartment*, UA

1961

Thomas Stanford for *West Side Story*, UA

1962

Anne Coates for *Lawrence of Arabia*, Columbia

1963

Harold F. Kress for *How the West Was Won*, MGM, Cinerama

1964

Cotton Warburton for *Mary Poppins*, Walt Disney

1965

William Reynolds for *The Sound of Music*, 20th C.-Fox

1966

Fredric Steinkamp, Henry Berman, Stewart Linder, and **Frank Santillo** for *Grand Prix*, MGM

1967

Hal Ashby for *In the Heat of the Night*, UA

1968

Frank P. Keller for *Bullitt*, Warner Bros.-Seven Arts

1969

Françoise Bonnot for *Z*, Cinema V

1970

Hugh S. Fowler for *Patton*, 20th C.-Fox

1971

Jerry Greenberg for *The French Connection*, 20th C.-Fox

1972

David Bretherton for *Cabaret*, Allied Artists

Best Film Editing

Robert De Niro starred as Jake La Motta in *Raging Bull* (1980). The film's Oscars included the Film Editing award.

1973
William Reynolds for *The Sting*, Universal

1974
Harold F. Kress and **Carl Kress** for *The Towering Inferno*, 20th C.-Fox-Warner Bros.

1975
Verna Fields for *Jaws*, Universal

1976
Richard Halsey and **Scott Conrad** for *Rocky*, UA

1977
Paul Hirsch, Marcia Lucas, and **Richard Chew** for *Star Wars*, 20th C.-Fox

1978
Peter Zinner for *The Deer Hunter*, Universal

1979
Alan Heim for *All That Jazz*, 20th C.-Fox

1980
Thelma Schoonmaker for *Raging Bull*, UA

1981
Michael Kahn for *Raiders of the Lost Ark*, Paramount

1982
John Bloom for *Gandhi*, Columbia (British)

1939

E. H. Hansen and **Fred Sersen** for *The Rains Came*, 20th C.-Fox

1940

Lawrence Butler (Photographic) and **Jack Whitney** (Sound) for *The Thief of Bagdad*, United Artists

1941

Farciot Edouart and **Gordon Jennings** (Photographic) and **Louis Mesenkop** (Sound) for *I Wanted Wings*, Paramount

1942

Farciot Edouart, Gordon Jennings, and **William L. Pereira** (Photographic) and **Louis Mesenkop** (Sound) for *The Wild Wind*, Paramount

1943

Fred Sersen (Photographic) and **Roger Heman** (Sound) for *Crash Dive*, 20th C.-Fox

1944

A. Arnold Gillespie, Donald Jahraus, and **Warren Newcombe** (Photographic) and **Douglas Shearer** (Sound) for *Thirty Seconds over Tokyo*, Metro-Goldwyn-Mayer

1945

John Fulton (Photographic) and **A. W. Johns** (Sound) for *Wonder Man*, Samuel Goldwyn Studio-RKO Radio

1946

Thomas Howard (Visual) for *Blithe Spirit*, Rank-UA (British)

1947

A. Arnold Gillespie and **Warren Newcombe** (Visual) and **Douglas Shearer** and **Michael Steinore** (Audible) for *Green Dolphin Street*, MGM

1948

Paul Eagler, J. McMillan Johnson, Russell Shearman, and **Clarence Slifer** (Visual) and **Charles Freeman** and **James G. Stewart** (Audible) for *Portrait of Jennie*, Selznick Studio

1949

Mighty Joe Young, Arko-RKO Radio

1950

Destination Moon, Eagle-Lion Classics

1951

When Worlds Collide, Paramount

1952

Plymouth Adventure, MGM

1953

The War of the Worlds, Paramount

1954

20,000 Leagues under the Sea, Walt Disney Studios

1955

The Bridges at Toko-Ri, Paramount

1956

John Fulton for *The Ten Commandments*, Paramount

1957

Walter Rossi (Audible) for *The Enemy Below*, 20th C.-Fox

1958

Tom Howard (Visual) for *Tom Thumb*, MGM

1959

A. Arnold Gillespie and **Robert MacDonald** (Visual) and **Milo Lory** (Audible) for *Ben Hur*, MGM

1960

Gene Warren and **Tim Baar** (Visual) for *The Time Machine*, MGM

1961

Bill Warrington (Visual) and **Vivian C. Greenham** (Audible) for *The Guns of Navarone*, Columbia

1962

Robert MacDonald (Visual) and **Jacques Maumont** (Audible) for *The Longest Day*, 20th C.-Fox

(In 1963 the Special Effects Award was discontinued, and the Special Visual Effects Award and the Sound Effects Award were created.)

1963

(Special Visual Effects)

Emil Kosa, Jr., for *Cleopatra*, 20th C.-Fox

(Sound Effects)

Walter G. Elliott for *It's a Mad, Mad, Mad, Mad World*, UA

1964

(Special Visual Effects)

Peter Ellenshaw, Hamilton Luske, and **Eustace Lycett** for *Mary Poppins*, Walt Disney Prods.

(Sound Effects)

Norman Wanstall for *Goldfinger*, UA

1965

(Special Visual Effects)

John Stears for *Thunderball*, UA

(Sound Effects)

Tregoweth Brown for *The Great Race*, Warner Bros.

1966

(Special Visual Effects)

Art Cruickshank for *Fantastic Voyage*, 20th C.-Fox

(Sound Effects)

Gordon Daniel for *Grand Prix*, MGM

1967

(Special Visual Effects)

L. B. Abbott for *Doctor Dolittle*, 20th C.-Fox

(Sound Effects)

John Poyner for *The Dirty Dozen*, MGM

(Sound Effects award not given after 1967.)

1968

(Special Visual Effects)

Stanley Kubrick for *2001: A Space Odyssey*, MGM

Best Special Effects

Stanley Kubrick's *2001: A Space Odyssey* won the 1968 Oscar for Special Visual Effects.

1969

(Special Visual Effects)

Robbie Robertson for *Marooned*, Columbia

1970

(Special Visual Effects)

A. D. Flowers and **L. B. Abbott** for *Tora! Tora! Tora!*, 20th C.-Fox

1971

(Special Visual Effects)

Alan Maley, Eustace Lycett, and **Danny Lee** for *Bedknobs and Broomsticks*, Walt Disney Prods.

(Special Achievement Awards were begun in 1972 and took the place of the Special Visual Effects and Sound Effects Awards.)

1972

L. B. Abbott and **A. D. Flowers** for *The Poseidon Adventure*, 20th C.-Fox

1973

None

1974

(Visual Effects)

Frank Brendel, Glen Robinson, and **Albert Whitlock** for *Earthquake*, Universal

1975

(Sound Effects)

Peter Berkos for *The Hindenburg*, Universal

1976

Carlo Rambaldi, Glen Robinson, and **Frank Van Der Veer** for *King Kong*, Paramount

L. B. Abbott, Glen Robinson, and **Matthew Yuricich** for *Logan's Run*, MGM

1977

(Sound Effects)

Benjamin Burtt, Jr. for *Star Wars*, 20th C.-Fox

(Sound Effects Editing Award)

Close Encounters of the Third Kind, Columbia: **Frank Warner**, Supervising Sound Effects Editors

(Visual Effects)

Star Wars, 20th C.-Fox: **John Stears, John Dykstra, Richard Edlund, Grant McCune**, and **Robert Blalack**

1978

(Visual Effects)

Les Bowie, Colin Chilvers, Denys Coop, Roy Field, Derek Meddings, and **Zoran Perisic** for *Superman the Movie*

1979

(Visual Effects)

H. R. Giger, Carlo Rambaldi, Brian Johnson, Nick Allder, and **Denys Ayling** for *Alien*

(Sound Effects Editing Award)

Alan Splet for *The Black Stallion*

1980

(Visual Effects)

Richard Edlund, Kit West, Bruce Nicholson, and **Joe Johnston** for *The Empire Strikes Back*, 20th C.-Fox

1981

(Visual Effects)

Richard Edlund, Kit West, Bruce Nicholson, and **Joe Johnston** for *Raiders of the Lost Ark*, Paramount

(Sound Effects)

Richard L. Anderson and **Benjamin P. Burtt, Jr.**, for *Raiders of the Lost Ark*, Paramount

1982

(Visual Effects)

Charles L. Campbell and **Ben Burtt** for *E. T. — the Extra-Terrestrial*, Universal

(Sound-Effects Editing)

Carlo Rambaldi, Dennis Muren, and **Kenneth F. Smith** for *E. T. — the Extra-Terrestrial*, Universal

Costumes

1948

(Black and White)

Roger K. Furse for *Hamlet*, Universal-International (British)

(Color)

Dorothy Jeakins and **Karinska** for *Joan of Arc*, RKO Radio

1949

(Black and White)

Edith Head and **Gile Steele** for *The Heiress*, Paramount

(Color)

Leah Rhodes, Travilla, and **Marjorie Best** for *Adventures of Don Juan*, Warner Brothers

1950

(Black and White)

Edith Head and **Charles LeMaire** for *All about Eve*, 20th Century-Fox

(Color)

Edith Head, Dorothy Jeakins, Elois Jenssen, Gile Steele, and **Gwen Wakeling** for *Samson and Delilah*, Paramount

1951

(Black and White)

Edith Head for *A Place in the Sun*, Paramount

(Color)

Orry-Kelly, Walter Plunkett, and **Irene Sharaff** for *An American in Paris*, Metro-Goldwyn-Mayer

1952

(Black and White)

Helen Rose for *The Bad and the Beautiful*, MGM

(Color)

Marcel Vertes for *Moulin Rouge*, United Artists

1953

(Black and White)

Edith Head for *Roman Holiday*, Paramount

(Color)

Charles LeMaire and **Emile Santiago** for *The Robe*, 20th C.-Fox

1954

(Black and White)

Edith Head for *Sabrina*, Paramount

(Color)

Sanzo Wada for *Gate of Hell*, Edward Harrison (Japanese)

1955

(Black and White)

Helen Rose for *I'll Cry Tomorrow*, MGM

(Color)

Charles LeMaire for *Love Is a Many-Splendored Thing*, 20th C.-Fox

1956

(Black and White)

Jean Louis for *The Solid Gold Cadillac*, Columbia

(Color)

Irene Sharaff for *The King and I*, 20th C.-Fox

1957

Orry-Kelly for *Les Girls*, MGM

1958

Cecil Beaton for *Gigi*, MGM

1959

(Black and White)

Orry-Kelly for *Some Like It Hot*, UA

(Color)

Elizabeth Haffenden for *Ben-Hur*, MGM

1960

(Black and White)

Edith Head and **Edward Stevenson** for *The Facts of Life*, UA

(Color)

Valles and **Bill Thomas** for *Spartacus*, U-I

1961

(Black and White)

Piero Gherardi for *La Dolce Vita*, Astor Pictures, Inc. (Italian)

(Color)

Irene Sharaff for *West Side Story*, UA

1962

(Black and White)

Norma Koch for *What Ever Happened to Baby Jane?*, Warner Bros.

(Color)

Mary Wills for *The Wonderful World of the Brothers Grimm*, MGM-Cinerama

1963

(Black and White)

Piero Gherardi for *Federico Fellini's 8½*, Embassy (Italy)

(Color)

Irene Sharaff, Vittorio Nino Novarese, and **Renie** for *Cleopatra*, 20th C.-Fox

1964

(Black and White)

Dorothy Jeakins for *The Night of the Iguana*, MGM

(Color)

Cecil Beaton for *My Fair Lady*, Warner Bros.

1965

(Black and White)

Julie Harris for *Darling*, Embassy

(Color)

Phyllis Dalton for *Doctor Zhivago*, MGM

1966

(Black and White)

Irene Sharaff for *Who's Afraid of Virginia Woolf?*, Warner Bros.

(Color)

Elizabeth Haffenden and **Joan**

Best Costume Design
Best Makeup

Anthony Powell's costumes for *Tess* won a 1980 Oscar. The film, which starred Natassia Kinski (right) and Leigh Lawson, also received awards for Art Direction and Cinematography.

Bridge for *A Man for All Seasons*, Columbia

1967

John Truscott for *Camelot*, Warner Bros.-Seven Arts

1968

Danilo Donati for *Romeo & Juliet*, Paramount

1969

Margaret Furse for *Anne of the Thousand Days*, Universal

1970

Nino Novarese for *Cromwell*, Columbia

1971

Yvonne Blake and **Antonio Castillo** for *Nicholas and Alexandra*, Columbia

1972

Anthony Powell for *Travels with My Aunt*, MGM

1973

Edith Head for *The Sting*, Universal

1974

Theoni V. Aldredge for *The Great Gatsby*, Paramount

1975

Ulla-Britt Soderlund and **Milena Canonero** for *Barry Lyndon*, Warner Bros.

1976

Danilo Donati for *Fellini's Casanova*, Universal

1977

John Mollo for *Star Wars*, 20th C.-Fox

1978

Anthony Powell for *Death on the Nile*

1979

Albert Wolsky for *All That Jazz*, 20th C.-Fox

1980

Anthony Powell for *Tess*, Columbia

1981

Milena Canonero for *Chariots of Fire*, Ladd Co./Warner Bros. (British)

1982

John Mollo and **Bhanu Athaiya** for *Gandhi*, Columbia (British)

Makeup

1981

Rick Baker for *An American Werewolf in London*

1982

Sarah Monzani and **Michele Burke** for *Quest for Fire*

CHAPTER 11

Best Foreign Language Film Awards

The Academy began giving special awards to foreign language films in 1947 and regular, annual awards in 1956. For the regular awards, each country is allowed to submit one film. From these entries, an average of 16 per year, an Academy committee picks five nominees. Final voting is limited to Academy members who have seen all the nominees.

Over the years, the nations to receive the most Best Foreign Language Film awards have been France, which has won eight Oscars and 22 nominations, and Italy, with seven Oscars and 19 nominations. France and Italy also each received three of the special awards before 1956.

No other nation has come close to that record. Films from the Soviet Union have won three Oscars; Czechoslovakia and Sweden have each won twice; and Algeria, Hungary, Ivory Coast, Spain, and West Germany each have won once. Japan has had 10 nominations but never won an Oscar, although the Japanese were honored three times in the pre-1956 special awards.

Among American moviemakers, French and Italian films are the most appreciated and influential of all imports. The first French film to win the Best Foreign Language Film award was *My Uncle* (1958), a warm comedy written, produced, directed, and acted by Jacques Tati. Director Claude Lelouch won the 1966 award with his popular, romantic *A Man and a Woman*. The outspoken and surrealist director Luis Buñuel won for *The Discreet Charm of the Bourgeoisie* in 1972. New Wave director François Truffaut, the most popular director with American audiences (he played the French scientist in *Close Encounters of the Third Kind*, 1977) won with *Day for Night* (1973). France won back-to-back awards in 1977 and 1978 with *Madame Rosa* (directed by Moshe Mizrahi) and *Get Out*

Italian director Federico Fellini has received four Best Foreign Film Oscars.

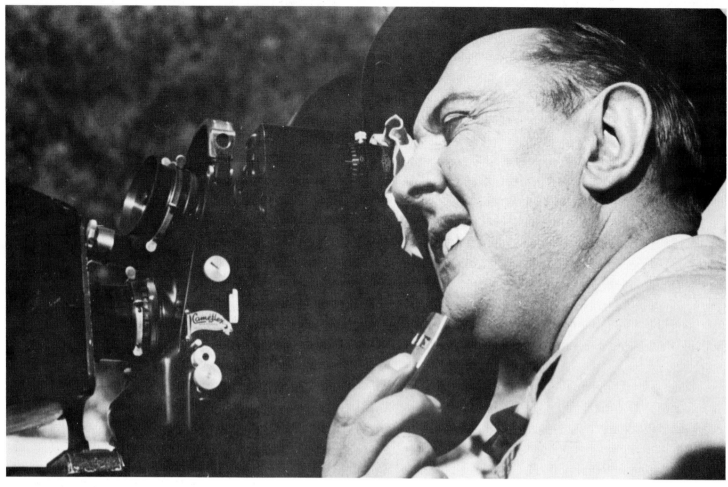

Jacques Tati produced and starred in his film, *My Uncle* (1958).

French producer-director Claude Lelouch accepted the 1966 Oscar from Patricia Neal for his film, *A Man and a Woman.*

French director Francois Truffaut is very popular with American audiences. His film *Day for Night* was chosen Best Foreign Film of 1973.

Fellini and his wife, Italian actress Guilietta Masina, returned to Rome in the spring of 1957 with the Oscar for the Best Foreign Film of 1956, *La Strada*.

Guilietta Masina and Anthony Quinn starred in Fellini's first Oscar winner, *La Strada* (1956).

Brazilian actress Florinda Bolkan starred in the Italian film, *Investigation of a Citizen above Suspicion,* **the 1970 Oscar winner directed by Elio Petri.**

Your Handkerchiefs (directed by Bertrand Blier).

Two directors account for most of the Italian honors. Vittorio De Sica won special awards for his postwar neorealist films, *Shoeshine* (1946) and *The Bicycle Thief* (1948). The gritty, documentary naturalism of these films was hailed as an exciting departure from studio polish and artifice. De Sica won regular Oscars for *Yesterday, Today and Tomorrow* (1964) and *The Garden of the Finzi-Continis* (1971). The sensationally expressive Federico Fellini won four Oscars — for *La Strada* (1956), *The Nights of Cabiria* (1957), *8½* (1963), and *Amarcord* (1974). The other Italian winner was *Investigation of a Citizen above Suspicion* (1970), directed by Elio Petri.

Foreign politics has regularly been suspected of playing a part in deciding which films are submitted by different countries. And critics like Andrew Sarris of the *Village Voice* have repeatedly expressed disappointment over the nominees in this category.

The positive side is that the awards have helped, as Academy President Jean Hersholt hoped in 1947, "promote a closer relationship between American film craftsmen and those of other countries." And the winners have been respectable, innovative films, deserving of wider attention than a few art house and college campus showings. American audiences have benefited from the increased exposure that winners receive as a result of their honors.

French director Luis Buñuel is shown here with actress Catherine Deneuve during the filming of *Belle de Jour* **(1967). Buñuel's 1972 film,** *The Discreet Charm of the Bourgeoisie,* **was an Oscar winner.**

1956

La Strada, a Ponti-De Laurentiis Production. Dino De Laurentiis and Carlo Ponti, Producers (Italy)
The Captain of Kopenick, Real-Film. Gyula Trebitsch and Walter Koppel, Producers (Germany)
Gervaise, Agnes Delahaie Productions Cinematographiques & Silver Film. Annie Dorfmann, Producer (France)
Harp of Burma, Nikkatsu Corporation. Masayuki Takagi, Producer (Japan)
Qivitoq, A/S Nordisk Films Kompagni. O. Dalsgaard-Olson, Producer (Denmark)

1957

The Nights of Cabiria, Dino De Laurentiis Production (Italy)
The Devil Came at Night, Gloria Film (Germany)
Gates of Paris, Filmsonor S.A. Production (France)
Mother India, Mehboob Productions (India)
Nine Lives, Nordsjofilm (Norway)

1958

My Uncle, Specta-Gray-Alter Films in association with Films du Centaure (France)
Arms and the Man, H. R. Sokal-P. Goldbaum Production, Bavaria Filmkunst A.G. (Germany)
La Venganza, Guion Producciones Cinematograficas (Spain)
The Road a Year Long, Jadran Film (Yugoslavia)
The Usual Unidentified Thieves, Lux-Vides-Cinecitta (Italy)

1959

Black Orpheus, Dispatfilm & Gemma Cinematografica (France)
The Bridge, Fono Film (Germany)
The Great War, Dino De Laurentiis Cinematografica (Italy)
Paw, Laterna Film (Denmark)
The Village on the River, N. V. Nationale Filmproductie Maatschappij (The Netherlands)

1960

The Virgin Spring, A. B. Svensk Filmindustri (Sweden)
Kapo, Vides-Zebrafilm-Cineriz (Italy)

La Verité, Han Productions (France)
Macario, Clasa Films Mundiales, S.A. (Mexico)
The Ninth Circle, Jadran Film Production (Yugoslavia)

1961

Through a Glass Darkly, A. B. Svensk Filmindustri (Sweden)
Harry and the Butler, Bent Christensen Production (Denmark)
Immortal Love, Shochiku Co., Ltd. (Japan)
The Important Man, Peliculas Rodriguez, S.A. (Mexico)
Placido, Jet Films (Spain)

1962

Sundays and Cybele, Terra-Fides-Orsay-Trocadero Films (France)
Electra, a Michael Cacoyannis Production (Greece)
The Four Days of Naples, Titanus-Metro (Italy)
Keeper of Promises (The Given Word), Cinedistri (Brazil)
Tlayucan, Producciones Matouk, S.A. (Mexico)

1963

Federico Fellini's 8½, a Cineriz Production (Italy)
Knife in the Water, a Kamera Unit of Film Polski Production (Poland)
Los Trantos, Tecisa-Films R.B. (Spain)
The Red Lanterns, Th. Damaskinos & V. Michaelides A.E. (Greece)
Twin Sisters of Kyoto, Shochiku Co., Ltd. (Japan)

1964

Yesterday, Today and Tommorrow, a Champion-Concordia Production (Italy)
Raven's End, AB Europa Film (Sweden)
Sallah, a Sallah Film Ltd. Production (Israel)
The Umbrellas of Cherbourg, a Parc-Madeleine-Beta Films Production (France)
Woman in the Dunes, a Teshigahara Production (Japan)

1965

The Shop on Main Street, a Ceskoslovensky Film Production (Czechoslovakia)

Blood on the Land, Th. Damaskinos & V. Michaelides, A.E.-Finos Film (Greece)
Dear John, A.B. Sandrew-Ateljeerna (Sweden)
Kwaidan, a Toho Company, Ltd., Production (Japan)
Marriage Italian Style, a Champion-Concordia Production (Italy)

1966

A Man and a Woman, Les Films 13 Production (France)
The Battle of Algiers, Igor Film-Casbah Film Production (Italy)
Loves of a Blonde, Barrandov Film Production (Czechoslovakia)
Pharaoh, Kadr Film Unit Production (Poland)
Three, Avala Film Production (Yugoslavia)

1967

Closely Watched Trains, Barandov Film Studio Production (Czechoslovakia)
El Amor Brujo, Films R.B., S.A. Production (Spain)
I Even Met Happy Gypsies, Avala Film Production (Yugoslavia)
Live for Life, Les Films Ariane-Les Productions Artistes Associes-Vides Films Production (France)
Portrait of Chieko, Shochiku Co., Ltd., Production (Japan)

1968

War and Peace, Mosfilm Production (Russia)
The Boys of Paul Street, Bohgros Films-Mafilm Studio I Production (Hungary)
The Firemen's Ball, Barrandov Film Studio Production (Czechoslovakia)
Stolen Kisses, Les Films du Carrosse-Les Productions Artistes Associes Production (France)

1969

Z, Reggane-O.N.C.I.C. Production (Algeria)
Adelen '31, AB Svensk Filmindustri Production (Sweden)
The Battle of Neretva, United Film Producers-Igor Film-Eichberg Film-Commonwealth United Production (Yugoslavia)
The Brothers Karamazov, Mosfilm Production (U.S.S.R.)
My Night with Maud, Films du

Best Foreign Language Films

Italy was a winner in 1964 with Vittorio De Sica's *Yesterday, Today and Tomorrow*, starring Sophia Loren and Marcello Mastroianni.

Brilliant young Czech director Jiri Menzel's *Closely Watched Trains*, starring actress Jitka Bandova (right), won the Best Foreign Film Oscar for 1967.

Losange-F.F.P.-Films du Carrosse-Films des Deux Mondes-Films de la Pleiade-Gueville-Renne-Simar Films Production (France)

1970

Investigation of a Citizen above Suspicion, Ver Films Prod. (Italy)

First Love, Alfa Prods.-Seitz Film Prod. (Switzerland)
Hoa-Binh, Madeleine-Parc-La Gueville-C.A.P.A.C. Prod. (France)
Paix sur les Champs, Philippe Collette-E.G.C. Prod. (Belgium)
Tristana, Forbes Films, Ltd.-United Cineworld-Epoca Films-Talia Film-Les Films Corona-Selenia Cinematografica Prod. (Spain)

1971

The Garden of the Finzi-Continis, a Gianni Hecht Lucari-Arthur Cohn Prod. (Italy)
Dodes'ka-den, a Toho Company, Ltd.-Yonki no Kai Prod. (Japan)
The Policeman, an Ephi-Israeli Motion Picture Studios Prod. (Israel)
Tchaikovsky, a Dimitri Tiomkin-Mosfilm Studios Prod. (U.S.S.R.)

1972

The Discreet Charm of the Bourgeoisie, a Serge Silberman Prod. (France)
The Dawns Here Are Quiet, a Gorky Studios Prod. (U.S.S.R.)
I Love You Rosa, a Noah Films Ltd. Prod. (Israel)
My Dearest Senorita, an El Iman Prod. (Spain)
The New Land, a Svensk Filmindustria Prod. (Sweden)

1973

Day for Night, a Les Films du Carrosse-P.E.C.F. (Paris) - P.I.C. (Rome) Prod. (France)
The House on Chelouche Street, a Noah Films Prod. (Israel)
L'Invitation, a Groupe 5 Geneve-Television Suisse Romande-Citel Films-Planfilm (Paris) Prod. (Switzerland)
The Pedestrian, an ALFA Glarus-MFG-Seitz-Zev Braun Prod. (West Germany)
Turkish Delight, a Rob Houwer Film Prod. (The Netherlands)

Footage being shot for the first Soviet film to receive an Oscar, *War and Peace* (1968)

Soviet director Serguei Bondartchouk (right) and his actress wife Irma Skobtseva (left) are shown arriving at the Paris premiere of their film, *War and Peace*. Viatcheslav Tikhonov and Ludmilla Saveliva (center) starred in the film.

1974

Amarcord, an F.C. (Rome)-P.E.C.F. (Paris) Prod. (Italy)
Catsplay, a Hunnia Studio Prod. (Hungary)
The Deluge, a Film Polski Prod. (Poland)
Lacombe, Lucien, an NEF-UPF (Paris)-Vides Film (Rome)-Hallelujah Film (Munich) Prod. (France)
The Truce, a Tamames-Zemborain Prod. (Argentina)

1975

Dersu Uzala, a Mosfilms Studios Production (U.S.S.R.)
Land of Promise, a Film Polski Production (Poland)
Letters from Marusia, a Conacine Productoni (Mexico)
Sondakan No. 8, a Toho-Haiyuza Production (Japan)
Scent of a Woman, a Dean Film Production (Italy)

1976

Black and White in Color, an Arthur Cohn Production/Société Ivoirienne de Cinema (Ivory Coast)
Cousin, Cousine, Les Films Pomereu-Gaumont Production (France)
Jacob, the Liar, a VEB/DEFA Production (East Germany)
Nights and Days, a Polish Corporation for Film-"KADR" Film Unit Production (Poland)
Seven Beauties, a Medusa Distribuzione Production (Italy)

1977

Madame Rosa, a Lira Films Production (France)
Iphigenia, a Greek Film Centre Production (Greece)
Operation Thunderbolt, a Golan-Globus Production (Israel)
A Special Day, a Canafox Films Production (Italy)
That Obscure Object of Desire, a Greenwich-Les Films Galaxie-In Cine Production (Spain)

Director Constantin Costa-Gavras (left) and stars Irene Papas and Yves Montand are shown attending the American premiere of their film, *Z*. In 1969 the Algerian film won the Best Foreign Film award and was nominated for the Best Picture Award.

1978

Get Out Your Handkerchiefs, (France)
The Glass Cell, (W. Germany)
Hungarians (Hungary)
Viva Italia (Italy)
White Bim Black Ear (U.S.S.R.)

1979

The Tin Drum (Germany)
The Maids of Wilko (Poland)
Mama Turns a Hundred (Spain)
A Simply Story (France)
To Forget Venice (Italy)

1980

Moscow Does Not Believe in Tears (U.S.S.R.)

Confidence (Hungary)
Kagemusha (Japan)
The Last Metro (France)
The Nest (Spain)

1981

Mephisto (Hungary)
The Boat Is Full (Switzerland)
Man of Iron (Poland)
Muddy River (Japan)
Three Brothers (Italy)

1982

Volver a Empezar (To Begin Again) (Spain)
Alfino and the Condor (Nicaragua)
Coup de Torchon (France)
The Flight of the Eagle (Sweden)
Private Life (U.S.S.R.)

CHAPTER 12

Best Short Film Awards

*I*n the days before television, movie-goers expected not only a feature and some previews but a full program of entertainment and information. Cartoons, travelogues, documentaries, nature films, newsreels, or short fictional films filled out the evening's offerings.

The Academy established a category for most of these films in the fifth year of the awards (1931-32). (Newsreels were not included, and documentaries had their own category beginning in 1941.) The rulebook specifies that to qualify as a short film, a film's running time must not be more than 33⅓ minutes. The Academy Short Films Branch nominates films from submissions by producers, and voting is limited to members who have seen all nominees.

At times, the boundary between Live Action Short Films and Documentary Short Subjects has been blurred. The National Film Board of Canada submitted the staged film *Neighbours* (1952) in both categories and won as a documentary. After *Sentinels of Silence* won both categories in 1971, the rules were changed to prohibit consideration of documentaries for Short Film awards.

For about three decades, when shorts were being shown in theaters, the Hollywood studios dominated this category. (As described in the following section, Walt Disney Productions was particularly successful in these awards.) Among the Live Action winners in this period were *Bored of Education* (1936), an *Our Gang* comedy from Metro-Goldwyn-Mayer; *Declaration of Independence* (1938), an historical featurette from Warner Brothers; and *Climbing the Matterhorn* (1947), a travel-adventure film from Monogram. In the cartoon competition, Disney creations were the most frequent winners, followed by Warner Brothers' *Tom & Jerry* series, a five-time winner. Other winning characters included *Tweetie Pie* (1947), *Gerald*

The Oscar-winning animated Short Film of 1978 was *Special Delivery*, a wacky tale of what could happen when one doesn't shovel the snow off the front steps. This combination detective story and soap opera includes a dead mailman, an estranged wife, and an unusual trial.

Mr. Magoo first won an Oscar in the Short Film category in 1954 for *When Magoo Flew*. He remained a cartoon favorite in the ensuing years.

McBoing-Boing (1950), *Mr. Magoo* (1954, 1956), and *Speedy Gonzales* (1955).

When the short film became less a theatrical staple and more an experimental and personal medium, the awards reflected the change. Independent and university productions won awards. The animated films became less cartoonish and more abstract.

Winning films in the last two decades included *An Occurrence at Owl Creek Bridge* (1963), a haunting Civil War story directed by Frenchman Robert Enrico; *Frank Film* (1973), an offbeat, animated autobiography by Frank Mouris; *Closed Mondays* (1974), a clay animation film; and *Bread and Board* (1979), a glimpse into the life of a Down's syndrome victim directed by her brother.

Photo courtesy of the National Film Board of Canada

I'll Find a Way, the story of a girl coping with a physical handicap, was the Best Live-Action Short Film of 1977. The 23-minute film was produced and distributed by the National Film Board of Canada.

Photo courtesy of the National Film Board of Canada

The sand creatures in *The Sand Castle* were shaped from foam rubber and wire and coated with sand. The animated short film won a 1977 Oscar.

Every Child, **named Best Animated Short Film of 1979, was Canada's contribution to an hour-long UNICEF film composed of 10 six-minute segments in celebration of the International Year of the Child.**

Walt Disney (center), winner of 30 Academy Awards, received a gold plaque from a Belgian publisher for "outstanding merit for the production of *Dumbo* (1941) and *Bambi* (1942) in French." Belgian actress Annette De Lattre is to the left of Disney.

*W*alt Disney—the champion Oscar winner. Before his death in 1966, he personally collected 30 Academy Awards, including the Thalberg Award and three honorary citations. Members of his studio, Walt Disney Productions, have won numerous other Oscars. The category he most dominated was Short Films. Disney and his organization won 19 Oscars and 30 other nominations in this field.

Twelve of the Disney winners were cartoons. Disney animations won in 10 of the category's first 13 years. His first Oscar was for *Flowers and Trees* (1931-32), the first film made in the three-color Technicolor process. Such classics as *The Three Little Pigs* (1932-33), *Ferdinand the Bull* (1938), *The Ugly Duckling* (1939), and the wartime Donald Duck cartoon *Der Fuehrer's Face* (1942) also won. *The Old Mill* (1937) was the only Mickey Mouse cartoon to win an Oscar, though the 1931-32 Academy Awards included a special statuette that went to Disney for creating the beloved character.

The seven Live Action winners from the Disney studios included four of the True Life Adventure films: *In Beaver Valley* (1950);

Disney's Dominance

Ferdinand the Bull (1938), a Disney classic, was one of his first award-winning cartoons.

In 1938 Disney won the Documentary/Short Subject award for *Ferdinand the Bull,* and his production of *Snow White and the Seven Dwarfs* received an Honorary Award for "significant screen innovation."

Nature's Half Acre (1951); *Water Birds* (1952); and *Bear Country* (1953). In other years, similar Disney nature films won in the documentary category, accounting for seven more Oscars won by the organization.

One of history's greatest showmen and a man with an unsurpassed gift for knowing what would appeal to family audiences, Disney is the most appropriate person to top the Oscar lists. His contributions to motion picture entertainment and education are so many and varied that it is hard to summarize them all. His 1938 special award for *Snow White and the Seven Dwarfs* simply described his work as "significant screen innovation which has charmed millions." That—along with 29 other Oscars—probably says it all.

1931-32

(Cartoons)

Flowers and Trees, Walt Disney,
  United Artists
Mickey's Orphans, Walt Disney, Co-
  lumbia
It's Got Me Again, Warner Brothers

(Comedy)

The Music Box, Metro-
  Goldwyn-Mayer
The Loud Mouth, Mack Sennett
Stout Hearts and Willing Hands,
  RKO Radio

(Novelty)

Wrestling Swordfish, Mack Sennett
Screen Souvenirs, Paramount
Swing High, MGM

1932-33

(Cartoons)

The Merry Old Soul, Universal
The Three Little Pigs, Walt Disney,
  UA
Building a Building, Walt Disney,
  UA

(Comedy)

So This Is Harris, RKO Radio
Mister Mugg, Universal
Preferred List, RKO Radio

(Novelty)

Krakatoa, Educational
Menu, MGM
The Sea, Educational

1934

(Cartoons)

The Tortoise and the Hare, Walt Dis-
  ney
Holiday Land, Columbia
Jolly Little Elves, Universal

(Comedy)

La Cucaracha, RKO Radio
Men in Black, Columbia
What, No Men!, Warner Bros.

(Novelty)

City of Wax, Educational
Bosom Friends, Educational
Strikes and Spares, MGM

1935

(Cartoons)

Three Orphan Kittens, Walt Disney,
  UA
The Calico Dragon, MGM
Who Killed Cock Robin?, Walt Dis-
  ney, UA

(Comedy)

How to Sleep, MGM
Oh, My Nerves, Columbia
Tit for Tat, MGM

(Novelty)

Wings over Mt. Everest, Educational
Audioscopiks, MGM
Camera Thrills, Universal

1936

(Cartoons)

Country Cousin, Walt Disney-UA
Old Mill Pond, MGM
Sinbad the Sailor, Paramount

(One-Reel)

Bored of Education, MGM
Moscow Moods, Paramount
Wanted, a Master, MGM

(Two-Reel)

The Public Pays, MGM
Double or Nothing, Warner Bros.
Dummy Ache, RKO Radio

(Color)

Give Me Liberty, Warner Bros.
La Fiesta de Santa Barbara, MGM
Popular Science J-6-2, Paramount

1937

(Cartoons)

The Old Mill, Walt Disney-RKO
  Radio
Educated Fish, Paramount
The Little Match Girl, Columbia

(One-Reel)

Private Life of the Gannets, Educa-
  tional
A Night at the Movies, MGM
Romance of Radium, MGM

(Two-Reel)

Torture Money, MGM
Deep South, RKO Radio
Should Wives Work, RKO Radio

(Color)

Penny Wisdom, MGM
The Man without a Country, Warner
  Bros.
Popular Science J-7-1, Paramount

1938

(Cartoons)

Ferdinand the Bull, Walt Disney-
  RKO Radio
Brave Little Tailor, Walt Disney-
  RKO Radio
Mother Goose Goes to Hollywood,
  Walt Disney-RKO Radio
Good Scouts, Walt Disney-RKO
  Radio
Hunky and Spunky, Paramount

(One-Reel)

That Mothers Might Live, MGM
The Great Heart, MGM
Timber Toppers, 20th C.-Fox

(Two-Reel)

Declaration of Independence, Warner
  Bros.
Swingtime in the Movies, Warner
  Bros.
They're Always Caught, MGM

1939

(Cartoons)

The Ugly Duckling, Walt Disney-
  RKO Radio
Detouring America, Warner Bros.
Peace on Earth, MGM
The Pointer, Walt Disney-RKO
  Radio

(One-Reel)

Busy Little Bears, Paramount
Information Please, RKO Radio
Prophet without Honor, MGM
Sword Fishing, Warner Bros.

(Two-Reel)

Sons of Liberty, Warner Bros.
Drunk Driving, MGM
Five Times Five, RKO Radio

1940

(Cartoons)

Milky Way, MGM
Puss Gets the Boot, MGM
A Wild Hare, Warner Bros.

Best Short Films

(One-Reel)

Quicker 'n a Wink, MGM
London Can Take It, Warner Bros.
More about Nostradamus, MGM
Siege, RKO Radio

(Two-Reel)

Teddy, the Rough Rider, Warner Bros.
Eyes of the Navy, MGM
Service with the Colors, Warner Bros.

1941

(Cartoons)

Lend a Paw, Walt Disney-RKO Radio
Boogie Woogie Bugle Boy of Company B, Universal
Hiawatha's First Rabbit Hunt, Warner Bros.
How War Came, Columbia
The Night before Christmas, MGM
Rhapsody in Rivets, Warner Bros.
The Rookie Bear, MGM
Rhythm in the Ranks, Paramount
Superman No. 1, Paramount
Truant Officer Donald, Walt Disney-RKO Radio

(One-Reel)

Of Pups and Puzzles, MGM
Army Champions, MGM
Beauty and the Beach, Paramount
Down on the Farm, Paramount
Forty Boys and a Song, Warner Bros.
Kings of the Turf, Warner Bros.
Sagebrush and Silver, 20th C.-Fox

(Two-Reel)

Main Street on the March, MGM
Alive in the Deep, Woodard Productions, Inc.
Forbidden Passage, MGM
The Gay Parisian, Warner Bros.
The Tanks Are Coming, Warner Bros.

1942

(Cartoons)

Der Fuehrer's Face, Walt Disney-RKO Radio
All Out for V, 20th C.-Fox
The Blitz Wolf, MGM
Juke Box Jamboree, Universal
Pigs in a Polka, Warner Bros.
Tulips Shall Grow, Paramount

(One-Reel)

Speaking of Animals and Their Families, Paramount
Desert Wonderland, 20th C.-Fox
Marines in the Making, MGM
United States Marine Band, Warner Bros.

(Two-Reel)

Beyond the Line of Duty, Warner Bros.
Don't Talk, MGM
Private Smith of the U.S.A., RKO Radio

1943

(Cartoons)

Yankee Doodle Mouse, MGM
The Dizzy Acrobat, Universal
The Five Hundred Hats of Bartholomew Cubbins, Paramount
Greetings, Bait, Warner Bros.
Imagination, Columbia
Reason and Emotion, Walt Disney-RKO Radio

(One-Reel)

Amphibious Fighters, Paramount
Cavalcade of the Dance with Veloz and Yolanda, Warner Bros.
Champions Carry On, 20th C.-Fox
Hollywood in Uniform, Columbia
Seeing Hands, MGM

(Two-Reel)

Heavenly Music, MGM
Letter to a Hero, RKO Radio
Mardi Gras, Paramount
Women at War, Warner Bros.

1944

(Cartoons)

Mouse Trouble, MGM
And to Think that I Saw It on Mulberry Street, Paramount
The Dog, Cat and Canary, Columbia
Fish Fry, Universal
How to Play Football, Walt Disney-RKO Radio
My Boy, Johnny, 20th C.-Fox
Swooner Crooner, Warner Bros.

(One-Reel)

Who's Who in Animal Land, Paramount
Blue Grass Gentlemen, 20th C.-Fox

Jammin' the Blues, Warner Bros.
Movie Pests, MGM
50th Anniversary of Motion Pictures, Columbia

(Two-Reel)

I Won't Play, Warner Bros.
Bombalera, Paramount
Main Street Today, MGM

1945

(Cartoons)

Quiet Please, MGM
Donald's Crime, Walt Disney-RKO Radio
Jasper and the Beanstalk, Paramount
Life with Feathers, Warner Bros.
Mighty Mouse in Gypsy Life, 20th C.-Fox
Poet and Peasant, Universal
Rippling Romance, Columbia

(One-Reel)

Stairway to Light, MGM
Along the Rainbow Trail, 20th C.-Fox
Screen Snapshots 25th Anniversary, Columbia
Story of a Dog, Warner Bros.
White Rhapsody, Paramount
Your National Gallery, Universal

(Two-Reel)

Star in the Night, Warner Bros.
A Gun in His Hand, MGM
The Jury Goes Round 'n Round, Columbia
The Little Witch, Paramount

1946

(Cartoons)

The Cat Concerto, MGM
Chopin's Musical Moments, Universal
John Henry and the Inky Poo, Paramount
Squatter's Rights, Walt Disney-RKO Radio
Walky Talky Hawky, Warner Bros.

(One-Reel)

Facing Your Danger, Warner Bros.
Dive-Hi Champs, Paramount
Golden Horses, 20th C.-Fox
Smart as a Fox, Warner Bros.
Sure Cures, MGM

(Two-Reel)

A Boy and His Dog, Warner Bros.
College Queen, Paramount
Hiss and Yell, Columbia
The Luckiest Guy in the World, MGM

1947

(Cartoons)

Tweetie Pie, Warner Bros.
Chip an' Dale, Walt Disney-RKO Radio
Dr. Jekyll and Mr. Hyde, MGM
Pluto's Blue Note, Walt Disney-RKO Radio
Tubby the Tuba, Paramount

(One-Reel)

Goodbye Miss Turlock, MGM
Brooklyn, U.S.A., Universal-International
Moon Rockets, Paramount
Now You See It, MGM
So You Want to Be in Pictures, Warner Bros.

(Two-Reel)

Climbing the Matterhorn, Monogram
Champagne for Two, Paramount
Fight of the Wild Stallions, U-I
Give Us the Earth, MGM
A Voice Is Born, Columbia

1948

(Cartoons)

The Little Orphan, MGM
Mickey and the Seal, Walt Disney-RKO Radio
Mouse Wreckers, Warner Bros.
Robin Hoodlum, Columbia
Tea for Two Hundred, Walt Disney-RKO Radio

(One-Reel)

Symphony of a City, 20th C.-Fox
Annie Was a Wonder, Warner Bros.
Cinderella Horse, Warner Bros.
So You Want to Be on the Radio, Warner Bros.
You Can't Win, MGM

(Two-Reel)

Seal Island, Walt Disney-RKO Radio
Calgary Stampede, Warner Bros.
Going to Blazes, MGM
Samba-Mania, Paramount
Snow Capers, U-I

1949

(Cartoons)

For Scent-imental Reasons, Warner Bros.
Hatch Up Your Troubles, MGM
Magic Fluke, Columbia
Toy Tinkers, Walt Disney, RKO Radio

(One-Reel)

Aquatic House-Party, Paramount
Roller Derby Girl, Paramount
So You Think You're Not Guilty, Warner Bros.
Spills and Chills, Warner Bros.
Water Trix, MGM

(Two-Reel)

Van Gogh, Canton-Weiner
Boy and the Eagle, RKO Radio
Chase of Death, Irving Allen Productions
The Grass Is Always Greener, Warner Bros.
Snow Carnival, Warner Bros.

1950

(Cartoons)

Gerald McBoing-Boing, Columbia
Jerry's Cousin, MGM
Trouble Indemnity, Columbia

(One-Reel)

Grandad of Races, Warner Bros.
Blaze Busters, Warner Bros.
Wrong Way Butch, MGM

(Two-Reel)

In Beaver Valley, Walt Disney-RKO Radio
Grandma Moses, Falcon Films, Inc.
My Country 'tis of Thee, Warner Bros.

1951

(Cartoons)

Two Mouseketeers, MGM
Lambert, the Sheepish Lion, Walt Disney-RKO Radio
Rooty Toot Toot, Columbia

(One-Reel)

World of Kids, Warner Bros.
Ridin' the Rails, Paramount
The Story of Time, Cornell Film Company (British)

(Two-Reel)

Nature's Half Acre, Walt Disney-RKO Radio

Balzac, Les Films du Compass (French)
Danger under the Sea, U-I

1952

(Cartoons)

Johann Mouse, MGM
Little Johnny Jet, MGM
Madeline, Columbia
Pink and Blue Blues, Columbia
Romance of Transportation, Natl. Film Board of Canada (Canadian)

(One-Reel)

Light in the Window, 20th C.-Fox
Athletes of the Saddle, Paramount
Desert Killer, Warner Bros.
Neighbours, Natl. Film Board of Canada (Canadian)
Royal Scotland, British Information Services (British)

(Two-Reel)

Water Birds, Walt Disney-RKO Radio
Bridge of Time, British Information Services, (British)
Devil Take Us, Theatre of Life
Thar She Blows!, Warner Bros.

1953

(Cartoons)

Toot, Whistle, Plunk and Boom, Walt Disney
Christopher Crumpet, Columbia
From A to Z-Z-Z-Z, Warner Bros.
Rugged Bear, Walt Disney-RKO Radio
The Tell Tale Heart, Columbia

(One-Reel)

The Merry Wives of Windsor Overture, MGM
Christ among the Primitives, IFE Releasing Corp. (Italian)
Herring Hunt, National Film Board of Canada (Canadian)
Joy of Living, 20th C.-Fox
Wee Water Wonders, Paramount

(Two-Reel)

Bear Country, Walt Disney-RKO Radio
Ben and Me, Walt Disney
Return to Glennascaul, Mayor-Kingsley Inc.
Vesuvius Express, 20th C.-Fox
Winter Paradise, Warner Bros.

1954

(Cartoons)

When Magoo Flew, Columbia
Crazy Mixed-Up Pup, U-I
Pigs Is Pigs, Walt Disney-RKO
  Radio
Sandy Claws, Warner Bros.
Touché, Pussy Cat, MGM

(One-Reel)

This Mechanical Age, Warner Bros.
The First Piano Quartette, 20th C.-
  Fox
The Strauss Fantasy, MGM

(Two-Reel)

A Time Out of War, Carnival Pro-
  ductions
Beauty and the Bull, Warner Bros.
Jet Carrier, 20th C.-Fox
Siam, Walt Disney, Buena Vista

1955

(Cartoons)

Speedy Gonzales, Warner Bros.
Good Will to Men, MGM
The Legend of Rock-a-Bye Point, U-I
No Hunting, Walt Disney-RKO
  Radio

(One-Reel)

Survival City, 20th C.-Fox
Gadgets Galore, Warner Bros.
3rd Avenue El, Ardee Films
Three Kisses, Paramount

(Two-Reel)

The Face of Lincoln, Cavalcade Pic-
  tures
The Battle of Gettysburg, MGM
On the Twelfth Day, Go Pictures, Inc.
Switzerland, Walt Disney
Twenty-Four Hour Alert, Warner
  Bros.

1956

(Cartoons)

Mister Magoo's Puddle Jumper, Co-
  lumbia
*Gerald McBoing-Boing on Planet
  Moo*, Columbia
The Jaywalker, Columbia

(One-Reel)

Crashing the Water Barrier, Warner
  Bros.
I Never Forget a Face, Warner Bros.
Time Stood Still, Warner Bros.

(Two-Reel)

The Bespoke Overcoat, Romulus
  Films
Cow Dog, Walt Disney
The Dark Wave, 20th C.-Fox
Samoa, Walt Disney

1957

(Cartoons)

Birds Anonymous, Warner Bros.
The Droopy Knight, MGM
Tabasco Road, Warner Bros.
Trees and Jamaica Daddy, Columbia
The Truth about Mother Goose, Walt
  Disney

(Live Action Subjects)

The Wetback Hound, Walt Disney
A Chairy Tale, Natl. Film Board of
  Canada
City of Gold, Natl. Film Board of
  Canada
Foothold on Antarctica, World Wide
  Pictures
Portugal, Walt Disney

1958

(Cartoons)

Knighty Knight Bugs, Warner Bros.
Paul Bunyan, Walt Disney
Sidney's Family Tree, 20th C.-Fox

(Live Action Subjects)

Grand Canyon, Walt Disney
Journey into Spring, British Trans-
  port Films (British)
The Kiss, Continental Dist., Inc.
Snows of Aorangi, New Zealand
  Screen Board
T Is for Tumbleweed, Continental
  Dist., Inc.

1959

(Cartoons)

Moonbird, Storyboard, Inc.
Mexicali Shmoes, Warner Bros.
Noah's Ark, Walt Disney
The Violinist, Kingsley Intl. Pictures
  Corp.

(Live Action Subjects)

The Golden Fish, Columbia (French)
Between the Tides, British Transport
  Films (British)
Mysteries of the Deep, Walt Disney
*The Running, Jumping and
  Standing-Still Film*, Kingsley-
  Union Films (British)
Skyscraper, Joseph Burstyn Film En-
  terprises, Inc.

1960

(Cartoons)

Munro, Rembrandt Films
Goliath, Walt Disney
High Note, Warner Bros.
Mouse and Garden, Warner Bros.
A Place in the Sun, Go Pictures, Inc.
  (Czechoslovakian)

(Live Action Subjects)

Day of the Painter, Kingsley-Union
  Films
The Creation of Woman, Trident
  Films, Inc. (Indian)
Islands of the Sea, Walt Disney
A Sport Is Born, Paramount

1961

(Cartoons)

Ersatz (The Substitute), Zagreb Film
Aquamania, Walt Disney
Beep Prepared, Warner Bros.
Nelly's Folly, Warner Bros.
Pied Piper of Guadalupe, Warner
  Bros.

(Live Action Subjects)

Seawards the Great Ships, Lester A.
  Schoenfeld Films
Ballon Vole (Play Ball!), Kingsley In-
  tl. Pictures Corp.
The Face of Jesus, Harry Stern, Inc.
Rooftops of New York, McCarty-
  Rush Productions
Very Nice, Very Nice, Natl. Film
  Board of Canada

1962

(Cartoons)

The Hole, Storyboard Inc.
Icarus Montgolfier Wright, UA
Now Hear This, Warner Bros.
Self Defense—for Cowards, Rem-
  brandt Films
Symposium on Popular Songs, Walt
  Disney

(Live Action Subjects)

Heureux Anniversaire, Atlantic Pic-
  tures Corp. (French)
Big City Blues, Mayfair Picture Co.
The Cadillac, United Producers
  Releasing Org.
The Cliff Dwellers, Lester A. Schoen-
  feld Films
Pan, Mayfair Picture Co.

1963

(Cartoons)

The Critic, Columbia
Automania 2000, Pathe Contemporary Films
The Game, Zagreb Film, Rembrandt Films
My Financial Career, Natl. Film Board of Canada
Pianissimo, Cinema 16

(Live Action Subjects)

An Occurrence at Owl Creek Bridge, Cappagariff-Janus Films
The Concert, Go Pictures
Home-Made Car, Lester A. Schoenfeld Films
Six-Sided Triangle, Lion Intl. Films
That's Me, Pathe Contemporary Films

1964

(Cartoons)

The Pink Phink, UA
Christmas Cracker, Natl. Film Board of Canada
How to Avoid Friendship, Rembrandt Films
Nudnik #2, Rembrandt Films

(Live Action Subjects)

Casals Conducts: 1964, Beckman Film Corp.
Help! My Snowman's Burning Down, Pathe Contemporary Films
The Legend of Jimmy Blue Eyes, Topaz Film Corp.

1965

(Cartoons)

The Dot and the Line, MGM
Clay or the Origin of Species, Pathe Contemporary Films
The Thieving Magpie, Allied Artists

(Live Action Subjects)

The Chicken, Pathe Contemporary Films
Fortress of Peace, Cinerama
Skaterdater, UA
Snow, British Transport Films
Time Piece, Muppets, Inc.

1966

(Cartoons)

Herb Alpert and the Tijuana Brass Double Feature, Paramount
The Drag, Natl. Film Board of Canada
The Pink Blueprint, UA

(Live Action Subjects)

Wild Wings, British Transport Films
Turkey the Bridge, Lester A. Schoenfeld Films
The Winning Strain, Paramount

1967

(Cartoons)

The Box, Brandon Films
Hypothese Beta, Pathe Contemporary Films
What on Earth!, Columbia

(Live Action Subjects)

A Place to Stand, Columbia
Paddle to the Sea, Natl. Film Board of Canada
Sky over Holland, Seneca Intl.
Stop, Look and Listen, MGM

1968

(Cartoons)

Winnie the Pooh and the Blustery Day, Walt Disney
The House that Jack Built, Natl. Film Board of Canada
The Magic Pear Tree, Murakami-Wolf Productions
Windy Day, Paramount

(Live Action Subjects)

Robert Kennedy Remembered, Natl. General
The Dove, Schoenfeld Film Dist.
Duo, Columbia
Prelude, Prelude Company

1969

(Cartoons)

It's Tough to Be a Bird, Walt Disney
Of Men and Demons, Paramount
Walking, Columbia

(Live Action Subjects)

The Magic Machines, Fly-By-Night Productions
Blake, Natl. Film Board of Canada
People Soup, Columbia

1970

(Cartoons)

Is It Always Right to Be Right?, Lester A. Schoenfeld Films
The Further Adventures of Uncle Sam: Part Two, Goldstone Films
The Shepherd, Brandon Films

(Live Action Subjects)

The Resurrection of Broncho Billy, Universal

Shut Up . . . I'm Crying, Lester A. Schoenfeld Films
Sticky My Fingers . . . Fleet My Feet, American Film Institute

1971

(Animated Films)

The Crunch Bird, Regency Film Dist. Corp.
Evolution, Columbia
The Selfish Giant, Pyramid Films

(Live Action Films)

Sentinels of Silence, Paramount
Good Morning, E/G Films
The Rehearsal, Cinema Verona

1972

(Animated Films)

A Christmas Carol, ABC Film Services
Kama Sutra Rides Again, Lion Intl. Films
Tup Tup, Zagreb Film

(Live Action Films)

Norman Rockwell's World . . . an American Dream, Columbia
Frog Story, Gidron Productions
Solo, Pyramid Films

1973

(Animated Films)

Frank Film, Frank Mouris
The Legend of John Henry, Pyramid Films
Pulcinella, Luzzati-Gianini

(Live Action Films)

The Bolero, Allan Miller
Clockmaker, James Street Prod. Ltd.
Life Times Nine, Insight Prod.

1974

(Animated Films)

Closed Mondays, Lighthouse Prod.
The Family that Dwelt Apart, Natl. Film Board of Canada
Hunger, Natl. Film Board of Canada
Voyage to Next, Hubley Studio
Winnie the Pooh and Tigger Too, Walt Disney

(Live Action Films)

One-Eyed Men Are Kings, C.A.P.A.C. Productions (Paris)
Climb, Dewitt Jones Productions
The Concert, Black and White Colour Film Co., Ltd.
Planet Ocean, Graphic Films
The Violin, Sincinkin, Ltd.

1975

(Animated Films)

Great, Granstern Ltd.-British Lion Films Ltd.
Kick Me, Robert Swarthe Productions
Monsieur Pointu, Natl. Film Board of Canada
Sisyphus, Hungarofilms

(Live Action)

Angel and Big Joe, Bert Salzman Prod.
Conquest of Light, Louis Marcus Films Ltd.
Dawn Flight, Lawrence M. Lansburgh Prod.
A Day in the Life of Bonnie Consolo, Barr Films
Doubletalk, Beattie Prod.

1976

(Animated Films)

Leisure, Film Australia
Dedalo, Cineteam Realizzazioni
The Street, Natl. Film Board of Canada

(Live Action)

In the Region of Ice, American Film Institute
Kudzu, Short
The Morning Spider, Black and White Colour Film Co.
Night Life, Opus Films, Ltd.
Number One, Number One Prod.

1977

(Animated Films)

Sand Castle, Natl. Film Board of Canada
The Dead Game, Natl. Film Board of Canada
The Doonesbury Special, Hubley Studio

Jimmy the C, Motionpicker

(Live Action)

I'll Find a Way, Natl. Film Board of Canada
The Absent-Minded Waiter, Aspen Film Society
Floating Free, A Trans World International Production
Notes on the Popular Arts, Saul Bass Films
Spaceborne, Lawrence Hall of Science, NASA

1978

(Animated Films)

Special Delivery, Natl. Film Board of Canada
Oh My Darling, Nico Crama Prod.
Rip Van Winkle, a Will Vinton-Billy Budd film

(Live Action)

Teenage Father, New Visions
A Different Approach, Brookfield Prod.
Mandy's Grandmother, Illumination
Strange Fruit, Amer. Film Inst.

1979

(Animated Films)

Every Child, Natl. Film Board of Canada
Dream Doll, Halas Batchelor Film Wright
It's So Nice to have a Wolf around the House, AR & T Prod.

(Live Action)

Board and Care, Learning Corp. of Amer.
Bravery in the Field, Natl. Film Board of Canada
Oh Brother My Brother, Pyramid Film
The Solar Film, Wildwood

Solly's Diner, Mathias, Zuckerman-Henkin Prod.

1980

(Animated Films)

The Fly, Pannonia Films, Budapest
All Nothing, Radio Canada
History of the World in Three Minutes Flat, Michael Mills Prod. Ltd.

(Live Action)

The Dollar Bottom, Rocking Horse Films Ltd.
Fall Line, Sports Imagery, Inc.
A Jury of Her Peers, Sally Heckel Prod.

1981

(Animated Films)

CRAC, Associate Radio-Canada
The Creation, Will Vinton Prod.
The Tender Tale of Cinderella Penguin, Natl. Film Board of Canada

(Live Action)

Violet, Amer. Film Institute
Couples and Robbers, Flamingo Pictures Ltd.
First Winter, Natl. Film Board of Canada

1982

(Animated Films)

Tango, Film Polski
The Great Cognito, Will Vinton Prod.
The Snowman, Snowman Enterprises

(Live Action)

A Shocking Accident, Flamingo Pictures Ltd.
The Silence, Amer. Film Inst.
Split Cherry Tree, Learning Corp. of Amer.
Sredni Vashtar, Laurentic Film Prod.

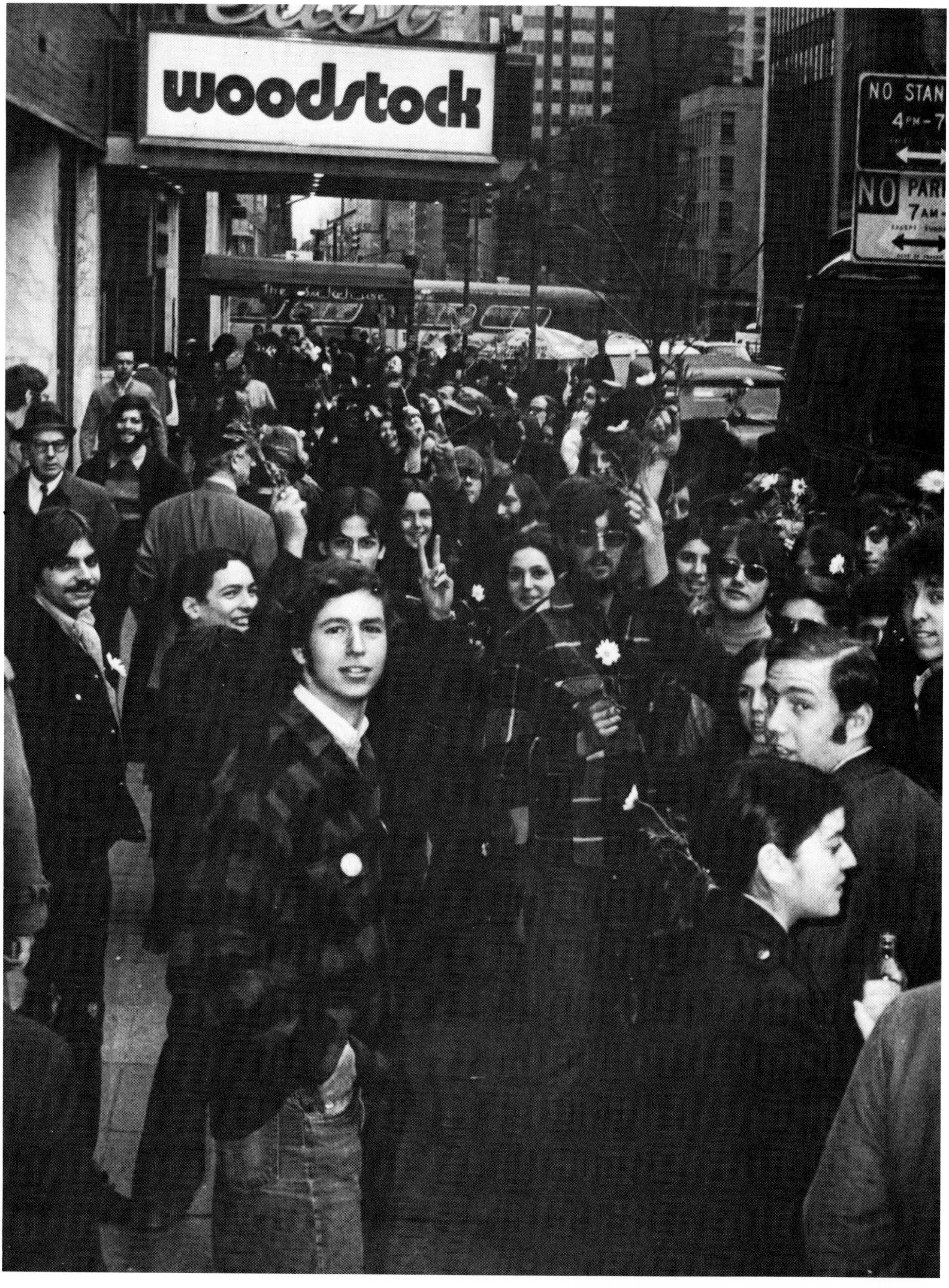
woodstock
NO STAN
4PM-7
NO PAR
7AM-

CHAPTER 13

Best Documentary Awards

*T*he Documentary awards were born during World War II, the period when the factual film first came into its own as a significant form. From 1941 until 1974 the Academy would consider only films available in 35 millimeter prints. The restriction meant that many smaller-budget productions did not qualify, and most of the winners were products of major studios or government agencies. Since 1975 16 millimeter films have been acceptable, provided they were previously honored by acceptance at noncompetitive international film festivals, or by winning best-in-category prizes at competitive festivals. The Academy has no documentary branch, so the nominations in this category are made by a committee composed of members of various other branches who have seen all the nominated documentaries.

For the first six years every winner was

a war film sponsored by the United States or an Allied government. These documentaries were general audience reports on the progress of the war designed to be shown in theaters. In 1942 four winners were recognized: the American films *Battle of Midway* and *Prelude to War*, the Australian *Kokoda Front Line*, and the Russian film *Moscow Strikes Back*.

Beginning in 1943 the category was subdivided into Documentary Short Subjects and Documentary Features, and two awards were given annually—except in 1946 when no Features were nominated, in 1949 when a third prize was given, and in 1957 when no Short Subjects were nominated.

For the first 20 years, documentaries generally were shot without synchronous sound. Narration, music, and sound effects were added in the editing room. The development of highly portable syn-

The Trans-Lux East Theatre in Manhattan wasn't big enough to house the crowd that flocked there to see *Woodstock* in 1970, and Warner Brothers opened the film at a second theatre across town the following week. The film was chosen Best Documentary of 1970.

The 1951 Oscar-winning documentary feature, *Kon-Tiki,* **followed the trek of Thor Heyerdahl's raft Kon-Tiki as it crossed the Pacific Ocean.**

chronous sound systems in the 1960s meant that small crews with handheld cameras could be part of an event as they recorded its sights and sounds. Often, no narrator was needed.

The new style, known as *cinema verité,* accounted for the very different way that the Vietnam War was filmed, compared with World War II. The 1967 Feature winner, *The Anderson Platoon,* was a French Broadcasting System portrait of an American unit struggling against a largely unseen enemy in Vietman and is an example of *cinema verité.* Barbara Kopple applied the style to a portrait of another kind of struggle involving striking Kentucky coal miners in *Harlan County, U.S.A.* (1976).

All the Documentary winners are portraits—most of them positive—of fascinating people, events, places, or processes around the world. *Kon-Tiki* (1951) traces Thor Heyerdahl's crossing of the Pa-

The great pianist Arthur Rubinstein was the subject of the Best Documentary Feature of 1969, *Arthur Rubinstein—Love of Life.*

Photo courtesy of the National Film Board of Canada

Photo courtesy of the National Film Board of Canada

Neighbours **was named the Best Short-Subject Documentary of 1952. It was also nominated for the Best Short Film award. The film told the story of two neighbors who end up killing each other over a flower budding between their houses.**

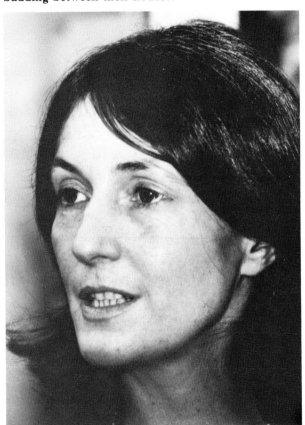

Photo courtesy of the National Film Board of Canada

Dr. Helen Caldicott called for disarmament and painted a frightening picture of the aftermath of nuclear war in the 1982 Oscar-winning Documentary, *If You Love This Planet***. A production of the National Film Board of Canada, the film was termed "political propaganda" by the U.S. Dept. of Justice.**

cific by raft. *Thursday's Children* (1954), narrated by Richard Burton, profiles the enchanting students of one British school for the deaf. *The Silent World* (1956), the first feature by Jacques-Yves Cousteau, reveals a universe beneath the sea. *Glass* (1959) tunefully and playfully portrays the artistry of glass blowers in a Dutch factory. *The War Game* (1966) uses staged scenes to depict the horrifying effects of a nuclear war on neighborhoods in England. *Why Man Creates* (1968) is Saul Bass's nonfiction homage to the imagination of scientists and artists. *Woodstock* (1970) celebrates the music and other pleasures of the era's greatest rock concert. *Close Harmony* (1981) shows how making music together bridged a gap between New York school children and senior citizens.

As the preceding list of Oscar-winning documentaries reveals, their emphasis is on factual content, but the approach taken by their creators may vary.

1941

Churchill's Island, Canadian Film
Board, United Artists
Adventures in the Bronx, Film As-
socs.
Bomber, U.S. Office of Emergency
Management Film Unit
Christmas under Fire, British Minis-
try of Information, Warner Bros.
Letter from Home, British Ministry
of Information
Life of a Thoroughbred, 20th C.-Fox
Norway in Revolt, RKO Radio
Soldiers of the Sky, 20th C.-Fox
War Clouds in the Pacific, Canadian
Film Board

1942

Battle of Midway, U.S. Navy, 20th
C.-Fox
Kokoda Front Line, Australian News
Information Bureau
Moscow Strikes Back, Artkino (Rus-
sian)
Prelude to War, U.S. Army Special
Services
A Ship Is Born, U.S. Merchant Ma-
rine, Warner Brothers
Africa, Prelude to Victory, 20th C.-
Fox
Combat Report, U.S. Army Signal
Corps
Conquer by the Clock, Office of War
Information, RKO Pathe
The Grain that Built a Hemisphere,
Walt Disney
Henry Browne, Farmer, U.S. Depart-
ment of Agriculture, Republic
High over the Borders, Canadian Na-
tional Film Board
High Stakes in the East, Netherlands
Information Bureau
Inside Fighting China, Canadian Na-
tional Film Board
It's Everybody's War, Office of War
Information, 20th C.-Fox
Listen to Britain, British Ministry of
Information
Little Belgium, Belgian Ministry of
Information
Little Isles of Freedom, Warner Bros.
Mr. Blabbermouth, Office of War In-
formation, Metro-Goldwyn-Mayer
Mr. Gardenia Jones, Office of War
Information, MGM
New Spirit, U.S. Treasury Depart-
ment: Walt Disney
The Price of Glory, Office of War In-
formation, Paramount
Twenty-One Miles, British Ministry
of Information
We Refuse to Die, Office of War In-
formation, Paramount
White Eagle, Cocanen Films

Winning Your Wings, U.S. Army Air
Force, Warner Bros.

1943

(Short Subjects)

December 7th, U.S. Navy
Children of Mars, RKO Radio
Plan for Destruction, MGM
Swedes in America, Overseas Motion
Picture Bureau
To the People of the United States,
U.S. Public Health Service
Tomorrow We Fly, U.S. Navy
Youth in Crisis, 20th C.-Fox

(Features)

Desert Victory, British Ministry of
Information
Battle of Russia, War Department
Baptism of Fire, U.S. Army
Report from the Aleutians, U.S. Army
Pictorial Service
War Department Report, Office of
Strategic Services

1944

(Short Subjects)

With the Marines at Tarawa, U.S.
Marine Corps
Arturo Toscanini, Office of War In-
formation
New Americans, RKO Radio

(Features)

The Fighting Lady, 20th C.-Fox and
U.S. Navy
Resisting Enemy Interrogation, U.S.
Army Air Force

1945

(Short Subjects)

Hitler Lives?, Warner Bros.
Library of Congress, Office of War
Information
To the Shores of Iwo Jima, U.S. Ma-
rine Corps

(Features)

The True Glory, Governments of
Great Britain and U.S.A.
The Last Bomb, U.S. Army Air Force

1946

(Short Subjects)

Seeds of Destiny, U.S. War Depart-
ment
Atomic Power, 20th C.-Fox
Life at the Zoo, Artkino
Paramount News Issue #37, Para-
mount
Traffic with the Devil, MGM

1947

(Short Subjects)

First Steps, United Nations
Passport to Nowhere, RKO Radio
School in the Mailbox, Australian
News and Information Bureau

(Features)

Design for Death, RKO Radio
Journey into Medicine, U.S. Department of State
The World Is Rich, British Information Services

1948

(Short Subjects)

Toward Independence, U.S. Army
Heart to Heart, Fact Film Organiza-
tion
Operation Vittles, U.S. Army Air
Force

(Features)

The Secret Land, U.S. Navy, MGM
The Quiet One, Mayer-Burstyn

1949

(Short Subjects)

A Chance to Live, 20th C.-Fox
So Much for so Little, Warner Bros.
Cartoons, Inc.
1848, A. F. Films, Inc.
The Rising Tide, National Film
Board of Canada

(Features)

Daybreak in Udi, British Information
Services
Kenji Comes Home, Protestant Film
Commission

1950

(Short Subjects)

Why Korea?, 20th C.-Fox Movietone
The Fight: Science Against Cancer,
National Film Board of Canada
with the Medical Film Institute of
the Association of American

Best Documentaries

Medical Colleges
The Stairs, Film Documents, Inc.

(Features)

The Titan: Story of Michelangelo, Classic Pictures, Inc.
With These Hands, Promotional Films Co., Inc.

1951

(Short Subjects)

Benjy, Fred Zinnemann with Paramount Pictures Corp.
One Who Came Back, sponsored by the Disabled American Veterans with the U.S. Department of Defense and the Association of Motion Picture Producers

(Features)

Kon-Tiki, RKO Radio (Norwegian)
I Was a Communist for the FBI, Warner Bros.

1952

(Short Subjects)

Neighbours, National Film Board of Canada (Canadian)
Devil Take Us, Theatre of Life Prod.
The Garden Spider (Epeira Diadema), Cristallo Films (Italian)
Man Alive!, United Productions of America for the American Cancer Society

(Features)

The Sea Around Us, RKO Radio
The Hoaxters, MGM
Navajo, Lippert Pictures, Inc.

1953

(Short Subjects)

The Alaskan Eskimo, Walt Disney Prods., RKO Radio
The Living City, Encyclopaedia Britannica Films, Inc.
Operation Blue Jay, U.S. Army Signal Corps.
They Planted a Stone, World Wide

Pictures, British Information Services (British)
The Word, 20th C.-Fox

(Features)

The Living Desert, Walt Disney Prods.
The Conquest of Everest, United Artists (British)
A Queen Is Crowned, Universal-International (British)

1954

(Short Subjects)

Thursday's Children, British Information Services (British)
Jet Carrier, 20th C.-Fox
Rembrandt: A Self-Portrait, Distributors Corp. of America

(Features)

The Vanishing Prairie, Walt Disney Prods.
The Stratford Adventure, National Film Board of Canada (Canadian)

1955

(Short Subjects)

Men against the Arctic, Walt Disney Prods.
The Battle of Gettysburg, MGM
The Face of Lincoln, Cavalcade Pictures, Inc.

(Features)

Helen Keller in Her Story, Nancy Hamilton Presentation
Heartbreak Ridge, Tudor Pictures (French)

1956

(Short Subjects)

The True Story of the Civil War, Camera Eye Pictures, Inc.
A City Decides, Charles Guggenheim & Assocs., Inc., Prod.
The Dark Wave, 20th C.-Fox
The House without a Name, U-I
Man in Space, Walt Disney Prods.

(Features)

The Silent World, A Filmad-F.S.J.Y.C. Prod., Columbia (French)
The Naked Eye, Camera Eye Pictures, Inc.
Where Mountains Float, Brandon Films, Inc. (Danish)

1957

(Features)

Albert Schweitzer, Hill and Anderson Prod., Louis de Rochemont Assocs.
On the Bowery, Lionel Rogosin Prods., Film Representations, Inc.
Torero!, Producciones Barbachano Ponce, Columbia (Mexican)

1958

(Short Subjects)

Ama Girls, Walt Disney Prods.
Employees Only, Hughes Aircraft Co.
Journey into Spring, British Transport Films, Lester A. Schoenfeld Films
The Living Stone, National Film Board of Canada
Overture, United Nations Film Service

(Features)

White Wilderness, Walt Disney Prods.
Antarctic Crossing, World Wide Pictures, Lester A. Schoenfeld Films
The Hidden World, Small World Co.
Psychiatric Nursing, Dynamic Films, Inc.

1959

(Short Subjects)

Glass, Netherlands Government (The Netherlands)
Donald in Mathmagic Land, Walt Disney Prods.
From Generation to Generation, Cullen Assocs., Maternity Center Assoc.

(Features)

Serengeti Shall Not Die, Transocean
  Film (German)
The Race for Space, Wolper, Inc.

1960

(Short Subjects)

Giuseppina, Lester A. Schoenfeld
  Films (British)
Beyond Silence, U.S. Information
  Agency
A City Called Copenhagen, Danish
  Government Film Office (Danish)
George Grosz' Interregnum, Educa-
  tional Communications Corp.
Universe, National Film Board of
  Canada (Canadian)

(Features)

The Horse with the Flying Tail, Walt
  Disney Prods.
Rebel in Paradise, Tiare Co.

1961

(Short Subjects)

Project Hope, MacManus, John &
  Adams, Inc., Ex-Cell-O Corp.
Breaking the Language Barrier, U.S.
  Air Force
Cradle of Genius, Plough Prods.
  (Irish)
Kahl, Dido-Film GmbH., AEG-
  Filmdienst (German)
*L'Uomo in Grigio (The Man in
  Gray)*, (Italian)

(Features)

***Le Ciel et la Boue (Sky Above and
  Mud Beneath)***, Ardennes Films
  and Michael Arthur Film Prods.,
  Rank Film Distrs., Ltd. (French)
*La Grande Olimpiade (Olympic
  Games 1960)*, Cineriz (Italian)

1962

(Short Subjects)

Dylan Thomas, Janus Films (Welsh)
The John Glenn Story, Department
  of the Navy, Warner Bros.
The Road to the Wall, CBS Films,
  Inc., Department of Defense

(Features)

Black Fox, Heritage Films, Inc.
Alvorada (Brazil's Changing Face),
  MW Filmproduktion (German)

1963

(Short Subjects)

Chagall, Auerbach Film Enterprises,
  Ltd.-Flag Films
The Five Cities of June, U.S. In-
  formation Agency
The Spirit of America, Spotlite News
Thirty Million Letters, British Trans-
  port Films
To Live Again, Wilding Inc.

(Features)

***Robert Frost: A Lover's Quarrel with
  the World***, WGBH Educational
  Foundation
*Le Maillon et La Chaine (The Link
  and the Chain)*, Films du
  Centaure-Filmartic
The Yanks Are Coming, David L.
  Wolper Prods.

1964

(Short Subjects)

Nine from Little Rock, U.S. Informa-
  tion Agency, Guggenheim
  Productions
Breaking the Habit, American Can-
  cer Society
Children Without, National Educa-
  tion Association, Guggenheim
  Productions
Kenojuak, National Film Board of
  Canada
140 Days under the World, New Zea-
  land National Film Unit, Rank
  Film Distributors of New Zealand

(Features)

***Jacques-Yves Cousteau's World with-
  out Sun***, Columbia
The Finest Hours, Le Vien Films,
  Ltd., Columbia
Four Days in November, UA
The Human Dutch, Haanstra
  Filmproductie
Over There, 1914-18, Pathe Contem-
  porary Films

1965

(Short Subjects)

To Be Alive!, Johnson Wax
Mural on Our Street, Pathe Contem-
  porary Films
Ouverture, Hungarofilm-Pathe Con-
  temporary Films
Point of View, National Tuberculosis
  Assoc.
Yeats Country, Aengus Films Ltd. for
  the Department of External Affairs
  of Ireland

(Features)

The Eleanor Roosevelt Story, Ameri-
  can Intl.
*The Battle of the Bulge . . . The Brave
  Rifles*, Mascott Prods.
The Forth Road Bridge, Random
  Film Prods., Ltd., Shell-Mex and
  B.P. Film Library
Let My People Go, Wolper Prods.
To Die in Madrid, Ancinex Prods.,
  Altura Films Intl.

1966

(Short Subjects)

A Year Toward Tomorrow, Sun Dial
  Films, Inc., Prod. for Office of Eco-
  nomic Opportunity
Adolescence, M.K. Prods.
Cowboy, U.S. Information Agency
The Odds Against, Vision Associates
  Prod. for the American Founda-
  tion Institute of Corrections
Saint Matthew Passion, Mafilm Stu-
  dio, Hungarofilm

(Features)

The War Game, BBC Prod. for the
  British Film Institute, Pathe
The Face of Genius, WBZ-TV,
  Group W, Boston
Helicopter Canada, National Film
  Board of Canada
*Le Volcan Interdit (The Forbidden
  Volcano)*, Cine Documents
  Tazieff, Athos Films
The Really Big Family, David L.
  Wolper Prod.

1967

(Short Subjects)

The Redwoods, King Screen Prods.
Monument to the Dream, Guggenheim Prods.
A Place to Stand, T.D.F. Prod. for the Ontario Department of Economics and Development
See You at the Pillar, Associated British-Pathe Prod.
While I Run This Race, Sun Dial Films for VISTA

(Features)

The Anderson Platoon, French Broadcasting System
Festival, Patchke Prods.
Harvest, U.S. Information Agency
A King's Story, Jack Le Vien Prod.
A Time for Burning, Quest Prods. for Lutheran Film Associates

1968

(Short Subjects)

Why Man Creates, Saul Bass & Associates
The House that Ananda Built, Government of India
The Revolving Door, Vision Associates for the American Foundation Institute of Corrections
A Space to Grow, Project Upward Bound
A Way Out of the Wilderness, John Sutherland Prods.

(Features)

Journey into Self, Western Behavioral Sciences Institute
A Few Notes on our Food Problem, U.S. Information Agency
The Legendary Champions, Turn of the Century Fights
Other Voices, DHS Films
Young Americans, The Young Americans Prod. (Declared ineligible May 7, 1969, because first released during 1967)

1969

(Short Subjects)

Czechoslovakia 1968, Sanders-Fresco Film Makers for U.S. Information Agency
An Impression of John Steinbeck: Writer, Donald Wrye Prods. for U.S. Information Agency
Jenny Is a Good Thing, A.C.I. Prod. for Project Head Start
Leo Beuerman, Centron Prod.
The Magic Machines, Fly-By-Night Prods.

(Features)

Arthur Rubinstein—The Love of Life, Midem Prod.
Before the Mountain Was Moved, Robert K. Sharpe Prods. for the Office of Economic Opportunity
In the Year of the Pig, Emile de Antonio Prod.
The Olympics in Mexico, Film Section of the Organizing Committee for the XIX Olympic Games
The Wolf Men, MGM Documentary

1970

(Short Subjects)

Interviews with My Lai Veterans, Laser Film Corp.
The Gifts, Richter McBride Prods. for the Water Quality Office of the Environmental Protection Agency
A Long Way from Nowhere, Robert Aller Prods.
Oisin, an Aengus Film
Time Is Running Out, Gesellschaft fur bildende Filme

(Features)

Woodstock, a Wadleigh-Maurice Ltd. Prod.
Chariots of the Gods, Terra Filmkunst GmbH.
Jack Johnson, The Big Fights
King: A Filmed Record . . . Montgomery to Memphis, Commonwealth United Prod.
Say Goodbye, A Wolper Prod.

1971

(Short Subjects)

Sentinels of Silence, Producciones Concord, Paramount
Adventures in Perception, Han van Gelder Filmproduktie for Netherlands Information Service
Art Is . . ., Henry Strauss Associates for Sears Roebuck Foundation
The Numbers Start with the River, a WH Picture for U.S. Information Agency
Somebody Waiting, Snider Prods. for U. of California Medical Film Library

(Features)

The Hellstrom Chronicle, David L. Wolper Prods., Cinema 5, Ltd.
Alaska Wilderness Lake, Alan Landsburg Prods.
On Any Sunday, Bruce Brown Films-Solar Prods., Cinema 5, Ltd.
The Ra Expeditions, Swedish Broadcasting Co., Interwest Film Corp.
The Sorrow and the Pity, Television Rencontre-Norddeutscher Rundfunk-Television Swiss Romande, Cinema 5, Ltd.

1972

(Short Subjects)

This Tiny World, a Charles Huguenot van der Linden Production
Hundertwasser's Rainy Day, an Argos Films-Peter Schamoni Film Prod.
K-Z, a Nexus Film Production
Selling Out, a Unit Productions Film
The Tide of Traffic, a BP-Greenpark Production

(Features)

Marjoe, a Cinema X Production, Cinema 5, Ltd.
Ape and Super Ape, Netherlands Ministry of Culture
Malcolm X, Warner Bros.
Manson, Merrick International Pictures
The Silent Revolution, a Leonaris Film Production

1973

(Short Subjects)

Princeton: A Search for Answers, Krainin-Sage Prods.
Background, D'Avino and Fucci-Stone Prods.
Children at Work, (Paisti Ag Obair), Gael-Linn Films
Christo's Valley Curtain, a Maysles Films Prod.
Four Stones for Kanemitsu, a Tamarind Prod.

(Features)

The Great American Cowboy, Keith Merrill Associates-Rodeo Film Prods.
Always a New Beginning, Goodell Motion Pictures
Battle of Berlin, Chronos Film
Journey to the Outer Limits, the National Geographic Society and Wolper Prods.
Walls of Fire, Mentor Prods.

1974

(Short Subjects)

Don't, R. A. Films
City Out of Wilderness, Francis Thompson Inc.
Exploratorium, a Jan Boorstin Prod.
John Muir's High Sierra, DeWitt Jones Prods.
Naked Yoga, a Filmshop Prod.

(Features)

Hearts and Minds, a Touchstone-Audjeff-BBS Prod., Howard Zucker/Henry Jaglom-Rainbow Pictures Presentation
Antonia: A Portrait of the Woman, Rocky Mountain Prods.
The Challenge . . . a Tribute to Modern Art, a World View Prod.
The 81st Blow, a Film by Ghetto Fighters House
The Wild and the Brave, E.S.J. Prods. with Tomorrow Entertainment Inc. & Jones/Howard Ltd.

1975

(Short Subjects)

The End of the Game, Opus Films Ltd.
Arthur and Lillie, Dept. of Communication, Stanford U.
Millions of Years ahead of Man, BASF

Probes in Space, Graphic Films
Whistling Smith, National Film Board of Canada

(Features)

The Man Who Skied Down Everest, a Crawley Films Presentation
The California Reich, Yasny Talking Pictures
Fighting for Our Lives, a Farm Worker Film
The Incredible Machine, the National Geographic Society and Wolper Prods.
The Other Half of the Sky: A China Memoir, MacLaine Productions

1976

(Short Subjects)

Number Our Days, Community Television of Southern California
American Shoeshine, Titan Films
Blackwood, National Film Board of Canada
The End of the Road, Pelican Films
Universe, Graphic Films Corp. for NASA

(Features)

Harlan County, U.S.A., Cabin Creek Films
Volcano: An Inquiry into the Life and Death of Malcolm Lowry, National Film Board of Canada
Hollywood on Trial, October Films/Cinema Associates Production
Off the Edge, Pentacle Films
People of the Wind, Elizabeth E. Rogers Productions

1977

(Short Subjects)

Gravity Is My Enemy, A John Joseph Production
Agueda Martinez: Our People, Our Country, a Moctesuma Esparza Production
First Edition, D. L. Sage Productions
Of Time, Tombs and Treasure, a Charlie/Papa Production
The Shetland Experience, Balfour Films

(Features)

Who Are the DeBolts? And Where Did They Get Nineteen Kids? Korty Films and Charles M. Schulz Crea-

tive Associates with Sanrio Films
The Children of Theatre Street, Mack-Vaganova Company
High Grass Circus, National Film Board of Canada
Homage to Chagall—The Colours of Love, a CBC Production
Union Maids, a Klein, Reichert, Mogulescu Production

1978

(Features)

Scared Straight!, Golden West Television Prod.
The Lovers' Wind, Ministry of Culture and Arts of Iran
Mysterious Castles of Clay, Survival Anglia Ltd. Prod.
Raoni, Franco Brazilian Prod.
With Babies and Banners—Story of the Women's Emergency Brigade, Women's Labor History Film Project Prod.

(Short Subjects)

The Flight of the Gossamer Condor, Shedd Prod.
The Divided Trail: A Native American Odyssey, Jerry Aronson Prod.
An Encounter with Faces, Film Div. of Govt. of India
Goodnight, Miss Ann, August Cinquegrana
Squires of San Quentin, J. Gary Mitchell Film Co.

1979

(Features)

Best Boy, Only Child Motion Pix, Inc.
Generation on the Wind, More than One Medium
Going the Distance, Natl. Film Board of Canada
The Killing Ground, ABC News Close-up Unit
The War at Home, Catalyst Films-Madison Film Prod. Co.

(Short Subjects)

Paul Robeson: Tribute to an Artist, Janus Films Inc.
Dae, Vardar Films-Skopje
Koryo Celadon, Charlie-Papa Prod.
Nails, Natl. Film Board of Canada
Remember Me, Vic Young Prod., Ltd.

1980

(Features)

From Mao to Mozart: Isaac Stern in China, Hopewell Found.
Agee, James Agee Film Project
The Day after Trinity, Jon Else Prod.
Front Line, David Bradbury Prod.
The Yellow Star—the Persecution of the Jews in Europe 1933-45, a Chronos Film

(Short Subjects)

Karl Hess: Toward Liberty, Halle/Ladue, Inc.
Don't Mess with Bill, Inside Prod., Inc.
The Eruption of Mount St. Helens, Graphic Films Corp.
It's the Same World, Dick Young Prod. Ltd.
Luther Metke at 94, UCLA Ethnographic Film Program

1981

(Features)

Genocide, Arnold Schwartzman Prod. Inc.
Against Wind and Tide, Seven League Prod. Inc.
Brooklyn Bridge, Florentine Film
Eight Minutes to Midnight: A Portrait of Dr. Helen Caldicott, Caldicott Project
El Salvador: Another Vietnam, Catalyst Media Prod.

(Short Subjects)

Close Harmony, a Noble Enterprise
Americas in Transition, Americas in Transition, Inc.
Journey for Survival, Dick Young Prod., Inc.
See What I Say, Michigan Women Filmmakers Prod.
Urge to Build, Roland-Halle Prod., Inc.

1982

(Features)

Just Another Missing Kid, Canadian Broadcast Corp.
After the Axe, Natl. Film Board of Canada
Ben's Mill, Public Broadcasting Associates-ODYSSEY
In Our Water, Foresight Prod.
A Portrait of Giselle, ABC Video Enterprises, Inc.

(Short Subjects)

If You Love This Planet, Natl. Film Board of Canada
Gods of Metal, Richter Prod. Film
The Klan—A Legacy of Hate in America, Guggenheim Prod., Inc.
To Live or Let Die, Amer. Film Found.
Traveling Hopefully, Arnuthfonyus Films, Inc.

Photo courtesy of Eastman Kodak Company

CHAPTER 14

Scientific or Technical Awards

*T*he Academy has functioned in several ways as the kind of scholarly body that its name implies. It has sponsored technical research, educational programs, scholarships, publications, film preservation work, the Margaret Herrick Library, and the annual Scientific or Technical awards.

The awards recognize those individuals and corporations responsible for "devices, methods, formulas, discoveries or inventions" that aid in any step of movie production and exhibition. For example, United Artists Studio Corporation won in 1936 for developing a quiet, efficient wind machine; the Motion Picture Research Council won in 1957 for improving the reflectance of drive-in theater screens.

The Scientific or Technical Academy Awards were first given in 1930-31, the fourth year of the Oscars, and are divided into three classes. Class I awards, very prestigious and rarely given, are for "basic achievements." Class II awards are for "achievements which exhibit a high level of engineering or technical merit," and Class III awards are for "valuable contributions." Class I award winners receive statuettes; Class II, plaques; and Class III, certificates. The winners are chosen by the Board of Governors, acting on recommendations of the Scientific or Technical Awards Committee appointed by the Academy president.

Sound recording and reproducing equipment has won the most awards. In the 1930s, the first full decade of sound movies, 25 awards recognized equipment that achieved higher fidelity, reduced noise, controlled music levels under voices, and in other ways improved film sound.

Early awards were primarily for mechanical and electrical devices. In recent years more and more winning projects have involved electronics and computers.

Many Oscars for Scientific or Technical Achievement have gone to the Eastman Kodak Company.

Star Wars **cleaned up at the 1977 Academy Awards show, with Oscars for Art Direction, Sound, Film Editing, Music, Costume Design, and Visual Effects as well as a Special Achievement Award for Sound Effects. In addition, a Class II Scientific or Technical Award went to John Dykstra for his use of a computerized camera in** *Star Wars.*

Star Wars **stars Mark Hamill, CP3O, and R2-D2 at the 1977 Academy Awards show**

Three winners of an Academy Award of Merit for Scientific or Technical Achievement are shown with Best Actress Maggie Smith and Best Supporting Actress nominee Maureen Stapleton at the 1978 ceremonies: Kenneth Mason of Eastman Kodak Company (left), Stefan Kudelski of Nagra Magnetic Recorders, Inc. (center), and Robert E. Gottschalk of Panavision, Inc.

This trend is especially apparent in the second largest group of winners—those involving special effects. The Academy has honored the inventors of a variety of mechanisms to simulate such effects as clouds, fog, and machine-gun fire. Several other awards have recognized improvements in composite, traveling-matte and rear-projection photography. A 1977 award recognized John Dykstra for his computer-controlled animation camera used in *Star Wars*. A 1981 award saluted the development of a motion picture figure mover for animation photography by Dennis Muren, Stuart Ziff, and Industrial Light and Magic Incorporated.

Other awards have recognized improvements in laboratory developing and printing equipment; in cameras, lenses, and accessories; in lighting and electrical equipment; in projectors and screens; in control systems and meters; in editing systems; and in color processes. Eastman Kodak Company has won 12 awards for improvements in film stock and film processing. In the 1950s, five wide-screen processes were recognized; awards went to Camera 65, CinemaScope, Cinerama, Todd-AO and VistaVision—but not for any 3-D process.

What the Scientific or Technical Awards lack in glamour—compared with the other Oscars—they make up for in significance. They have helped keep the industry moving ahead technologically.

1930-31

Class I

Electrical Research Products, Inc., RCA-Photophone, Inc., and RKO Radio Pictures, Inc. DuPont Film Manufacturing Corp. and Eastman Kodak Co.

Class II

20th Century-Fox Film Corp.

Class III

Electrical Research Products, Inc. RKO Radio Pictures, Inc. RCA-Photophone, Inc.

1931-32

Class II

Technicolor Motion Picture Corp.

Class III

Eastman Kodak Co.

1932-33

Class II

Electrical Research Products, Inc. RCA-Victor Co., Inc.

Class III

20th C.-Fox Film Corp., Fred Jackman, Warner Brothers Pictures, Inc., and Sidney Sanders of RKO Studios, Inc.

1934

Class II

Electrical Research Products, Inc.

Class III

Columbia Pictures Corp. Bell and Howell Co.

1935

Class II

Agfa Ansco Corp. Eastman Kodak Co.

Class III

Metro-Goldwyn-Mayer Studio William A. Mueller of Warner Bros. Mole-Richardson Co.

Douglas Shearer and MGM Studio Sound Dept. Electrical Research Products, Inc. Paramount Productions, Inc. Nathan Levinson of Warner Bros.

1936

Class I

Douglas Shearer and MGM Studio Sound Dept.

Class II

E. C. Wente and Bell Telephone Laboratories RCA Manufacturing Co., Inc.

Class III

RCA Manufacturing Co., Inc. (2 awards) Electrical Research Products, Inc. United Artists Studio Corp.

1937

Class I

Agfa Ansco Corp.

Class II

Walt Disney Prods., Ltd. Eastman Kodak Co. Farciot Edouart and Paramount Pictures, Inc. Douglas Shearer and MGM Studio Sound Dept.

Class III

John Arnold and MGM Studio Camera Dept. John Livadary of Columbia Pictures Corp. Thomas T. Moulton and UA Studio Sound Dept. RCA Manufacturing Co., Inc. Joseph E. Robbins and Paramount Pictures, Inc. Douglas Shearer and MGM Studio Sound Dept.

1938

Class III

John Aalberg and RKO Sound Dept. Byron Haskin and Warner Bros. Special Effects Dept.

1939

Class III

George Anderson of Warner Bros. John Arnold of MGM Thomas T. Moulton, Fred Albin, and Samuel Goldwyn Studio Sound Dept. Farciot Edouart, Joseph E. Robbins, William Rudolph, and Paramount Pictures, Inc. Emery Huse and Ralph B. Atkinson of Eastman Kodak Co. Harold Nye of Warner Bros. A. J. Tondreau of Warner Bros. F. R. Abbott, Haller Belt, Alan Cook, and Bausch & Lomb Optical Co. Mitchell Camera Co. Mole-Richardson Co. Charles Handley, David Joy, and National Carbon Co. Winton Hoch and Technicolor Motion Picture Corp. Don Musgrave and Selznick Intl. Pictures, Inc.

1940

Class I

20th C.-Fox Film Corp.

Class III

Anton Grot and Warner Bros. Art Dept.

1941

Class II

Electrical Research Products Div. of Western Electric Co., Inc. RCA Manufacturing Co.

Class III

Ray Wilkinson and Paramount Studio Laboratory Charles Lootens and Republic Studio Sound Dept. Wilbur Silvertooth and Paramount Studio Engineering Dept. Paramount Pictures, Inc., and 20th C.-Fox Film Corp. Douglas Shearer, MGM Studio Sound Dept., and Loren Ryder and Paramount Studio Sound Dept.

Scientific or Technical Awards

1942

Class II

Carroll Clark, F. Thomas Thompson, and the RKO Art and Miniature Dept.

Daniel B. Clark and 20th C.-Fox Film Corp.

Class III

Robert Henderson and Paramount Studio Engineering and Transparency Depts.

Daniel J. Bloomberg and Republic Studio Sound Dept.

1943

Class II

Farciot Edouard, Earle Morgan, Barton Thompson, and Paramount Studio Engineering and Transparency Depts.

Photo Products Dept. of E. I. DuPont de Nemours and Co., Inc.

Class III

Daniel J. Bloomberg and Republic Studio Sound Dept.

Charles Galloway Clarke and 20th C.-Fox Camera Dept.

Farciot Edouard and Paramount Studio Transparency Dept.

Willard H. Turner and RKO Sound Dept.

1944

Class II

Stephen Dunn, RKO Sound Dept., and Radio Corp. of America

Class III

Linwood Dunn, Cecil Love, and Acme Tool Manufacturing Co.

Grover Laube and 20th C.-Fox Camera Dept.

Western Electric Co.

Russell Brown, Ray Hinsdale, and Joseph E. Robbins

Gordon Jennings

Radio Corp. of America and RKO Sound Dept.

Daniel J. Bloomberg and Republic Studio Sound Dept.

Bernard B. Brown and John P. Livadary

Paul Zeff, S. J. Twining, and George Seid of Columbia Studio Laboratory

Paul Lerpae

1945

Class III

Loren L. Ryder, Charles R. Daily, and Paramount Studio Sound Dept.

Michael S. Leshing, Benjamin C. Robinson, Arthur B. Chatelain, and Robert C. Stevens of 20th C.-Fox Studio and John G. Capstaff of Eastman Kodak Co.

1946

Class III

Harlan L. Baumbach and Paramount West Coast Laboratory

Herbert E. Britt

Burton F. Miller and Warner Bros. Sound and Electrical Depts.

Carl Faulkner of 20th C.-Fox Sound Dept.

Mole-Richardson Co.

Arthur F. Blinn, Robert O. Cook, C. O. Slyfield, and Walt Disney Studio Sound Dept.

Burton F. Miller and Warner Bros. Sound Dept.

Marty Martin and Hal Adkins of RKO Miniature Dept.

Harold Nye and Warner Bros. Studio Electrical Dept.

1947

Class II

C. C. Davis and Electrical Research Products div. of Western Electric Co.

C. R. Daily and Paramount Studio Film Laboratory, Still and Engineering Depts.

Class III

Nathan Levinson and Warner Bros. Sound Dept.

Farciot Edouart, C. R. Daily, Hal Corl, H. G. Cartwright, and Paramount Studio Transparency and Engineering Depts.

Fred Ponedel of Warner Bros.

Kurt Singer and RCA-Victor Div. of the Radio Corp. of America

James Gibbons of Warner Bros.

1948

Class II

Victor Caccialanza, Maurice Ayers, and Paramount Studio Set Construction Dept.

Nick Kalten, Louis J. Witti, and 20th C.-Fox Mechanical Effects Dept.

Class III

Marty Martin, Jack Lannon, Russell Shearman, and RKO Special Effects Dept.

A. J. Moran and Warner Bros. Studio Electrical Dept.

1949

Class I

Eastman Kodak Co.

Class III

Loren L. Ryder, Bruce H. Denny, Robert Carr, and Paramount Studio Sound Dept.

M. B. Paul

Herbert Britt

André Coutant and Jacques Mathot

Charles R. Daily, Steve Csillag and Paramount Studio Engineering, Editorial, and Music Depts.

International Projector Corp.

Alexander Velcoff

1950

Class II

James B. Gordon and 20th C.-Fox Camera Dept.

John P. Livadary, Floyd Campbell, L. W. Russell, and Columbia Studio Sound Dept.

Loren L. Ryder and Paramount Studio Sound Dept.

1951

Class II

Gordon Jennings, S. L. Stancliffe, and Paramount Studio Special Photographic and Engineering Depts.
Olin L. Dupy of MGM
Radio Corp. of America, Victor Div.

Class III

Richard M. Haff, Frank P. Herrnfeld, Garland C. Misener, and the Ansco Film Div. of General Aniline and Film Corp.
Fred Ponedel, Ralph Ayers, and George Brown of Warner Bros.
Glen Robinson and MGM Construction Dept.
Jack Gaylord and MGM Construction Dept.
Carlos Rivas of MGM

1952

Class I

Eastman Kodak Co.
Ansco Division, General Aniline and Film Corp.

Class II

Technicolor Motion Picture Corp.

Class III

Projection, Still Photographic, and Development Engineering Depts. of MGM Studio
John G. Frayne, R. R. Scoville, and Westrex Corp.
Photo Research Corp.
Gustav Jirouch
Carlos Rivas of MGM

1953

Class I

Professor Henry Chretien, Earl Sponable, Sol Halprin, Lorin Grignon, Herbert Bragg, and Carl Faulkner of 20th C.-Fox
Fred Waller

Class II

Reeves Soundcraft Corp.

Class III

Westrex Corp.

1954

Class I

Loren L. Ryder, John R. Bishop, and Paramount Pictures, Inc.

Class III

David S. Horsley and Universal-International Studio Special Photographic Dept.
Karl Freund and Frank Crandell of Photo Research Corp.
Wesley C. Miller, J. W. Stafford, K. M. Frierson, and MGM Sound Dept.
John P. Livadary, Lloyd Russell, and Columbia Studio Sound Dept.
Roland Miller and Max Goeppinger of Magnascope Corp.
Carlos Rivas, G. M. Sprague, and MGM Sound Dept.
Fred Wilson of Samuel Goldwyn Studio Sound Dept.
P. C. Young of MGM Projection Dept.
Fred Knoth and Orien Ernest of U-I Studio Technical Dept.

1955

Class I

National Carbon Co.

Class II

Eastman Kodak Co.
Farciot Edouart, Hal Corl, and Paramount Studio Transparency Dept.

Class III

20th C.-Fox Studio and Bausch & Lomb Co.
Walter Jolley, Maurice Larson, and R. H. Spies of 20th C.-Fox
Steve Krilanovich
Dave Anderson of 20th C.-Fox
Loren L. Ryder, Charles West, Henry Fracker, and Paramount Studio
Farciot Edouart, Hal Corl, and Paramount Studio Transparency Dept.

1956

Class III

Richard H. Ranger of Rangertone, Inc.
Ted Hirsch, Carl Hauge, and Edward Reichard of Consolidated Film Industries
Technical Departments of Paramount Pictures Corp.
Roy C. Stewart and Sons of Stewart-TransLux Corp., C. R. Daily, and Paramount Pictures Corp. Transparency Dept.
MGM Construction Dept.
Daniel J. Bloomberg, John Pond, William Wade, and Republic Studio Engineering and Camera Depts.

1957

Class I

Todd-AO Corp. and Westrex Corp.
Motion Picture Research Council

Class II

Societé d'Optique et de Mecanique de Haute Precision
Harlan L. Baumbach, Lorand Wargo, Howard M. Little, and Unicorn Engineering Corp.

Class III

Charles E. Sutter, William B. Smith, Paramount Pictures Corp., and General Cable Corp.

1958

Class II

Don W. Prideaux, LeRoy G. Leighton, and General Electric Co. Lamp Division
Panavision, Inc.

Class III

Willy Borberg of General Precision Laboratory, Inc.
Fred Ponedel, George Brown, and Conrad Boye of Warner Bros. Special Effects Dept.

1959

Class II

Douglas G. Shearer of MGM and Robert E. Gottschalk and John R. Moore of Panavision, Inc.
Wadsworth E. Pohl, William Evans, Werner Hopf, S. E. Howse, Thomas P. Dixon, Stanford Research Institute, and Technicolor Corp.
Wadsworth E. Pohl, Jack Alford, Henry Imus, Joseph Schmit, Paul Fassnacht, Al Iofquist, and Technicolor Corp.
Howard S. Coleman, A. Francis Turner, Harold H. Schroeder, James R. Benford, and Harold E. Rosenberger of Bausch & Lomb Optical Co.
Robert P. Gutterman of General Kinetics, Inc., and Lipsner-Smith Corp.

Class III

Ub Iwerks of Walt Disney Prods.
E. L. Stones, Glen Robinson, Winfield Hubbard, and Luther Newman of MGM Construction Dept.

1960

Class II

Ampex Professional Products Co.

Class III

Arthur Holcomb, Petro Vlahos, and **Columbia Studio Camera Dept.**
Anthony Paglia and **20th C.-Fox Mechanical Effects Dept.**
Carl Hauge, Robert Grubel, and **Edward Reichard** of Consolidated Film Industries

1961

Class II

Sylvania Electric Products, Inc.
James Dale, S. Wilson, H. E. Rice, John Rude, Laurie Atkin, Wadsworth E. Pohl, H. Peasgood, and **Technicolor Corp.**
20th C.-Fox Research Dept. (under direction of **E. I. Sponable** and **Herbert E. Bragg**) and **Deluxe Laboratories, Inc.**, with the assistance of **F. D. Leslie, R. D. Whitmore, A. A. Alden, Endel Pool,** and **James B. Gordon**

Class III

Electric Eye Equipment Div. of Hurletron, Inc.
Wadsworth E. Pohl and **Technicolor Corp.**

1962

Class II

Ralph Chapman
Albert S. Pratt, James L. Wassell, and **Hans C. Wohlrab** of Bell & Howell Co.
North American Philips Co., Inc.
Charles E. Sutter, William Bryson Smith, and **Louis C. Kennell** of Paramount Pictures Corp.

Class III

Electro-Voice, Inc.
Louis G. MacKenzie

1963

Class III

Douglas G. Shearer and **A. Arnold Gillespie** of MGM

1964

Class I

Petro Vlahos, Wadsworth E. Pohl, and **Ub Iwerks**

Class II

Sidney P. Solow, Edward H. Reichard, Carl W. Hauge, and **Job Sanderson** of Consolidated Film Industries
Pierre Angenieux

Class III

Milton Forman, Richard B. Glickman, and **Daniel J. Pearlman** of ColorTran Industries
Stewart Filmscreen Corp.
Anthony Paglia and **20th C.-Fox Mechanical Effects Dept.**
Edward H. Reichard and **Carl W. Hauge** of Consolidated Film Industries
Edward H. Reichard, Leonard L. Sokolow, and **Carl W. Hauge** of Consolidated Film Industries
Nelson Tyler

1965

Class II

Arthur J. Hatch of Strong Electric Corp.
Stefan Kudelski

1966

Class II

Mitchell Camera Corp.
Arnold & Richter KG

Class III

Panavision, Inc.
Carroll Knudson
Ruby Raksin

1967

Class III

Kollmorgen Corp., Electro-Optical Division
Panavision, Inc.
Fred R. Wilson of Samuel Goldwyn Studio Sound Dept.
Waldon O. Watson and **Universal City Studio Sound Dept.**

1968

Class I

Philip V. Palmquist of Minnesota Mining and Manufacturing Co., **Herbert Meyer** of Motion Picture and Televison Research Center, and **Charles D. Staffell** of Rank Org.
Eastman Kodak Co.

Class II

Donald W. Norwood
Eastman Kodak Co. and **Producers Service Co.**
Edmund M. DiGiulio, Niels G. Petersen, and **Norman S. Hughes** of Cinema Product Development Co.
Optical Coating Laboratories, Inc.
Eastman Kodak Co.
Panavision, Inc.
Todd-AO Co. and **Mitchell Camera Co.**

Class III

Carl W. Hauge and **Edward H. Reichard** of Consolidated Film Industries, **E. Michael Meahl** and **Roy J. Ridenour** of Ramtronics
Eastman Kodak Co. and **Consolidated Film Industries**

1969

Class II

Hazeltine Corp.
Fouad Said
Juan de la Cierva and **Dynasciences Corp.**

Class III

Otto Popelka of Magna-Tech Electronics Co., Inc.
Fenton Hamilton of MGM
Panavision, Inc.
Robert M. Flynn and **Russell Hessy** of Universal City Studios

1970

Class II

Leonard Sokolow and **Edward H. Reichard** of Consolidated Film Industries

Class III

Sylvania Electric Products Inc.
B. J. Losmandy
Eastman Kodak Co. and **Photo Electronics Corp.**
Electro Sound Inc.

1971

Class II

John N. Wilkinson of Optical Radiation Corp.

Class III

Thomas Jefferson Hutchinson, James R. Rochester, and **Fenton Hamilton**
Photo Research, division of Kollmorgen Corp.

Robert D. Auguste and Cinema Products Co.
Producers Service Corp., Consolidated Film Industries, Cinema Research Corp. and Research Products, Inc.
Cinema Products Co.

1972

Class II

Joseph E. Bluth
Edward H. Reichard and Howard T. La Zare of Consolidated Film Industries and Edward Efron of IBM
Panavision, Inc.

Class III

Photo Research, division of Kollmorgen Corp. and PSC Technology, Inc.
Carter Equipment Company, Inc., and Ramtronics
David Degenkolb, Harry Larson, Manfred Michelson, and Fred Scobey of DeLuxe General Inc.
Jiro Mukai and Ryusho Hirose of Canon, Inc., and Wilton R. Holm of AMPTP Motion Picture and Television Research Center
Philip V. Palmquist and Leonard L. Olson of 3M Co. and Frank P. Clark of AMPTP Motion Picture and Television Research Center
E. H. Geissler and G. M. Berggren of Wil-Kin Inc.

1973

Class II

Joachim Gerb and Erich Kastner of Arnold and Richter Co.
Magna-Tech Electronic Co., Inc.
William W. Valliant of PSC Technology, Inc., Howard F. Ott of Eastman Kodak Co., and Gerry Diebold of Richmark Camera Service Inc.
Harold A. Scheib, Clifford H. Ellis, and Roger W. Banks of Research Products Inc.

Class III

Rosco Laboratories, Inc.
Richard H. Vetter of Todd-AO Corp.

1974

Class II

Joseph D. Kelly of Glen Glenn Sound
Burbank Studios Sound Dept.
Samuel Goldwyn Studios Sound Dept.

Quad-Eight Sound Corp.
Waldon O. Watson, Richard H. Stumpf, Robert J. Leonard, and Universal City Studios Sound Dept.

Class III

Elemack Co.
Louis Ami of Universal City Studios

1975

Class II

Chadwell O'Connor of O'Connor Engineering Laboratories
William F. Miner of Universal City Studios and Westinghouse Electric Corp.

Class III

Lawrence W. Butler and Roger Banks
David J. Degenkolb and Fred Scobey of DeLuxe General Inc., and John C. Dolan and Richard Dubois of Akwaklame Company
Joseph Westheimer
Carter Equipment Co., Inc., and Ramtronics
The Hollywood Film Co.
Bell & Howell
Fredrik Schlyter

1976

Class II

Consolidated Film Industries and Barnebey-Cheney Co.
William L. Graham, Manfred G. Michelson, Geoffrey F. Norman, and Siegfried Seibert of Technicolor

Class III

Fred Bartscher of Kollmorgen Corp. and Glenn Berggren of Schneider Corp.
Panavision, Inc.
Hiroshi Suzukawa of Canon and Wilton R. Holm of AMPTP Motion Picture and Television Research Center
Carl Zeiss Co.
Photo Research, division of Kollmorgen Corp.

1977

Class I

Garrett Brown and Cinema Products Corp.

Class II

Joseph D. Kelly, Barry K. Henley, Hammond H. Holt, and Glen Glenn Sound

Panavision, Inc.
N. Paul Kenworthy, Jr., and William R. Latady
John C. Dykstra, Alvah J. Miller, and Jerry Jeffress
Eastman Kodak Co.
Stefan Kudelski of Nagra Magnetic Recorders, Inc.

Class III

Ernst Nettmann of Astrovision Div. of Continental Camera Systems, Inc.
Electronic Engineering Co. of California
Bernard Kuhl and Werner Block of Osram, GmbH
Panavision, Inc. (2 awards)
Piclear, Inc.

1978

(Academy Award of Merit)

Eastman Kodak Co.
Stefan Kudelski of Nagra Magnetic Recorders, Inc.
Panavision, Inc.

(Scientific and Engineering Award)

Ray Dolby, Ioan Allen, David Robinson, Stephen Katz, and Philip S. J. Boole of Dolby Laboratories, Inc.

(Technical Achievement Award)

Karl Macher and Glenn Berggren of Isco Opticschen Werke
David Degenklob, Arthur Ford, and Fred Scobey of DeLuxe General, Inc.
Kiichi Sekigucki of Cine-Fi Intl.
Leonard Chapman of Leonard Equipment Co.
James Fisher of J. L. Fisher, Inc.
Robert Stindt of Prod. Grip Equipment Co.

1979

(Academy Award of Merit)

Mark Serrurier

(Scientific and Engineering Award)

Neiman-Tillar Associates
Mini-Micro Systems, Inc.

(Technical Achievement Award)

Michael V. Chewey, Walter G. Eggers, and Alan Hecht of MGM Laboratories
Irwin Young, Paul Kaufman, and Frederick Schlyter of Do Art Film Laboratories, Inc.
James Stanfield and Paul Trester

Zorin Perisic of Courier Films, Ltd.
A. D. Flowers and Logan Frazee
Photo Research Div. of Kollmorgen Corp.
Bruce Lyon and John Lamb
Ross Lowell of Lowel-Light Manuf., Inc.

1980

(Academy Award of Merit)

Linwood Dunn, Cecil Love, and Acme Tool and Manuf. Co.

(Scientific and Engineering Award)

Jean-Marie Lazalou, Alain Masseron, and David Samuelson of Samuelson Alga Cinema S.A. and Samuel Film Service Ltd.
Edward B. Krause of Filmline Corp.
Ross Taylor
Ernhardt Kühl and Werner Block of Osram GmbH
David Graston

(Technical Achievement Award)

Carter Equipment Co.
Hollywood Film Co.
André DeBrie, S.A.
Charles Vaughn and Eugene Nottingham of Cinetron Computer Systems, Inc.

John Lang, Walter Hrastnik, and Charles Watson of Bell & Howell Co.
Worth Baird of LaVezzi Machine Works, Inc.
Peter Regla and Dan Slater of Elicon

1981

(Academy Award of Merit)

Fuji Photo Film Co. Ltd.

(Scientific and Engineering Award)

Nelson Tyler
Leonard Sokolow and Howard La-Zare
Richard Edlund and Industrial Light and Magic, Inc. (2 awards)
Edward Blasko and Roderick Ryan of Eastman Kodak Co.

(Technical Achievement Award)

Hal Landaker and Alan Landaker
Bill Hogan, Richard Stumpf, and Daniel Braver of Universal City Studio
John DeMuth
Ernst Nettmann of Continental Camera Systems, Inc.
Bill Taylor of Universal City Studio
Peter Parks of Oxford Scientific Films

Louis Stankiewicz and H. L. Blachford
Dennis Muren and Stuart Ziff of Industrial Light and Magic, Inc.

1982

(Academy Award of Merit)

August Arnold and Erich Kaestner of Arnold and Reichert GmbH

(Scientific and Engineering Award)

Colin Mossman and the Research and Development Group of Rank Film Laboratories
Sante Zelli and Salvatore Zellie of Elemack Italia
Leonard Chapman
Mohammad Nozari of Minnesota Mining and Manuf. Co.
Brianne Murphy and Donald Schisler of Mitchell Insert Systems, Inc.
Jacobus Dimmers

(Technical Achievement Award)

Richard Deats
Constant Tresfon and Adriaan De Rooy Egripment and Ed Phillips and Carlos De Mattos of Matthews Studio Equipment
Bran Ferren of Associates and Ferren
Christie Electric Corp. and LaVezzi Machine Works, Inc.

CHAPTER 15

Honorary, Thalberg, and Hersholt Awards

The Honorary, Thalberg, and Hersholt Awards are special awards that need not be given every year. They are voted on and awarded by the Academy's Board of Governors.

HONORARY AWARDS

Honorary Awards, called Special Awards until 1950, allow the Academy to honor individuals whose achievements, for one reason or another, might not be recognized in the standard, annual categories. A few people have won Honorary Oscars in addition to traditional awards—Laurence Olivier and Gary Cooper for example—but for most winners the Honorary Award is their only one.

Honorary Oscars have gone to silent-film pioneers who did most of their work before the Academy Awards began in 1927. Charlie Chaplin (who won in 1927-28 and 1971), Lillian Gish (1970), D. W. Griffith (1935), Buster Keaton (1959),

Harold Lloyd (1952), Mary Pickford (1975), and Mack Sennett (1937) were recognized for their early contributions to the art of the motion picture.

Other winners were sound-era film greats who never won regular Oscars but whose contributions could not be overlooked. These winners include Fred Astaire (1949), Greta Garbo (1954), Cary Grant (1969), director Howard Hawks (1974), Danny Kaye (1954), Gene Kelly (1951), and Barbara Stanwyck (1981). The most frequent winner has been Bob Hope, who received Honorary Awards in 1940, 1944, 1952, and 1965.

Child actors and actresses sometimes have received Honorary Awards recognizing outstanding performances. Winning youngsters have included Judy Garland (1939), Hayley Mills (1960), Mickey Rooney (1938)—who won another Honorary Oscar in 1982— and Shirley Temple (1934).

Buster Keaton received an Honorary Award in 1959 for "unique talent which brought immortal comedies to the screen."

Charlie Chaplin received an Honorary Award for his "versatility and genius in writing, acting, directing, and producing *The Circus*," a 1928 silent film. Forty-three years later he received a second Honorary Award, this one for "the incalculable effect he has had in making motion pictures the art form of this century."

Star hoofer Fred Astaire (right) accepted his 1949 Special Award from George Murphy. Astaire was commended for his contributions to musical motion pictures.

Cary Grant's only Oscar was an Honorary Award for his acting, given in 1969 "with the respect and affection of his colleagues."

Cited for bringing to the screen "the spirit and personification of youth," child star Mickey Rooney received an Honorary Award in 1938. The adult Mickey Rooney received another Honorary Award in 1982. Rooney is shown here (right) with co-stars Butch Jenkins and Elizabeth Taylor in *National Velvet* (1945).

On the same night that Shirley Temple presented the 1934 Best Actress award to Claudette Colbert (right), the child star received a Special Award for her "outstanding contribution to screen entertainment."

Master of suspense Alfred Hitchcock received the Irving G. Thalberg Award for 1967. Although nominated five times, Hitchcock never received a Best Director Oscar.

Still other Honorary Awards have served as precursors to regular awards later established for such categories as Foreign Language Films, Special Effects, and Makeup. The list of winners is completed by a miscellany of individuals (such as inventor Lee De Forest in 1959 and film editor Margaret Booth, 1977); organizations (the Museum of Modern Art in 1937 and the Society of Motion Picture and Television Engineers in 1957); and corporations (Bell and Howell in 1953 and Bausch & Lomb in 1954).

A few Honorary Awards have been specially tailored to suit the honorees. In 1937 ventriloquist Edgar Bergen received a wooden statuette for creating his dummy Charlie McCarthy. For *Snow White and the Seven Dwarfs* (1938), Walt Disney received a statuette for himself and seven miniatures for the dwarfs.

THE THALBERG AWARD

The Irving G. Thalberg Award recognizes "creative producers whose body of work reflects a consistently high quality of motion picture production." Thalberg (1899-1936) was the artistic supervisor at Metro-Goldwyn-Mayer from the company's formation in 1924 until his death. He helped build the prosperity of the studio during the time it boasted "more stars than there are in heaven."

THE HERSHOLT AWARD

The Jean Hersholt Humanitarian Award began in 1956. It honors "individuals whose humanitarian efforts have brought credit to the industry." An actor born in Denmark who appeared in hundreds of films, Hersholt (1886-1956) served as head of the Motion Picture Relief Fund for 18 years.

1927-28

Warner Brothers
Charles Chaplin

1928-29

None

1929-30

None

1930-31

None

1931-32

Walt Disney

1933

None

1934

Shirley Temple

1935

David Wark Griffith

1936

March of Time
W. Howard Greene and **Harold Rosson**

1937

Mack Sennett
Edgar Bergen
The Museum of Modern Art Film Library
W. Howard Greene

1938

Deanna Durbin and **Mickey Rooney**
Harry M. Warner
Walt Disney
Oliver Marsh and **Allen Davey**
Gordon Jennings, Jan Domela, Dev Jennings, Irmin Roberts, Art Smith, Farciot Edouart, Loyal Griggs, Loren Ryder, Harry Mills, Louis H. Mesenkop and **Walter Oberst**
J. Arthur Ball

1939

Douglas Fairbanks
Motion Picture Relief Fund: Jean Hersholt, President; **Ralph Morgan**, Chairman of the Executive Committee; **Ralph Block**, First Vice-President; and **Conrad Nagel**
Judy Garland
William Cameron Menzies
Technicolor Company

1940

Bob Hope
Colonel Nathan Levinson

1941

Rey Scott
The British Ministry of Information
Leopold Stokowski
Walt Disney, William Garity, John N. A. Hawkins, and **RCA Manufacturing Company**

1942

Charles Boyer
Noel Coward
Metro-Goldwyn-Mayer Studio

1943

George Pal

With four Honorary Awards, Bob Hope (right) holds the record. He is shown here receiving congratulations for his first Special Award from the Best Actor and Best Actress of 1940, Jimmy Stewart and Ginger Rogers.

1944

Margaret O'Brien
Bob Hope

1945

Walter Wanger
Peggy Ann Garner
The House I Live In
Republic Studio, Daniel J. Bloomberg, and **Republic Sound Department**

1946

Laurence Olivier
Harold Russell
Ernst Lubitsch
Claude Jarman, Jr.

1947

James Baskette
Bill and Coo
Shoe-Shine
Colonel William N. Selig, Albert E. Smith, Thomas Armat, and **George K. Spoor**

1948

Monsieur Vincent (French)
Ivan Jandl
Sid Grauman
Adolph Zukor
Walter Wanger

1949

The Bicycle Thief (Italian)
Bobby Driscoll
Fred Astaire
Cecil B. De Mille
Jean Hersholt

1950

George Murphy
Louis B. Mayer
The Walls of Malapaga (Franco-Italian)

1951

Gene Kelly
Rashomon (Japanese)

1952

George Alfred Mitchell
Joseph M. Schenck
Merian C. Cooper
Harold Lloyd
Bob Hope
Forbidden Games (French)

Honorary Awards

1953

Pete Smith
20th Century-Fox Corporation
Joseph I. Breen
Bell and Howell Company

1954

Bausch & Lomb Optical Company
Kemp R. Niver
Greta Garbo
Danny Kaye
Jon Whiteley
Vincent Winter
Gate of Hell (Japanese)

1955

Samurai, the Legend of Musashi (Japanese)

1956

Eddie Cantor

1957

Charles Brackett
B. B. Kahane
Gilbert M. ("Broncho Billy") Anderson
The Society of Motion Picture and Television Engineers

1958

Maurice Chevalier

1959

Lee De Forest
Buster Keaton

1960

Gary Cooper
Stan Laurel
Hayley Mills

1961

William L. Hendricks
Fred L. Metzler
Jerome Robbins

1962

None

1963

None

1964

William Tuttle

1965

Bob Hope

Gene Kelly (right), who won an Honorary Award in 1951, presented the 1961 Honorary Award to Jerome Robbins for Robbins' achievements in choreography on film. Robbins also received a 1961 Oscar for co-directing *West Side Story*.

1966

Y. Frank Freeman
Yakima Canutt

1967

Arthur Freed

1968

John Chambers
Onna White

1969

Cary Grant

1970

Lillian Gish
Orson Welles

1971

Charles Chaplin

1972

Charles S. Boren
Edward G. Robinson

1973

Henri Langlois
Groucho Marx

1974

Howard Hawks
Jean Renoir

1975

Mary Pickford

1976

None

1977

Margaret Booth
Gordon E. Sawyer and **Sidney P. Solow**

1978

Walter Lantz
Laurence Olivier
King Vidor
The Museum of Modern Art Film Department

1979

Alec Guinness
Hal Elias

1980

Henry Fonda

1981

Barbara Stanwyck

1982

Mickey Rooney

Irving G. Thalberg Memorial Awards

1937	*1949*	*1961*	*1973*
Darryl F. Zanuck	None	**Stanley Kramer**	**Lawrence Weingarten**
1938	*1950*	*1962*	*1974*
Hal B. Wallis	**Darryl F. Zanuck**	None	None
1939	*1951*	*1963*	*1975*
David O. Selznick	**Arthur Freed**	**Sam Spiegel**	**Mervyn Le Roy**
1940	*1952*	*1964*	*1976*
None	**Cecil B. De Mille**	None	**Pandro S. Berman**
1941	*1953*	*1965*	*1977*
Walt Disney	**George Stevens**	**William Wyler**	**Walter Mirisch**
1942	*1954*	*1966*	*1978*
Sidney Franklin	None	**Robert Wise**	None
1943	*1955*	*1967*	*1979*
Hal B. Wallis	None	**Alfred Hitchcock**	**Ray Stark**
1944	*1956*	*1968*	*1980*
Darryl F. Zanuck	**Buddy Adler**	None	None
1945	*1957*	*1969*	*1981*
None	None	None	**Albert R. (Cubby) Broccoli**
1946	*1958*	*1970*	*1982*
Samuel Goldwyn	**Jack L. Warner**	**Ingmar Bergman**	None
1947	*1959*	*1971*	
None	None	None	
1948	*1960*	*1972*	
Jerry Wald	None	None	

United Nations mediator Ralph Bunche (center) presented the 1950 Irving G. Thalberg Award to Darryl Zanuck (right), producer of that year's Best Picture, *All about Eve*. Joseph L. Mankiewicz (left) won both the Best Director and the Best Screenplay awards for the film.

234

Jean Hersholt Humanitarian Awards

1956

Y. Frank Freeman

1957

Samuel Goldwyn

1958

None

1959

Bob Hope

1960

Sol Lesser

1961

George Seaton

1962

Steve Broidy

1963

None

1964

None

1965

Edmond L. DePatie

1966

George Bagnall

1967

Gregory Peck

1968

Martha Raye

1969

George Jessel

1970

Frank Sinatra

1971

None

1972

Rosalind Russell

1973

Lew Wasserman

1974

Arthur B. Krim

1975

Jules C. Stein

1976

None

1977

Charlton Heston

1978

Leo Jaffe

1979

Robert S. Benjamin

1980

None

1981

Danny Kaye

1982

Walter Mirisch

Academy president Walter Mirisch, shown here helping Bob Hope light candles on a cake commemorating the Academy's 50th anniversary, received the Jean Hersholt Humanitarian Award in 1982.

CHAPTER 16

The Great Oscar Losers

K eep your eye on the losers tonight as they applaud the winners," Bob Hope advised at the beginning of one Oscar telecast. "You'll see great understanding, great sportsmanship—great acting."

Unsuccessful nominees such as Al Pacino, Deborah Kerr, and Alfred Hitchcock are not really losers, of course. Their nominations imply extraordinary achievements that have been noticed by their colleagues. Nor do other talented individuals who have never been nominated, but whose films have been applauded in many other ways—such as Mickey Rooney, Ethel Merman, and director George Sidney—deserve the label "loser."

The word is used here as shorthand for "those who did not win." Among them, doubtless, are some who deserved to win. This chapter records some of the individuals and films whose absence from the lists

of Oscar winners people have found surprising. It should be noted that some of them did receive Honorary Awards from the Academy or awards in categories other than those discussed here.

ACTORS AND ACTRESSES

Listed seven times on the ballot but never among the Oscar winners, Richard Burton led the pack of also-ran performers until 1982, when Peter O'Toole tied Burton's record by receiving his seventh nomination for Best Actor without a single win. Also in 1982, Paul Newman received his sixth nomination but still no Oscar. Arthur Kennedy and Al Pacino, nominated five times each, have never won; Montgomery Clift, four times; Kirk Douglas, three times; and Charlie Chaplin, Cary Grant, Basil Rathbone, and Peter Sellers, two times each. Gene Kelly, Robert Mitchum, and Orson Welles were each nominated once but received no Oscar for

Paul Newman, shown here in character from *The Hustler* (1961), has yet to win an Oscar after receiving six nominations.

Not winning the Best Actor Oscar in 1982 brought Peter O'Toole the bittersweet consolation of being tied with Richard Burton for receiving the most nominations without winning a single Oscar. A pensive O'Toole is shown here in *Under Milk Wood* (1973).

His famous dimple helped Kirk Douglas win three nominations but no Oscar.

Dance groundbreaker Gene Kelly was never elected the Best Actor, although he was nominated once (for the 1945 *Anchors Aweigh*). He pictured here with co-star Leslie Caron in *American in Paris* in 1951, the same year he received an Honorary Award.

Deborah Kerr, nominated six times and noted for her versatility as an actress, never won the coveted Oscar.

Judy Garland was favored to win the Oscar for her stunning comeback performance in *A Star Is Born* (1954) but was edged out by the newcomer Grace Kelly.

Best Actor. Fred Astaire's only (unsuccessful) nomination came not for a starring role in a musical, but for a supporting role in *The Towering Inferno* (1974).

Male performers never nominated for their acting include Alan Alda, John Barrymore, Joseph Cotten, Errol Flynn, Boris Karloff, Peter Lorre, E. G. Marshall, Edward G. Robinson, Donald Sutherland, and Ronald Reagan.

Deborah Kerr (*From Here to Eternity*, 1953) and Thelma Ritter (*All about Eve*, 1950) lead the actresses who have never won an Oscar with six nominations each. Irene Dunne and Agnes Moorehead each received five nominations without a win; Greta Garbo, Shirley MacLaine, Marsha Mason, and Barbara Stanwyck, four each; Gloria Swanson, three; Judy Garland, two; and Marlene Dietrich, Carole Lombard, and Lana Turner, one each. Actresses who have never been nominated include such popular figures as Jean Harlow, Betty Hutton, Dorothy Lamour, Marilyn Monroe, Raquel Welch, and Esther Williams.

DIRECTORS

In the directing category, Alfred Hitchcock never won an Oscar, though he was nominated for *Lifeboat* (1944), *Spellbound* (1945), *Rear Window* (1954), and *Psycho* (1960). His film *Rebecca*, for which he was not nominated as director, did win the best Picture award in 1944.

Robert Stevenson, who worked for Walt Disney Productions, directed 12 top-grossing films but never won an Oscar and was nominated only for one of them, *Mary Poppins* (1964). Moneymaking champion Steven Spielberg did not win for *Jaws* (a nominee for Best Picture in 1975) or for *Close Encounters of the Third Kind* (1977), *Raiders of the Lost Ark* (1981), or *E.T.—the Extra-Terrestrial* (1982), all nominees for Best Director.

Robert Altman, Cecil B. De Mille, Howard Hawks, and Orson Wells have all been nominated once but received no Directing Oscar. The only woman ever nominated for the Best Director award, Lina Wertmuller (*Seven Beauties*, 1976), did not win. George Sidney, director of 12 top-grossing films including *Show Boat* (1951), was not nominated as Best Director, though two of his early short films, *Quicker 'n a Wink* (1940) and *Of Pups and Puzzles* (1941) won back-to-back Short Film Oscars.

BEST PICTURES

Among Best Picture also-rans, *Citizen Kane* (1941) stands out. Considered by many critics to be one of the greatest films of all time, today it is studied literally frame by frame in film schools. It was nominated but lost in the Oscar race to *How Green Was My Valley*. *Sunset Boulevard* (1950), *High Noon* (1952), *Dr. Strangelove* (1964), *The Graduate* (1967),

Orson Welles, shown with wife-to-be Dolores Del Rio in 1941, directed and starred in what many critics consider to be the best picture of all time, *Citizen Kane* (1941), but won an Oscar only for co-writing the screenplay.

The Turning Point (1977) and *Reds* (1981) are among other highly praised films that did not win the Best Picture award.

The 1939 nominees for Best Picture faced especially formidable competition. Ten nominees were permitted that year, and several of them might have been winners in ordinary years. But *Of Mice and Men, Mr. Smith Goes to Washington, The Wizard of Oz,* and *Wuthering Heights* all bowed before the overwhelming strength of *Gone with the Wind.*

Films that some critics and fans insist should have at least been nominated for Best Picture, though they were not, include *Laura* (1944); *The Third Man* (1950); *The African Queen* (1951); *Singin' in the Rain* (1952); *Psycho* (1960); *Long Day's Journey*

Although Warren Beatty won the Best Director award, his film *Reds* (1981) did not win the Best Picture award.

Laurence Olivier and Merle Oberon starred in *Wuthering Heights*. Although the film was nominated, it lost the Best Picture award to *Gone with the Wind*.

into Night (1962); *2001: A Space Odyssey* (1968); *Cabaret* (1972); and *Manhattan* (1979).

A Hollywood joke has it that late at night, after the Oscars have been dispensed, the losers stand in the parking lot and read to each other what would have been their acceptance speeches. It must be painful to come so close to a coveted honor and then miss it. But the losing nominees and others who deserved consideration have much to be proud of.

As Dustin Hoffman put it when he accepted the 1979 Best Actor award for *Kramer vs. Kramer*: "I refuse to believe that I beat Jack Lemmon, that I beat Al Pacino, that I beat Peter Sellers. I refuse to believe that Robert Duvall lost. We are part of an artistic family. In an artistic family that strives for excellence, none of you have ever lost."

A young Richard Burton in *My Cousin Rachel* (1952)

Welsh-born stage and screen actor Richard Burton has attained the not necessarily enviable record of being the first performer to receive as many as seven Oscar nominations without winning once. This serious actor's talents have been showcased in productions ranging from John Gielgud's *Hamlet* on Broadway to the horror film sequel *Exorcist II: The Heretic*. In his best work, critics and audiences found his presence as captivating and his speaking voice as sonorous as any living performer's. Meanwhile, a personal life that rivals the soap operas has kept him in the tabloids and tarnished his image as a rigorous artist.

Burton was nominated as Best Supporting Actor for his first American film, *My Cousin Rachel* (1952). Then he received six Best Actor nominations for roles in costume spectacles and contemporary dramas: *The Robe* (1953); *Becket* (1964); *The Spy Who Came in from the Cold* (1965); *Who's Afraid of Virginia Woolf?* (1966); *Anne of the Thousand Days* (1969); and *Equus* (1977).

His sometime wife and co-star Elizabeth Taylor, who won her second Oscar

Burton: Seven Times the Bridesmaid

Burton's title role in *Becket* (1964) won him a third Oscar nomination. In costume here, he chats with Elizabeth Taylor, who stopped by to watch the filming.

Both Burton and Taylor were nominated for their performances in *Who's Afraid of Virginia Woolf?* Taylor won an Oscar, but Burton did not.

As Dr. Martin Dysart, Burton attempted to console patient Alan Strang (Peter Firth) in *Equus* (1977). His performance brought Burton his seventh Best Actor nomination but no Oscar.

for *Who's Afraid of Virginia Woolf?*, found the fact that he did not also win for that film particularly disappointing. "It's nice to win," she said the next day, "but the edge is certainly taken off because Richard didn't win. And he *was* the best actor of the year." (Paul Scofield won that year for his performance in *A Man for All Seasons*.)

Peter O'Toole, who co-starred with Burton, in *Becket* nearly 20 years before, tied Burton's record when he received his seventh unsuccessful acting nomination for *My Favorite Year* (1982).

Perhaps Jack Nicholson and Louise Fletcher should not have been so happy to receive their Oscars for *One Flew over the Cuckoo's Nest* in 1975, for the "Oscar jinx" was soon to strike.

Was it the jinx that affected Rod Steiger's career after he was awarded a Best Supporting Actor Oscar in 1968?

Gene Hackman, clutching his "jinxed" Oscar at the 44th annual Academy Awards ceremony

When Milos Forman won Best Director of 1975 for *One Flew over the Cuckoo's Nest*, he warned the film's Oscar winning co-stars Jack Nicholson and Louise Fletcher: "You know, now we're all going to fail." As it turned out, their next films — Forman's *Hair*, Nicholson's *The Missouri Breaks*, and Fletcher's *Exorcist II: The Heretic* — were all indeed disappointments at the box office, with the critics, and to their makers.

What Forman was referring to was the so-called "Oscar jinx," which is said to have put the whammy on certain winners since the 1930s. In 1936 and 1937 Luise Rainer won back-to-back Best Actress awards. She then finished five mediocre movies in the next year and, except for one film in 1943, promptly disappeared from the screen. Some said it was a series of poor choices of movies that made her career collapse. Others blamed the mysterious jinx, and she herself said: "Those two Academy Awards I got were bad for me . . . I later did one bad film. I was treated as if I had never done anything good in my life."

Many winners, including

Is There an Oscar Jinx?

Jack Lemmon, Jane Fonda, and Glenda Jackson, have gone on to greater heights after winning their first Academy Award. But for others the awards represented a peak that proved impossible to match, at least immediately afterward. The list of those supposedly affected includes Olivia De Havilland, Marlon Brando, Rod Steiger, Liza Minnelli, and Gene Hackman.

Their downturns might be ascribed to the normal ups and downs that would be expected in anyone's career in a risky and creative business — except that a Temple University doctoral dissertation found statistical confirmation of it. In a study of biographical data that might relate to predicting box office revenues, prior Academy Awards were found to be *negative* predictors for people's next movies.

Even this finding, however, may have logical explanations. For one thing, Academy Awards often go to seasoned veterans at the peaks or near the ends of their careers instead of to rising newcomers. Also un-derstandable psychological grounds for reverses could exist: fear of success, un-realistic expectations, or perhaps an attempt to out-do one's self or belief in a self-fulfilling prophecy.

Some winners may price themselves out of desirable projects, appear to produc-ers to be too expensive, or find themselves typecast re-peatedly in roles similiar to those for which they won the Oscar. "Once you win," said Best Supporting Act-ress of 1966, Sandy Dennis, "people think you're going to ask so much more, they don't ask you. Besides, there's always a touch of en-vy." Gig Young said sourly: "It didn't help me to win or get nominated three times. Oh, it's a great thing to be appreciated by your peers. But the producers thought I was going to want more money and that I was going to be difficult. The Oscar doesn't give you a ticket to anything — not even to a theater." Bette Midler, a 1979 nominee, complained, "You should see the worth-less scripts I've been offered since *The Rose.*" And Di-ana Ross, nominated for her role *Lady Sings the Blues* (1972), said, "Scores of offers appeared that would have had me playing Billie Holliday over and over again."

Others who allegedly were jinxed may simply have shifted their interests. In the 1960s Rita Moreno was sometimes cited as a victim of Oscar's backspin because she made only one film in the seven years after winning Best Supporting Actress in *West Side Story* (1961). The reality is that one film was all she had time for; she was finding success in other fields of en-tertainment. Later in her career she made more mov-ies. She has become the only female performer to win all four prestige show business awards — the Os-car; the Tony (for *The Ritz*); the Emmy (for appearances on "*The Muppets*" and "*The Rockford Files*"); and the Grammy (for *The Elec-tric Company Album*).

The jinx is talked about enough in Hollywood and joked about enough on talk shows that some winners may believe in a psy-chological force that makes one's own best act hard to follow.

CHAPTER 17

For the Record

WINNERS OF THE MOST OSCARS IN EACH CATEGORY

Actor	Marlon Brando, Gary Cooper, Fredric March, Spencer Tracy (2 each)
Actress	Katharine Hepburn (4)
Art Direction	Cedric Gibbons (10)
Cinematography	Joseph Ruttenberg, Robert L. Surtees (3 each)
Costume Design	Edith Head (8)
Directing	John Ford (4)
Documentary	Walt Disney (4)
Film Editing	Ralph Dawson, Daniel Mandell (3 each)
Foreign Language Film	France (8)
Honorary Awards	Bob Hope (4)
Scientific or Technical	Paramount (28)
Scoring	Alfred Newman (9)
Set Decoration	Edwin B. Willis (8)
Short Film	Walt Disney (17)
Song	Sammy Cahn, Johnny Mercer (4 each)
Sound	Douglas Shearer (5)
Sound Effects	Douglas Shearer (2)
Special Effects and Special Visual Effects	L. B. Abbott, A. Arnold Gillespie (4 each)
Supporting Actor	Walter Brennan (3)
Supporting Actress	Shelley Winters (2)
Thalberg Award	Darryl F. Zanuck (3)
Writing	Billy Wilder (3)
Total Awards	Walt Disney (30)

Billy Wilder won his record three writing Oscars for the screenplays to *The Lost Weekend* (1945), *Sunset Boulevard* (1950), and *The Apartment* (1960). Wilder also won two Oscars for his directing talents.

GENERATION GAPS

Oldest Best Actor	Henry Fonda, 76
Youngest Best Actor	Richard Dreyfuss, 29
Oldest Best Actress	Katharine Hepburn, 74
Youngest Best Actress	Janet Gaynor, 22
Oldest Best Supporting Actor	George Burns, 80
Youngest Best Supporting Actor	Timothy Hutton, 19
Oldest Best Supporting Actress	Ruth Gordon, 72
Youngest Best Supporting Actress	Tatum O'Neal, 10

Richard Dreyfuss, happy to be the youngest winner of the Best Actor award, received the 1977 Oscar for his performance in *The Goodbye Girl.*

BEST PICTURE SUPERLATIVES

Highest grossing (in constant dollars)

Gone with the Wind (1939)

Longest running time

Lawrence of Arabia (1962) — 3 hours, 42 minutes

Most nominations

All About Eve (1950) — 14 nominations

Most Oscars

Ben-Hur (1959) — 11 Oscars

Fewest nominations

Grand Hotel (1931-32) — Nominated for Best Picture only

Fewest Oscars

Broadway Melody (1928-29); *Grand Hotel* (1931-32); and *Mutiny on the Bounty* (1935) — Each won Best Picture only

Longest title

One Flew over the Cuckoo's Nest (1975)

Shortest title

Gigi (1958)

First non-American winner

Hamlet (1948) — British

Only silent winner

Wings (1927-28)

First color winner

Gone with the Wind (1939)

Latest black-and-white winner

The Apartment (1960)

Billy Wilder (left) directed Jack Lemmon in *The Apartment* in 1960, the most recent black-and-white film to be named Best Picture.

IN THE FAMILY: WINNERS AND NOMINEES WHO ARE BLOOD RELATIVES

Lionel Barrymore, Best Actor (1930-31); and *Ethel Barrymore*, Best Supporting Actress (1944), the only brother and sister to win Oscars. Their younger brother, actor *John Barrymore*, was never nominated.

Francis Ford Coppola, Best Director (1974); his father, *Carmine Coppola*, Best Original Dramatic Score (1974); and his sister, *Talia Shire*, Best Actress nominee (1976).

Olivia De Havilland, Best Actress (1946, 1949), and her sister, *Joan Fontaine*, Best Actress (1941) were both nominated for Best Actress in 1941 films.

Henry Fonda, Best Actor (1981); daughter *Jane Fonda*, Best Actress (1971, 1978); son *Peter Fonda*, Best Screenplay nomination (1969).

James Goldman, Best Screenplay (1968); and his brother *William Goldman*, Best Screenplay (1969, 1976).

John Huston, Best Director (1948); and his father, *Walter Huston*, Best Supporting Actor (1948). It was the only time family members won Oscars the same evening.

Herman J. Mankiewicz, Best Original Screenplay (1941); his brother, *Joseph L. Mankiewicz*, Best Directing and Best Screenplay (1949) and Best Directing and Best Screenplay (1950); Herman's son, *Don Mankiewicz*, Best Screenplay nomination (1958).

Liza Minnelli, Best Actress (1972); her mother, *Judy Garland*, Honorary Award (1939); her father, *Vincente Minnelli*, Best Director (1958).

John Mills, Best Supporting Actor (1970); daughter *Hayley Mills*, Honorary Award (1960).

Ryan O'Neal, Best Actor nominee (1970); and his daughter *Tatum O'Neal*, Best Supporting Actress (1973).

Michael Redgrave, Best Actor nominee (1947); daughter *Vanessa Redgrave*, Best Supporting Actress (1977) and Best Actress nominee (1966, 1968, 1971); daughter *Lynn Redgrave*, Best Actress nominee (1966).

Francis Ford Coppola's 1974 Oscar for the direction of *The Godfather Part II* was a family matter.

Joseph L. Mankiewicz (right) joined his talented family of Oscar winners when he received the Best Director award of 1949 fpr *A Letter to Three Wives*. Ida Lupino presented the award, and Paul Douglas was master of ceremonies.

TITLE SONGS THAT WON BEST SONG*

"High Noon (Do Not Forsake Me, Oh My Darlin')," 1952

"Three Coins in the Fountain," 1954

"Love Is a Many-Splendored Thing," 1955

"Gigi," 1958

"Never on Sunday," 1960

"Days of Wine and Roses," 1962

"Born Free," 1966

"Theme from Shaft," 1971

"The Way We Were," 1973

"You Light Up My Life," 1977

"Fame," 1980

"Arthur's Theme (The Best that You Can Do)," 1981

*Note: "White Christmas." "White Christmas" won Best Song of 1942 in *Holiday Inn*, not in the movie *White Christmas* (1954). In *White Christmas* the song "Count Your Blessings Instead of Sheep" was nominated.

The 1981 Best Original Song, "Arthur's Song" from *Arthur* was a collaboration of (left to right) Burt Bacharach, Carole Bayer Sager, Christopher Cross, and Peter Allen.

STUDIO SWEEPSTAKES:
BEST PICTURE AWARDS PER STUDIO/DISTRIBUTOR

United Artists	11
Columbia	11
Metro-Goldwyn-Mayer	9
Paramount	7
20th Century-Fox	7
Universal	4
Warner Brothers	4
RKO Radio	2

Index